Food Security

Cross-country Policies and Experiences

FOOD SECURITY

Cross-country Policies and Experiences

Australia □ Austria □ Brazil □ Cuba □ Germany □ Indonesia □ Kenya □ Mexico □ New Zealand □ North Korea □ Norway □ Thailand □ United Kingdom □ Vietnam

Edited by

Ranita Nagar

•Professor of Economics, Dean of the Department of Research,
Head of the Department of Social Sciences,
Gujarat National Law University (GNLU),
Gandhinagar, Gujarat
•Director, GNLU Centre for Food Security and Agro Economy

Centre for Food Security and Agro Economy
Gujarat National Law University, Gandhinagar

in association with

New Century Publications
New Delhi, India

New Century Publications
4800/24, Bharat Ram Road,
Ansari Road, Daryaganj,
New Delhi - 110 002 (India)

Tel.: 011-2324 7798, 4358 7398, 6539 6605
Fax: 011-4101 7798
E-mail: indiatax@vsnl.com • info@newcenturypublications.com
www.newcenturypublications.com

Editorial office:
LG–7, Aakarshan Bhawan,
4754-57/23, Ansari Road, Daryaganj,
New Delhi – 110 002

Tel.: 011-4356 0919

First Published: **2016**

ISBN: **978-81-7708-417-7**

Published by New Century Publications and printed at Salasar Imaging Systems, New Delhi.

Designs: Patch Creative Unit, New Delhi.

PRINTED IN INDIA

About the Book

Food security is one of the major components of social security. It consists of ensuring that food is available at all times, that all persons have means of and access to it, that it is nutritionally adequate in terms of quantity, quality and variety, and that it is acceptable within the given culture. There are three elements in this definition, availability, accessibility and suitability. In recent years, nutrition has been considered as a part of food security.

Food security is a form of investment in human capital. It brings stability in people's lives and makes it easier for them to meet their basic needs, protect health, educate children, and take risks. Poverty, land degradation, climate change are some of the causes of food insecurity.

Each country, be it developed or developing, faces a specific challenge in meeting the food requirements of its population. The problem is more severe in developing countries which are agro economies and are heavily dependent on natural climate for a good yield. There are other problems also like food wastage by a section of the population while the rest go hungry.

No country could perhaps ever be 100 percent food secure in the holistic comprehension of the term. Yet there are some countries which have more successfully tackled their food requirements with effective economic and trade policies while others are failing.

This book comprises of 15 papers which provide critical and comparative analysis of food security policies and programmes in a cross-section of countries, developed and developing.

About the Editor

Dr. Ranita Nagar is Professor of Economics, Dean of the Department of Research and the Head of the Department of Social Sciences at Gujarat National Law University (GNLU), Gandhinagar, Gujarat. She also holds the post of Director at the GNLU Centre for Food Security and Agro Economy.

She has a Ph.D. in Economics from Gujarat University, Ahmedabad. In addition to academic publications, she has been instrumental in introducing courses on law and economics at the University. Recently, she attended the Coase-Sandor Summer School in Law and Economics at Chicago Law University, University of Chicago, USA.

Contents

Preface

One often imagines a malnourished two year old Saharan or Asian child when discussing the issue of food security. However, it is a gross misconception that poverty or a low GDP is the best indicator of food insecurity just as much as it is an error to believe that simply procuring or producing enough food for a country's population makes a country food secure.

Food security is one of the major components of social security. It consists of ensuring that food is available at all times, that all persons have means of and access to it, that it is nutritionally adequate in terms of quantity, quality and variety, and that it is acceptable within the given culture. There are three elements in this definition, availability, accessibility and suitability. In recent years, nutrition has been considered as a part of food security.

For proponents, food security is a form of investment in human capital. It will bring some security in people's lives and make it easier for them to meet their basic needs, protect their health, educate their children, and take risks. Poverty, increased food consumption, land degradation, climate change are some of the causes of food insecurity.

Food security is closely related to the development of technologies for increasing agriculture outputs through process innovations for land saving and water use. The question is how to develop and deploy new agro biotechnology tools and precision agriculture for increasing the output of agriculture sector in a country.

Food security is to be measured not only in terms of availability but also accessibility. Each country, be it developed or developing, faces a specific challenge in meeting the food requirements of its population. The most apparent of these issues is the one faced by low GDP countries which are agro economies and are heavily dependent on natural climate for a good yield. However, there are other problems like excessive food wastage by a section of the country while the rest go hungry.

No country could perhaps ever be 100 percent food secure in the holistic comprehension of the term. Yet there are scme countries which have more successfully tackled their food requirements with effective policies and trade while others are failing.

The book contains an exhaustive analysis of the food security issues and policies of 15 countries to provide the reader with an international overview of the problem of food security. The contributors to this volume all belong to Gujarat National Law University, Gandhinagar. The authors and the editor hope this book will aid in the quest for staving off hunger, as in the words of Jimmy Carter, "We know that a peaceful world cannot long exist, one-third rich and two-thirds hungry".

Gandhinagar **Ranita Nagar**

1

Australia: Agro Economy and Food Security

Aakanksha Parashar and Sudeepta Rao M

Socio-economic Profile of Australia

This chapter deals with an overview of the socio-economic profile of Australia, with the aid of different economic factors. The statistics of the same are obtained from the CIA World Factbook. [1] Each indicator about Australian data is compared with similar information regarding US and India.

Australia has a slightly lesser population of children, compared to India and US. The population of teenagers and adults is more or less the same across all the three countries. Australia has a greater population of aged which is perhaps a reflection of the advanced medical and health care facilities of Australia. Agriculture contributes to the greatest proportion of the GDP in India when compared to Australia and US. In Australia, the service sector plays a pivotal role while contributing in the GDP as compared to the agriculture sector.

Australia is today a well-established and prospering economy. With a relatively high-growth and low-inflation economy supported by robust political and economic institutions, and an internationally competitive business sector, Australia now ranks as the 13th largest economy in the world (measured by GDP), and the 3rd largest in the Asia-Pacific region. [2]

It is interesting how different geographic parts of Australia, contribute to different sectors of the economy. The Eastern parts of Australia concentrate on the service and financial industries, and the Western part contains majority of the natural resources. Australia is a highly industrialised economy, and the chief industries include mining and food processing, among others. Australia is self-sufficient in the production of food—agriculture and cattle-rearing have been staple occupations. [3]

Australia is a major agricultural producer and exporter. Australian farms and their closely related sectors generate $137 billion-a-year in production, or 12 percent of the GDP. Australian agriculture represents 1.6 million jobs and 20 percent of national exports. Major agricultural exports include wheat, barley, sugarcane, fruit, cattle, sheep and poultry as well as an increasing amount of processed or prepared food products, such as fish products, cheese and wine.

Agricultural productivity has exhibited a strong growth over the last three decades—more than twice the rate achieved in Australia's market sector as a whole. Between 1975 and 2004, Australian farms consistently achieved average multifactor productivity growth of 2.8 percent a year. No other industry, with the sole exception of telecommunications and information technology, comes close to this achievement.

Food Security in Australia

'The United Nation's Food and Agriculture Organization (FAO) estimates that nearly one billion people go hungry every day, with two-thirds living in the Asia-Pacific region...This on-going challenge has been compounded by the global food crises, which in 2008 pushed more than 130 million people back into poverty as the price of staple foods rose by between 50 and 200 percent. Prices abated somewhat in 2009, but since mid-2010 they have risen above even 2008 levels, pushing an estimated 44 million people back into poverty, according to the World Bank'. [4]

It is perhaps relevant to start this chapter with a brief introduction on what food security is. Food security, as the name suggests, is a security with regard to food—or, no insecurity or threat, in terms of accessibility or affordability or storage of food. Hence, it is clear that certain sections of society are more susceptible to food security. In Australia, these sections include indigenous people (24 percent); unemployed people (23 percent) and single parent households (23 percent).

The Australian government has developed a comprehensive approach to food security targeting the immediate needs of the poorest, while also strengthening the foundations of long-term global food security. This response includes emergency food assistance, increased funding for rural development and international collaboration to prioritise food security issues and pursue trade policy reforms.

The Australian Government has strongly and consistently pursued agricultural trade liberalisation through multilateral, bilateral and regional fora...In the 2003-2004 Budget, the Australian Government made a commitment of $16.5 million to the Global Crop Diversity Trust (GCDT). The GCDT is a joint initiative of the Food and Agriculture Organisation and the Consultative Group on International Agricultural Research to provide secure funding for gene banks to conserve plant genetic resources for food and agriculture around the world.

'The Standards in the Australia-New Zealand Food Standards Code are legislative instruments under the Legislative Instruments Act, 2003. The code is enforced by State and Territory and New Zealand agencies and the Australian Quarantine and Inspection Service (for imported food). The FSANZ Code provides unified food manufacture and handling standards, and concentrates on protecting public health and safety, whilst providing flexibility to permit industry innovation'. [5] It is very interesting to note that the role of the Australian government when it comes to food security is not limited to Australia alone.

Australia is in collaboration with countries like Indonesia, East Timor and many countries in Africa in order to enhance agricultural trade and productivity. The areas of action include better management of fisheries, developing export opportunities and enhancing private sector participation.

The Australian government is also actively involved in

spreading awareness on the advantages of open trade and efficient markets and to increase opportunities in developing countries to maximise returns on their outputs and better their incomes. The Doha Round of multilateral trade negotiations was in the same vein, as it aimed at lessening the distortion to global agricultural trade, especially production and export subsidies in developed countries, which disadvantage farmers in developing countries.

Australia rendered very significant support in the 2008 food crisis. On May 1, 2008, in lieu of the appeal of the World Food Programme, Australia contributed an additional $30 million.

In July 2008, the then Prime Minister Rudd announced a commitment of $50 million to a World Bank Trust Fund, part of the World Bank's Global Food Response Program, the focus of which was to render support to countries in dealing with the higher food prices.

A report commissioned by the Australian government found that foreigners are heavily investing in the country's agricultural companies such as those into sugar, grain and beef production. South Australian Senator Nick Xenophon warned of the impact of control of such foreign capital into Australia's food security.

'Reports said that the government officials are crafting a plan to ensure that foreign investments in the country's prime farming assets are more transparent.

The Australian Bureau of Agricultural and Resource Economics, which commissioned the report, made an announcement on plans to make foreign investments in the agro sector more transparent. The report would include the figures on how much of Australia's farming sector is now owned by foreign investors'. [6]

In response to the same, the government decided not to reduce foreign investment in Australia. 'Following an ABARES report on foreign investment in the agriculture sector, the Government decided not to tighten foreign investment controls in relation to the acquisition of Australian agricultural land and business. In particular, the monetary threshold for the notification of private acquisitions of farms remains the same as for Australian business generally'. [7]

International Treaties and Agencies

Perth Declaration on Food Security Principles: 'The commonwealth is uniquely placed to support global food security efforts through Commonwealth countries' membership in all major global and regional forums that are engaged on this issue. Commonwealth countries therefore commit to use their membership of these forums to advocate the Perth declaration on Food Security Principles to achieve outcomes that are relevant and meaningful to members...'.

The Perth Declaration on Food Security is a declaration entered into by select Commonwealth countries. The declaration reflects the Commonwealth members' collective attitude in addressing the goals of food security. They recognize the need of international co-operation and conducive efforts to overcome food insecurity, especially in light of the 2007 and 2008 food crises. The key factors that the member countries recognize in dealing with the concern of food security include, population growth, scarce land and water resources, the diversion of fertile land, the reduction in crop species and use of crops for non-food purposes, urbanisation, distorted markets and climate change. Above all, the principal belief of the member countries is that everyone has the right to, "safe sufficient and nutritious food, consistent with the progressive realisation of the right to adequate food in the context of national food security".

World Food Summit: The World Food Summit in 1996 set the goal of halving the number of people who live in absolute poverty and a state of severe under-nourishment by 2015. We all knew at the time that this was an ambitious but necessary goal. Some progress has been made, but much more needs to be done. The World Food Summit was started in the year 1996. The Honourable Warren Truss, Minister for Agriculture, Fisheries and Forestry of Australia, addressed the gathering and opined, "In view of the challenges indicated in 1996 Summit, the Australian Government, by means of overseas agricultural aid programmes and food security strategy, has worked to enable and support the development, particularly within the Asia-Pacific region". In the recent Summit, The Honourable Warren Truss opined, "that while improving production and technical assistance is important, international trade is of paramount significance in delivering economic growth and reducing poverty in developing countries. He further continued that growth in trade improves living standards, raises incomes and helps assure food security". [8]

Pacific Agreement on Closer Economic Relations: The Pacific Agreement on Closer Economic Relations (PACER) Plus negotiations offer an opportunity to help Pacific Islands Forum countries benefit from enhanced regional trade and economic integration. Pacific Islands Forum Leaders launched negotiations on PACER Plus at their fortieth meeting in August 2009.

Participants in the PACER Plus negotiations included Australia, Cook Islands, Federated States of Micronesia, Kiribati, Nauru, New Zealand, Niue, Palau, Papua New Guinea, Republic of Marshall Islands, Samoa, Solomon Islands, Tonga, Tuvalu, and Vanuatu.

Australia's approach to the PACER Plus negotiations was different to that taken in traditional free trade agreement negotiations. Australia's primary objective was to promote the economic development of Forum Island Countries through greater regional trade and economic integration.

Australia is conscious of the negotiating capacity constraints faced by Forum Island Countries and has committed to providing Forum Island Countries with appropriate capacity building and support. Australia, for instance, has already provided substantial funds for Forum Island Countries to commission independent research on PACER Plus and for training of Forum Island Country trade officials to strengthen their capacity in respect of the PACER Plus negotiations. Australia has provided funding for officials from Forum Island Countries to attend PACER Plus meetings and is also helping to fund the Office of the Chief Trade Adviser which provides independent support and advice to Forum Island Countries on PACER Plus matters.

Australia New Zealand Treaty: The Australia-New Zealand Closer Economic Relations Trade Agreement (known as ANZCERTA or the CER Agreement) is one of the most comprehensive bilateral free trade agreements in existence. It covers substantially all trans-Tasman trade in goods, including agricultural products, and was the first to include free trade in services.

'The Agreement's central provision is the creation of a World Trade Organization (WTO)-consistent free trade area encompassing Australia and New Zealand. Since ANZCERTA entered into force in 1983, the two way trade in goods between the two countries has expanded at an average annual growth rate of eight percent. The harmonisation of trans-Tasman food standards through the ANZFA Agreement of 1995 means lower compliance costs for industry, fewer regulatory barriers, and more consumer choice.' [9]

Food and Agriculture Organisation of the United Nations: The FAO was established in 1919 with a mandate to raise levels of nutrition and standards of living, to improve agricultural productivity, and to better the condition of rural populations. The FAO collects and maintains statistical data, disseminates information, provides a world centre for knowledge and expertise, provides a neutral forum for international policy dialogue, develops international norms, standards and conventions, and provides technical assistance. Australia, as a major world food producer and agricultural trading nation, is a founding member and has participated actively in it since its inception. Australia's main interest in FAO activities relate to facilitating the collection of data and information exchange on agriculture, fisheries and forestry industries, participating in FAO's work in codification of agricultural surplus disposals and food aid transactions. The FAO headquarters is located in Rome.

Australian Centre for International Agricultural Research: The Australian Centre for International Agricultural Research (ACIAR) is a statutory authority that operates as part of the Australian Government's development cooperation programs. The Centre encourages Australia's agricultural scientists to use their skills for the benefit of developing countries and Australia.

ACIAR funds research projects that are developed within a framework reflecting the priorities of Australia's aid program and national research strengths, together with the agricultural research and development priorities of partner countries.

The main functions of the ACIAR are as under:

- Commission research into improving sustainable agricultural production in developing countries.
- Fund project related training.
- Communicate the results of funded research.
- Conduct and fund development activities related to research programs.
- Administer the Australian Government's contribution to the international agricultural research centres.

Australian International Food Security Centre: The Australian International Food Security Centre (AIFSC) is an Australian Government initiative that sits within the Australian Centre for International Agricultural Research (ACIAR). The Australian Prime Minister Julia Gillard, announced the establishment of the AIFSC to strengthen the Australian Government's contribution to global food security at the Commonwealth Heads of Government Meeting (CHOGM) in October 2011.

Strategy for the AIFSC has been developed for the 10-year period 2012-2022. It identifies the scope and most effective areas of focus to deliver greatest impact for food security and the operations and delivery mechanisms to achieve these. The strategy is to outline and build responses to the priorities, gaps and research capabilities needs, identified through consultations with Australian, African and international stakeholders.

The programmes include:

- **Sustainable and Productive Farming Systems**—improving sustainable productivity in farming systems, including better natural resource management; enabling policies to enhance productivity.
- **Food Markets, Value Chains and Social Systems**--generating more income from cash crops, trees and livestock products and other enterprises to enable poor people to purchase food; enabling policies, improved market access for smallholder farmers; understanding barriers to adoption.
- **Food Nutrition and Safety**—improving nutrition, increasing diversity in diets, reducing post-harvest loss and adding value to food.
- **Communications and Knowledge Management**—innovations in information and knowledge delivery (e.g. ICT), bridging research and extension, fostering scaling out mechanisms, empowering farming communities.
- **Education, Training and Capacity Building**—building individual and institutional capacity; critical mass of women and men trained to address food security issues; strengthening trade negotiations; emerging issues; institutional partnerships.

Leading Judgements

- Steve Marsh is an organic farmer and lives in Kojonup, Western Australia. In December 2010, Mr. Marsh's genetically modified canola seeds were found in his farm, blown over from a neighbouring property. About 70 percent of his farm is now contaminated, and the National Association for Sustainable Agriculture Australia Limited, suspended his certification of organic farming. While Steve Marsh wants to pursue a suit against his neighbour, the same is being supported by many well-wishers, and the Steve Marsh Benefit Fund has been founded for the same.
- There has been considerable debate on the topic of coal seam gas in Australia. The farmers are opposed to the

mining of the same, and they joined with Friends of the Earth and other representatives in the 'Lock the gate' campaign. [10] Senate Inquiry recommendations has been made on the same.

- The Murray-Darling Basin is home to the largest river system in Australia. 3.2 million people rely on the Murray Darling base for drinking water, the basin also provides about 41 percent of the country's agriculture with water, for crops like cotton, rice and wheat. Many plant and animal species rely on the Murray-Darling Basin for survival. The problems now faced include the water crisis for industrial and domestic use and rise of salinity and chemical pollution. [11] The Murray-Darling Basin authority was to come up with a draft plan, to address the said issues. The Wentworth Group of concerned scientists on January 19, 2012, called for the Murray-Darling Basin authority to withdraw the drafted plan. 'The government should stop the process, instruct the authority to withdraw the draft plan, abandon the proposal for a 2015 review and instead take the time necessary to include the science and social science now'.

Comparison of Food Security in India and Australia

We have now understood that food security, simply means, enough food for everyone. There can be many impediments to *enough food*—from availability to affordability. How a country deal with such impediments to formulate the food security strategy of that country.

The main issues of food security in India among others include malnutrition due to inadequate supply of nutritious food and rising food prices.

India achieved self-sufficiency in food grains in 1970s, and has sustained it since then. However, this self-sufficiency did as not reflect totally on the households. Hence, the focus was later turned to food security at the household level and per capita food energy in-take, in view of the national malnutrition levels. The government has undertaken many welfare programmes, like public distribution system, 'Food for Work' programmes and Mid-Day meal schemes.

In India, the Central Government sponsors a scheme known as the National Food Security Mission. The scheme centres on enhancing agricultural production of rice and pulses. This can be achieved by increasing the cultivable area, at targeted districts, and improving soil fertility. The same will lead to greater employment opportunities and hence, a better economy. This outlines the main aims of the National Food Security Mission. To achieve these aims, the Mission adopts various mission programmes that involves stakeholders at all levels, promotion of improved technology, fixed targets for different districts and capacity building of farmers, among other strategies.

Australia seems to be in a comfortable position when it comes to food security, producing about twice as much food as it consumes. Hence, while Australia might not have an immediate concern of feeding all its citizens, it takes a humanitarian interest in food security around the world.

The Australian Government is very actively involved with other countries, with respect to agricultural research and trade. These relations are primarily focused on aiding the partner nations to become self-reliant in terms of food production and agriculture, and sustaining this self-dependence.

Hence, perhaps an observation could be made that when it comes to food security, the Indian government has a more welfare based approach, while the main postulate of the Australian Government seems to be on the emphasis in free trade and an open market system.

It might now be relevant to briefly deal with the relationship between Australia and India in agriculture in slightly greater detail.

The ACIAR is involved with agricultural activities in both Australia and other countries as well. In February 2011, a joint forum for Indian and Australian agricultural researchers was arranged by the ACIAR. Australian High Commissioner to India, Mr. Peter Varghese, said, "Australia and India have common agricultural research interests because of their similar environmental conditions and natural resource management issues, along with common crops such as heat, sorghum and pulses. Along with the prevalent areas of focus, water management, cropping system, wheat improvement and agricultural policy, other suggestions include application of competition law to food chains, a regulation framework to include a transparent review process and management of the buffer stock of the Food Corporation of India, to name a few". [12] Hence, the association of Australia and India in agricultural research seems to be a positive step, and steps must be taken to sustain the same.

Critical Analysis of Food Security in Australia

Hypothesis: 'Making healthy food affordable should be the aim of food security plans in Australia, as compared to enhancing agricultural productivity'.

It is now seen that Australia is in a comfortable position with respect to food production. Australia's active involvement in aiding agriculture development in other countries is perhaps a testament to the same. Hence, to say that Australia's main concern in agriculture need not be enhancing agricultural productivity is perhaps a safe conclusion.

Hence, simply put, there is food. There is food now, but will there be food in the coming years? The experts seem to think so. But is this food reaching everyone in the society? The definition of food security, as we have dealt with in the very beginning, is access to food. Is the food Australia produces, affordable by all sections of society, and hence is it accessible to everyone in the society?

Of course, these people do not live in desperate refugee camps; and most do not endure long periods of famine and destitution. Yet, a couple of years back, some two million Australians reported there have been times when they have run out of food and could not afford to buy more.

It may appear contradictory to write about hunger when a large proportion of the Australian population tries to reduce calorie intake. But a more perplexing question is why hunger, although a growing problem in Australia, is neglected in a country which in aggregate terms is food secure.

While expenditure on food perhaps is not a major issue for single persons who earn comfortably, what about families with a single earning person, or college students who fend for themselves, or aborigines and such communities? On one hand, there is enough food, but on the other hand, this food is perhaps not reaching everyone due to high prices.

The capitalist-open market system advocated by Australia seems to be working very well in one aspect. It has opened up trade relations for Australia, and Australia is beyond self-sufficient in agriculture production. Hence, the issue—if there is one—lies not in the production of food, but in making the same available to all sections of the society.

In the opinion of the authors, this is where the government should step in. The government could undertake welfare measures to ensure an egalitarian distribution of the food produced, by regulating prices. While a capitalist approach is maintained with respect to international trade in agriculture, a socialistic approach might aid closer home. Hence, the best of both worlds is achieved.

Endnotes

1. "The World Factbook", Central Intelligence Agency, accessed on 29-07-2013, available at: https://www.cia.gov/library/publications/the-world-factbook/geos/au.html.
2. "The Australian Market", The ASX Group, accessed on 20-05-2013, available at: http://www.asxgroup.com.au/the-australian-market.htm.
3. "Economy", Australia, accessed on 29-07-13, available at: http://www.infoplease.com/ce6/world/A0856772.html.
4. "Australian Aid", The Australian Agency for International Development; available at: www.ausaid.gov.au.

5. "Food Standards: Australia and New Zealand", SAI Global, accessed on 29-07-13, available at: http://www.saiglobal.com/Information/Legislation/Services.
6. Vittorio Hernandez, "Australia's Food Security May be Jeopardised by Foreign Investments into Agri Firms", *International Business Times, Realty and Investments*, January 4, 2013, accessed on 29-07-13, available at: http://au.ibtimes.com/articles/275944/20120104/australia-s-food-security-jeopardised-foreign-investments.htm.
7. Clayton Utz, accessed on 29-07-13, available at: www.claytonutz.com.
8. Food and Agricultural Organisation of the United Nations, accessed on 29-07-13, available at: www.fao.org.
9. "Pacific Agreement on Closer Economic Relations", Australian Government, Department of Foreign Affairs and Trade, accessed on 29-07-13, available at: http://www.dfat.gov.au/fta/pacer/index.html.
10. "Australia First Queensland"; accessed on 29-07-13, available at: http://afqld.blogspot.in.
11. "Murray-Darling Basin", accessed on 29-07-13, available at: http://www.actnow.com.au/Issues/MurrayDarling_Basin.aspx.
12. "India", Australian Centre for International Agricultural Research (ACIAR), accessed on 01-03-12, available at: http://aciar.gov.au/country/india.

2

Austria: National Nutrition Action Plan

Katyayini Surendran and Zahra Aziz

Socio-economic Profile

In terms of population, Austria is quite the melting pot. Some ethnic groups in Austria are Germans, Turks, Serbs, Croats, Slovenes and Bosnians. Other recognized minorities include Hungarians, Czechs, Slovaks, and Romans. During the annual census conducted in 2013, the population was estimated at 8.45 million, and the annual population growth rate was said to be 0.4 percent (in 2011). The literacy level in Austria is laudable. In a recent survey it was concluded that Austria has 98 percent literacy level. Education is mandatory up to 9 years of age. In terms of industry, iron and steel, chemicals, capital equipment and consumer goods are the main drivers of the economy.

Trade exports include iron and steel products, timber, paper, electro technical machinery, chemical products and food products, while imports include machinery, vehicles, chemicals, iron and steel, metal goods, fuels and raw materials. The principle trade partners of Austria are the European Union, Switzerland, China and the United States. In terms of food trade, the total merchandise exported till 2008 was 13.4 percent and the total merchandise imported was 12.9 percent. The net food product (food exported-food imported) in the total GDP was -2.3 percent.

Legislative Framework

Plant Protection Products Act, 1997: Integrated pest management was implemented into the national law with the 'Plant Protection Products Act, 1997' [2] in August 1997.

According to this Act, plant protection products have to be used taking into account the principles of integrated pest management.

Fertilizer Act, 1994: According to the Fertilizer Act, 1994, the marketing of fertilizer which endangers the fertility of the soil or the health of humans and animals is forbidden.

The implementation of the 1991 Master Transportation Concept is in progress, and transportation issues are an important part of the Austrian National Environment Plan. In order to have a less polluting and safer transportation system, issues such as relative cost-effectiveness of alternative systems, transportation technologies, mass transit systems, environmental impact assessment and safety have all been comprehensively addressed.

National Nutrition Action Plan (NAP): The Austrian National Nutrition Action Plan, which was launched recently, follows a horizontal "health in all policies" strategy and combines Austria's nutrition policies and strategies. [3] The primary goals of the NAP include a reduction of over-, under-malnutrition as well as the reduction in the rising overweight and obesity rates by 2020. It sets for Austria, food policy goals by offering an overview of international and European developments and identifies primary possible fields of action. The NAP is not a static document but a rolling strategy and action catalogue. It adapts annually the goals and issues as well as the review of existing measures to be updated.

One of the first initiatives of the NAP was the new national nutrition pyramid for Austria, which is to help consumers improve their eating behaviour. The focus of the NAP for the year 2011 was on the target groups of infants, children, juveniles and pregnant women. The project 'eat right from the beginning' (a cooperation of the Ministry of Health with the Federation of Austrian Social Insurance and the Agency for Health and Food Safety) was continued.

Organic Farming for Sustainable Development: One of the most important trends of recent decades in Austria was the strong development of environmental awareness. This is shown in particular by the widespread participation in the Agro-Environmental Programme available for Austrian agriculture since the accession to the EU in 1995.

More than 70 percent of all domestic farms and 90 percent of Austria's utilized agricultural area takes part in this programme. By doing so, agricultural enterprises make an important contribution to the protection of environment. Organic farming is by far the most important positive example of the eco-land Austria. Austrian agriculture is prepared to continue this path consistently in cooperation with farmer associations, processing enterprises and commerce. [4]

The principle of sustainability plays an important role in agricultural policy. Sustainability means careful dealing with natural resources, efficient replacement of limited and scarce commodities, reduction of the environmental stress resulting from industrial production, and reduction of the consumption of non-renewable resources. The intention to support the greening of the Austrian agriculture is recorded in national laws, special guidelines and a so called 'advisor contract'. This contract stipulates the subsidizing of personnel costs by the Federal Ministry for Agriculture and district chambers of agriculture. The further development of environmental awareness to promote sustainable agriculture practice is backed up by a well-organized education and training system.

Within the framework of integrated production also, the aspects of soil protection receive special attention in the authorization of plant protection products. The biggest measure included in the already mentioned Austrian Rural Development Programme is the Austrian Agro-Environmental Programme. It involves provisions concerning an obligatory soil analysis. Targeted fertilisation measures which are tailored to the relevant requirements make an important contribution to the "health" of the soil. Ensuring soil fertility in a sustainable manner is one of the primary objectives of the Austrian Agro-Environmental Programme, as it provides strong impulses towards ecology, landscape tending, and the protection against natural hazards, biodiversity, and wholesome food.

The great success of organic products in Austria can be attributed to the following factors.

Subsidies for Organic Farmers: Since 1991, Austria grants subsidies for organic farming. This government aid is aimed at restructuring agriculture on the basis of ecological criteria. After joining the EU, Austria was able to further increase aid to organic farmers. In 2000, Austria's organic farmers received 150 Mio EUR from the ÖPUL Agro-Environment Programme as compensation for their ecological contribution. Almost half of the money was provided by the European Union and the rest was divided among the Federal Government and the Provinces. In 2005, the number of subsidized organic farms rose to 20,104, which is a plus of 2.7 percent compared to 2004. The area under organic farming increased by 5 percent to a total of 360,369 hectares. An area of 141,594 hectares arable crops were cultivated according to organic criteria (+ 8.5 percent compared to 2004). The share of organic farms of the IACS enterprises amounted to 12.9 percent.

Trade Chains: Large trade chains were framed which began marketing organic products in 1995. [5] For the first time, large portions of the population were able to purchase products of organic farming in stores other than in specialized organic shops. This clearly demonstrates the Austrian philosophy. Contrary to many other European countries, organic products in Austria were not meant to become only niche products. The objective was rather to make this most ecologically compatible form of land use as widespread as possible in order to ensure that the good quality of soil, water and air be preserved for sustainable development.

Ecological Awareness among Consumers: It was the readiness of consumers to contribute to a better environment and to accept higher prices for organic products that encouraged the trade chains to begin selling organic products in the first place. In addition, Austria has taken a very precautionary approach with respect to GMOs in agriculture. No deliberate release with GMOs has taken place so far in Austria. A number of GMO-products which have gained EU-wide approval have been provisionally prohibited in Austria on scientific grounds (3 maize products, 1 oilseed rape). [6] These safeguard measures are still legally in force. As a consequence, no GMOs can be grown and commercialized legally in Austria so far.

Plant-Genetic Resources (PGR): PGR play a prominent part in Austrian environment program. Farmers receive a premium for cultivation of seldom species or land varieties or ecotypes. The aims are the preservation of genetic diversity *in situ* in the original habitat or ecosystem and the sustainable use of these old and valuable resources. [7] To safeguard old varieties, land varieties or ecotypes, Austria has also built up a couple of gene banks. In these gene banks, the plant genetic material is kept under controlled conditions and scientific work and documentation takes place. These measures are in line with the Global Plan of Action and the International Treaty on Plant Genetic Resources for Food and Agriculture. [8]

Insurance Schemes: Austrian Hail Insurance is a fund-partnership insurance scheme incorporating eight insurance companies. It is non-profit organization and was founded in 1946. The business organization is built on a mutual insurance association system. The corporate objectives include comprehensive risk management for agriculture systems and non-profit features. The farmers pay 50 percent of the insurance premium. The rest is compensated by the provinces (25 percent) and the federal government (25 percent). The target of the system is a comprehensive risk management system transferring private insurance from pure hail insurer to a full partner on multi-peril coverage. The arable crops and fruit and vegetable insurance coverage include hail, drought, storm, frost, drift, flood, slugs' damage, sprouting, excessive rain and crow damage. The grassland farmers incur damage from hail, flood, clamp silo foil, stillbirth and death of cattle.

Austrian Agriculture Policy: Since 1962, the Common Agricultural Policy (CAP) has established a comprehensive legal framework for European agriculture aiming to achieve the objectives set out in the Treaty of Rome. [9] The CAP is unique in the extent to which it is regulated and financed at EU level. Its common approach, in particular, to the single market, makes it possible to guarantee the functioning of internal market of agricultural products. The goals of the Austrian agricultural policy are given in the Federal Agricultural Act of 1992.

The policy is divided into two pillars: the first pillar consists of a framework for supporting the income of farmers through the payment of direct aid and a system for managing and supporting agricultural markets. The second pillar of the CAP provides a framework to support the development of rural areas of the EU. The first pillar is 100 percent financed by the EU budget, whereas the second pillar is co-financed by the UE budget and those of the Member States.

The community organic farming legislation underwent a profound revision process based on the European Action Plan for Organic Food and Farming. A milestone of this process is the new Council Regulation on organic production and labelling of organic products adopted in 2008.

Agencies that Work for Food Security

Organic production is a system of production of food and farm management that aims at sustainable agriculture, the production of high quality products and the use of processes that do not harm the environment health. The organic market has rapidly developed and experienced annual growth rates of more than 10 percent in the last two decades. The European market for organic food amounts to about € 20 billion annually, representing an estimated 1.5 percent share of the entire food market.

The EU legal framework governing the sector of organic production aims at providing the basis for the sustainable development of organic production while guaranteeing fair competition, ensuring consumer confidence and protecting consumer interests and ensuring the effective functioning of the internal market.

ARGE: ARGE Waste Prevention, Resource Protection and Sustainable Development Ltd., Austria, is a non-profit organization providing services in the fields of sustainable development and municipal waste management.

ARGE has been promoting sustainable development and waste management with strong cooperation and support from the Federal Ministry of Austria. Their subsidiary donor is a European Union (EU) programme [10] that encourages cooperation among the countries of central Europe to improve agriculture and environment.

ARGE has been a constant supporting system for sustainable development in Austria. This non-profit organization has provided solutions for major agricultural problems faced in Austria. With the help of the Federal Ministry and other international organizations, ARGE has implemented new ideas and technologies to improve agriculture and waste management.

Austrian Development Cooperation (ADC): ADC pursues its goals of reducing global poverty, ensuring peace and human security and preserving the environment in an international framework. To bring all this into place and to get the strategies right, the first basic thing they concentrate on is agriculture and sustainable development. They implement many policies and programs, which are agreed on with the EU and other international committees such as the UN, OECD, IFIS etc. ADC also supports countries in Africa, Asia and Central America. The operational unit of the ADC is Austrian Development Agency (ADA).

Through this organization, Austria conducts bilateral development cooperation with partner countries and provides multilateral assistance in different fields, namely agriculture. ADC also collaborates with NGOs that implement programs and projects which contribute to development of agriculture, education etc.

National Environmental Plan (NUP): Agricultural production and environment are closely linked. New technologies are used for agricultural purposes these days. Though these technologies are of great use and help for agriculture, they prove to be a threat to the environment. The end results of these modern technologies are pollution. To balance the development of agriculture and maintain the environment, the National Environmental Plan was started. Their main objectives were to avoid:

- Species loss and species impoverishment due to competition for habitat space and altered usages;
- Material inputs into agro ecosystems, with negative repercussions for soil, water and air parameters;
- Climate-relevant and other gaseous emissions in as yet undetermined quantities.

The NUP improved certain areas of agriculture and brought about changes in food security measures. They issued tenders and notices to the Government to bring a balance between food security and environment.

Food and Agriculture Organisation (FAO): The FAO is the largest specialized agency in the United Nations system. FAO has been fighting world poverty and hunger by working for agricultural development, improved nutrition and food security since its inception in 1945. It now has 194 member nations, two associate members and one member organization, the European Community (EC). Austria has been a member of FAO since 1955.

FAO has played a major role in Austria's agriculture and food security policies. The Organization collects, analyses and disseminates information; advises the Austrian government on policy and planning; serves as an international forum for discussing food and agricultural issues and approving international standards and agreements; and provides direct aid for development. It also intervenes in times of crisis when food production and distribution are disrupted by human or natural disasters such as war, drought and insect infestations.

In Austria, the FAO laid emphasis on sustainable agriculture and rural development. The aim was to satisfy the needs of the present and future generations through programmes that do not harm the environment and that are technically appropriate, economically viable and socially acceptable.

European Union: The European Union's main objectives are:

- To preserve a viable, economically sound, farm-based agriculture in an intact rural area;
- To promote the manifold earning and employment combinations between agriculture and other economic sectors;
- To encourage market-oriented production, processing and marketing;
- To support agriculture in order to enable it to balance natural disadvantages;
- To safeguard optimum supply of the population with high quality food and raw materials and the natural assets of soil, water and air, to preserve and shape the cultural and recreational landscape and to support the protection against natural hazards.

The legal basis is Regulation 2092/91—its Council Regulation (EEC) No. 2092/91 of June 24, 1991 on organic production of agricultural products and indications referring thereto on agricultural products and foodstuffs. Precisely, the regulation states:

"The demand from consumers for organically produced agricultural products and foodstuffs is increasing; and a new market for agricultural products is thus being created by this phenomenon; the market price for such products is higher, while the way in which they are produced involves less intensive use of land; therefore, in the context of the reorientation of the common agricultural policy, this type of production may contribute towards the attainment of a better balance between supply of, and demand for, agricultural products, the protection of the environment and the conservation of the countryside. In response to the rising demand, agricultural products and foodstuffs are being placed on the market with indications stating or implying to purchasers that they have been produced organically or without the use of synthetic chemicals".

In Austria, agriculture is given importance. The European Union plays an important role in Austrian agriculture. Sometimes imports, exports and agro-economic development inputs are given by the EU. The European Union makes sure to get the food security policies implemented and followed regularly. It organizes programmes where many countries participate and share agro-economic problems and inputs.

In Austria, the EU looks after the maintenance of family farms, the wide ecological orientation and that if further development of the economic capacity of agriculture is playing a key role. Attention is also paid to the growing importance of extra-agricultural income combinations, better compensation of non-productive services through direct payments as well as a stronger orientation towards entrepreneurial initiatives in the agricultural sector.

The EU follows the Food Regulation Act, 1998, to manage the legal framework of the food security. Some of it includes the regulation of food hygiene, contaminants, additives, fresh foods, farm foods etc.

As for other sectors of the economy, regulatory measures in agriculture are also for the greater part based on specific legislations. In addition, non-agricultural laws also have impacts on the margin of the agricultural policy. The second main pillar of agricultural policy is rural development, which, since Austria's accession to the European Union, is primarily designed within the framework of the Common Agricultural Policy.

Main Actors of the Austrian Agricultural Policy

Federal Ministry of Agriculture, Forestry, Environment and Water Management: In matters concerning the Common Agricultural Policy, the Republic of Austria is represented in the

EU Council by The Federal Ministry of Agriculture, Forestry, Environment and Water Management which is responsible for the all-European orientation and the integration of the agricultural policy within the framework of the Common Agricultural Policy of the European Union.

Its tasks are regulated in the Federal Ministries Act and comprises of activities in the fields of market organisation, trade policy, agricultural subsidisation, agricultural extension, education and research, etc.

The "Green Report", a separate report on the situation of agriculture published annually, provides information about the situation of agriculture within Austria's national economy, consequences of the Austrian agricultural policy, the agricultural subsidies as well as the economic situation of agriculture.

Federal Minister for Agriculture, Forestry, Environment and Water Management is the first and foremost person responsible for the national implementation of the agricultural market policy, the agricultural structural policy and the accompanying measures, and the remaining national subsidisation activities.

Offices of Provincial Governments: The Republic of Austria comprises nine autonomous provinces and more than 2,000 municipalities. [11] Due to this federalist structure, agricultural and forestry tasks are carried out by the Federal Provinces as well, especially by the agriculture departments of the offices of the Provincial Governments.

The main focus is on the implementation of support measures for agricultural and forestry enterprises and on the improvement of the infrastructure in rural areas.

Chambers of Agriculture: Austrian farm families have a legally established representation of interest in all Federal Provinces. The Federal Chambers of Agriculture are linked by an umbrella organisation, the Austrian Chamber of Agriculture, which acts as a coordination body. It focuses mainly on farm advice and tasks delegated by the national and regional governments, as well as the representation of interest, in particular vis-à-vis all Austrian institutions and at European level.

All self-employed persons active in agriculture and/or forestry as well as the members of their families working with them are by law, members of the Chambers of Agriculture. [12] They have the right to make use of the services of the Chambers without paying for them and to elect its representatives, and the duty to ensure the financing of the expenses of their Chambers by levy contributions.

The Austrian Chamber of Agriculture represents its members in various economic institutions, e.g. in the market organisation agency AgrarMarkt Austria, many commissions, advisory committees and scientific institutions. It represents the interests of Austria's agriculture and forestry throughout Europe as it is also a member of COPA, the Committee of Professional Agricultural Organisations in Europe.

AgrarMarkt Austria: In 1993, AgrarMarkt Austria (AMA) was founded with a dual purpose—to execute the agricultural market regulations and to carry out agricultural marketing. Furthermore, AMA is also responsible for the payment of premiums and subsidies.

Being a market organisation and intervention body, AMA is a corporation under public law and administers public funds. However, legislation also provides for AMA's task to enhance the marketing of domestic foods which is financed through marketing contributions. This task is carried out by a subsidiary of AMA, the Agrarmarkt Austria-Marketing GmBH. It develops marketing and advertising strategies for Austrian agricultural products in Austria and abroad and at the same time takes quality-enhancing measures like the "AMAGütezeichen" (AMA quality label).

Austrian Agency for Health and Food Safety (AGES): By order of the Republic of Austria, the Austrian Agency for Health and Food Safety, carries out diverse tasks related to food safety. [13] It inspects and issues appraisals in accordance with the Austrian Food Act and conducts investigations in the field of veterinary medicine and works to fight and prevent infectious diseases in humans. Federal institutes and federal offices working in the fields of food and feed control and inspection, bacteriology and serology, veterinary medicine and agriculture were merged under the Austrian Agency for Health and Food Safety. Austria is the only European country where the federal competences from most different technical fields along the food chain are bundled in one enterprise.

Federal Environment Agency: The Federal Environment Agency contributes to the environmental assessment of agricultural activities and promotes the use of environmentally friendly agricultural practices in Austria. The key intelligence lies in agro-environmental indicators for assessing relations between agriculture and environment, especially in the assessment of agricultural nutrient balances at farm level, regional level and national level, as well as in evaluation projects concerning effects of agri-environmental measures on biodiversity and landscape. They have also been working in the field of organic farming and quality of compost and slurry from biogas plants. Another important task is analyzing the regional and territorial development of rural and mountain areas, national emission projections for agriculture and assessments of emissions from land use, land use change and forestry. [14] Above all, it also contributes to the implementation of the national climate strategy.

Position of Austria with Regard to International Treaties

Convention on Biological Diversity (Rio Convention): Austria has been a member of the United Nations for a considerably long time. Austria is bound to follow various conventions and treaties. One such major convention which Austria follows is the Rio Convention (1993). The Convention on Biological Diversity (CBD), known informally as the Biodiversity Convention, is an international legally binding treaty. The Convention has three main goals:

- Conservation of biological diversity (or biodiversity).
- Sustainable use of its components.
- Fair and equitable sharing of benefits arising from genetic resources.

The Austrian Foreign Ministry has revealed some of the policies the country follows, which are under the guidelines of the Rio Convention. International environmental and sustainability policies promote environmental protection and sustainable development around the globe. International agreements define standards and targets for conserving nature and natural resources, which are subsequently discussed, reviewed and further developed at international conferences. The United Nations Conference on Environment and Development (Earth Summit) held in Rio de Janeiro (Brazil) in 1992 was one of the most important international conferences on environment of the last few decades. Many solutions and agendas were the result of this conference. One such agenda is the 'Agenda 21'.

Agenda 21: Sustainable development, commonly defined as development that 'meets the needs of the present without compromising the ability of future generations to meet their own needs' has since then developed into a central policy area. Ten years after the Rio Summit, the World Summit on Sustainable Development in Johannesburg (South Africa)—was specifically dedicated to this issue.

UN Conference on Sustainable Development: Sustainability is one of the overarching goals of the European Union. During Austria's EU Council Presidency, the Renewed EU Sustainable Development Strategy was adopted.

EU Sustainable Development Strategy: The Federal Ministry for European and International Affairs is involved in all ongoing developments in the field of international environmental and sustainability policy, and through its network of international representations makes available a valuable infrastructure in this field to other Austrian institutions, e.g. the Federal Ministry of Agriculture, Forestry, Environment and Water Management and the Austrian Development Agency.

Conclusion

The hypothesis of this research paper was to show that Austria has achieved high levels of food security along with achieving sustainable development through organic farming. More than 70 percent of all domestic farms and 90 percent of Austria's utilized agricultural area takes part in this programme. The intention to support the greening of the Austrian agriculture is recorded in national laws, special guidelines and a so called "advisor contract". The biggest measure is included in the Austrian Rural Development Programme—the Austrian Agro-environmental Programme (ÖPUL). The major reasons for the success of organic farming in Austria are trade chains, insurance schemes, plant-genetic resources, ecological awareness among consumers and subsidies for organic farmers.

Thus, Austria has combined high levels of food security with sustainable development.

Endnotes

1. "Land Area in Austria", *Trading Economics*, accessed on January 21, 2013, available at: http://www.tradingeconomics.com/austria/land-area-sq-km-wb-data.html.
2. "Company and Structure", Austrian Agency for Health and Food Safety, accessed on June 03, 2013, available at: http://www.ages.at/ages/en/ages-austrian-agency-for-health-and-food-safety.
3. "International Symposium on Nuclear and Related Techniques for Food Integrity, Traceability, Safety and Quantity", Agriculture Network Information Collaborative, accessed on June 03, 2013, available at: http://www.agnic.org/events/topics/foodsecurity?f percent5Bcountry percent5D percent5B percent5D=Austria.
4. "All Have a Right to Food", Agricultural Market Austria, accessed on December 21, 2012, available at: http://www.ama.at/Portal.Node/public?gentics.am=PCP&p.contenti

d=10007.35148.

5. "Biofuels and Food Security", OFID Pamphlet Series, accessed on May 26, 2013, available at: http://www.ofid.org/LinkClick.aspx?fileticket=O3FeeiHvu7U percent3D&tabid=109.
6. "Agricultural Transformations and Food Security", Food and Agriculture Organization, accessed on February 19, 2013, available at: http://www.foodsec.org/fileadmin/user_upload/eufao-fsi4dm/docs/Austria_1400_Bosc_Even.pdf.
7. "Food Defence", ISEKI Food Association, accessed on June 04, 2013, available at: https://www.iseki-food.net/node/3874.
8. "International Scientific Symposium on Food and Nutrition Security Information: From Valid Measurement to Effective Decision-making", Food and Agriculture Organization, accessed on March 17, 2013, available at: http://www.foodsec.org/fileadmin/user_upload/eufao-fsi4dm/docs/iss-abstract-book.pdf.
9. "Trade-off between Food Security, Climate Change Mitigation", The Meat Site, accessed on March 16, 2013, available at: http://www.themeatsite.com/meatnews/21898/tradeoff-between-food-security-climate-change-mitigation.
10. "Ethical Reflections: Why should the Fight against Global Hunger be one of the Top Priorities", *Caritas*, accessed on June 5, 2013, available at: http://www.caritas.org/includes/pdf/cardinalrodriguezcongresshunger2012.pdf.
11. "More Food for Fewer People?", The Poultry Site, accessed on June 15, 2013, available at: http://www.thepoultrysite.com/news/vars/country/at.
12. "Austrian Agency for Health and Food Safety", *Austrian Life Sciences*, accessed on June 14, 2013, available at: http://www.lifesciencesdirectory.at/index.php?file=show.php&ref=381&PHPSESSID=h3joihr95ino6m9vq5kcnvm5c6.
13. "Global Hunger and Food Security Initiative", US Department of State, accessed on January 14, 2013, available at: http://www.state.gov/s/globalfoodsecurity/129952.htm.
14. Bayer Crop Science and IFC, supported by Austria, to help small-scale Ukranian farmers increase agricultural productivity, Bayer

Crop Science, accessed on June 30, 2013, available at: http://www.cropscience.bayer.com/en/Media/Press-Releases/2013/Bayer-CropScience-IFC-supported-Austria-partner-small-scale-Ukrainian-farmers-increase-agricultural.aspx.

3

Brazil: Fome Zero (Zero Hunger) Programme

Anamika Ray

Introduction

The recent promulgation of the National Food Security Ordinance in India has seen the Opposition, and much of the nation, up in arms. This conflict, however, is only a microcosm for the larger domain of food politics, a domain which is now, more than ever before, in a state of flux. In countries on the higher end of the HDI ratings, the challenge with regard to food is not hunger, but obesity. The simple Indian notion of 'roti, kapda, makaan', as the only essentials for survival, has taken a complete U-turn with the demand for organic food on the rise. [1]

So now, consumers not only want food, they also want freshly-grown, scientifically-monitored food. Vagaries of the monsoons have led to a sharp incline in farmer suicides [2] and the use of harsh chemicals to enhance crop growth. Meanwhile, the possible amendment in the country's foreign direct investment policy on multi-brand retails threatens to drive local producers to bankruptcy.

In such volatile conditions, it becomes imperative for policy makers to delineate a reliable food security policy which will meet the needs of the population. This delineation has to be achieved in consonance with a thorough review of the existing policies and their effectiveness in nation-imposed restrictions. One could not find a better framework to review, than that of Brazil, which has one of the world's most remarkable food policies in place.

Brazil provides an extensive legislative framework for food and nutrition security, a result of a committed and concentrated political agenda. The crucial importance given to this field can be well assessed by the 2010 inclusion of the right to food as a social right in the country's constitution. [3] The object of this paper is to assess the Brazilian food security policy and prove that these achievements are the result of focused decision-making and extensive public participation.

Socio-economic Profile

Brazil, South America's largest country, is the sixth largest economy in the world. With a population of almost 200 million (2012), the country had an impressive GDP of around US$ 2 trillion (2012). Despite such prosperity, 21.4 percent (2009) of the Brazilian population, about 40 million people, lived in abject poverty. The large gap in income levels only exacerbates the matter.

Further, Brazil is the world's fourth-largest food exporter, and has been showing the fastest rate of food export growth as compared to the world's food producers. [4] The country, hence, obviously produces enough food to cater to the domestic and export requirements.

Even so, nearly a third of the Brazilian population is in a state of 'food insecurity', which means "consistent access to adequate food is limited by a lack of money and other resources at times during the year". [5]

Out of this, over 12 million are facing 'severe food insecurity' which, as opposed to the previous definition, means a consistent state of hunger.

As stated, Brazil produces enough to meet domestic demand at least. Hence, the problem lies not with the production, but with the accessibility. Since people do not earn enough, they don't have enough money to buy food. This is especially true in northern Brazil, as most of Brazil's food is grown in the central and southern regions. [6] Moreover, 60 percent of the country's food insecure population lives in the north. Such conditions do not bode well for uniform access to food.

Policy Framework to Support Food Security

SAN (Food and Nutritional Security): SAN, rather than being a policy, is the concept of food and nutrition security, as advanced by the Brazilian government. [7] The national directives and policies of SAN, as elaborated by an FAO report, are as follows:

1. To promote universal access to adequate food.
2. To structure fair archaeological and suitable systems for food production, extraction, processing and distribution.
3. To establish permanent processes of education and capacity training in food security and human right for adequate food.
4. To expand and coordinate food and nutrition security actions intended for the indigenous people and traditional communities.
5. To strengthen food and nutrition actions at all levels of health care, in articulation with the other food and nutrition security policies.
6. To promote food and nutrition sovereignty and security at the national level.
7. To promote access to water for human consumption and for the production of food.

The country's food security laws and policy initiatives are in pursuance of these objectives.

Fome Zero (Zero Hunger) Programme: Food security, or the lack of it, is a demon with many heads. It requires the participation and co-ordination of a large number of sectors and stakeholders. This imperative requirement is recognised and well-addressed by the Fome Zero policy of the Brazilian government.

The Fome Zero policy, meaning 'Zero Hunger', was initiated in 2003 under the aegis of the then-newly elected President LuizInácio Lula da Silva, amidst tremendous media hype. [8] It consists of 50 policy initiatives undertaken by the government, keeping in mind the prevalent Brazilian conditions. [9] The salient features of the policy are as follows.

Fome Zero's ambitious objective is not just to reduce food

insecurity, but to eliminate hunger altogether. It hopes to achieve this object by addressing four main issues plaguing the Brazilian situation: (i) uniformity in food access; (ii) unbridled support to small landholdings and family farms; (iii) generation of income to buy food resources; and (iv) coordination among distributors and middlemen.

The Fome Zero policy works under three main heads:

- *Implementation of Food Policies*: The Special Ministry of Food Security and Hunger Combat (MESA) is responsible for implementing structural, special and local policies.
- *Participatory Food and Nutritional Security Policy-Making*: The CONSEA, or the National Food and Nutritional Security Council guides the President regarding policy initiatives and civil society participation in the food security mechanism.
- *Solidarity against Hunger*: This is a major policy objective of the Fome Zero policy, and a national movement too. It includes the participation of civil society and the government sector.

The Fome Zero policy, while rather vast in its scope, has certain flagship programs, which have resulted in its phenomenal success. These are:

- **BolsaFamilia:** This is world's largest conditional cash transfer scheme, encompassing no less than 12 million of the nation's poorest. The conditions imposed, such as 85 percent attendance in school by the beneficiaries' children who are under 14, and the provision of proper vaccination and nutrition to the wards, achieve more than one objective. Not only does the scheme ensure that the citizenry has financial resources to procure food, it also ensures that the population is literate and healthy.
- **Alimentação Escolar:** The Alimentação Escolar, or the school meal programme, is similar to the Anganwadi scheme in India. Mid-day meals are provided to the children who attend school. In order to better the management of procurement and distribution of school

meals, about half of the 5,500 municipalities in Brazil have established School Feeding Communities or the CAEs. [10] These communities consist of parents, teachers and local officials. This move has resulted in an unprecedented improvement in the quality of the mid-day meals, a far cry from the mid-day meals in India, which once resulted in the death of 23 children in Bihar.

This programme was sanctioned as the National Schools Meal Programme (PNAE) in 2009.

CONSEA (National Food and Nutrition Security Council): The CONSEA is a consulting body formed in 2003 which advised the President on issues relating to food security and nutrition procurement. The body was envisaged as a bridge between the government and the civil society. Hence, the body consists of 57 counsellors (2012-2013), out of which, two-thirds are civil society representatives and one-third are State Ministers and Central Government representatives.

While usual public-government partnerships are doomed to failure, the CONSEA has proposed a number of crucial policy initiatives since its creation. These include an increase in the budget allotted for the school meal program. Upon CONSEA's recommendation, the Lula government allotted 14 percent of the nation's GDP to the programme, effectively allotting $820 million to the project in 2006. The creation of the Food Acquisition Programme (PAA), which has been discussed later, was also the result of the CONSEA's recommendation.

However, the body's magnum opus is said to be its role in the Brazil Congress passing the National Law on Food and Nutrition Security (LOSAN) in 2006, which established the National System for Food and Nutrition Security (SISAN). LOSAN also made CONSEA a permanent national institution with a mandatory role in the development of the SISAN, thereby empowering CONSEA.

CAISAN (Chamber on Food and Nutrition Security): The CAISAN is a body very similar to the CONSEA. While

CONSEA has the ear of the President, the CAISAN has the ear of the Minister for Social Development and Fight against Hunger (MDS). Hence, when CONSEA needs to get the government to implement the policies it recommends, it approaches the CAISAN.

Apart from implementing the CONSEA's policy recommendations, the CAISAN also has a duty to monitor the consequences of such policies. [11] Also, since the CAISAN is composed on senior government officials, and it is popular with the masses, it wields considerable power. Hence, irrespective of the government in power, and the authority of such government to challenge the CAISAN's activities, the decisions of the CAISAN are rarely questioned. This ensures that the nation's commitment to its food security directive remains uninterrupted. Apart from those mentioned, the CAISAN's duties [12] are:

- To elaborate, from the directives originated from the CONSEA, the National Policy and Plan of Food and Nutrition Security, pointing out directives, goals, sources of funds and follow up instruments, monitoring and evaluation of its implementation.
- To coordinate the execution of the policy and the plan.
- To articulate policies and plans from the state and federal district entities.

SISAN (National System for Food and Nutrition Security): The SISAN is a system which aims to integrate food security policies in Brazil with a special emphasis on civil society participation. It primarily promotes the evaluation and monitoring of food security initiatives in the country. [13] It has also established food security as a matter of public policy. [14] Hence, the state is now liable to provide its citizens with cheap, good quality food.

PNSAN (National Food and Nutrition Security Policy): The LOSAN mentioned earlier, also determined the formulation of the PNSAN, a national policy which involves all relevant stakeholders. Additionally, the 2010 decree establishing the PNSAN was the product of combined efforts by the Inter-Ministerial Chamber on Food and Nutritional Security (CAISAN), the National Council on Food and Nutritional Security (CONSEA), and the National Conferences on Food and Nutritional Security (CNSAN).

PNSAN's specific objectives are to:

- Identify, analyse, disseminate and act on the factors that influence food and nutritional insecurity in Brazil.
- Link the programmes and actions of various sectors to respect, protect, promote and provide the human right to adequate food, considering the variety of social, cultural, environmental, ethnic-racial, equity of gender and sexual orientation, as well as provide tools for its accountability.
- Promote sustainable agro-ecological systems for food production and distribution that respect biodiversity and strengthen family agriculture, indigenous people and traditional communities, and that ensure consumption and access to adequate and healthy food, respecting the diversity of national food culture.
- Include respect for food sovereignty and the guarantee of the human right to adequate food, including access to water, as a state policy, and to promote them in international negotiations and cooperation.

PNSAN's important contribution is to engrave food security as a state policy, much like the SISAN, such that the continuation of the Fome Zero programme by subsequent governments has no bearing on the state's liability in the field of food security.

PAA (Food Acquisition Programme): This programme was established in 2003 (decreed in 2008) in pursuance of the CONSEA's objective to promote small landholdings and family farming. In order to provide food supplies to food insecure regions, the programme enforces the procurement of such food supplies directly from family farmers. [15] Such massive acquisitions from small domestic producers not only promotes and encourages family farms, it also creates transactions between the earlier-marginalised family farms and the marginalized sections of the population, which is most in need of government aid.

Since the programme's establishment in 2003 and until its decree in 2008, around 3 million tonnes of food have been acquired through the PAA programme, and distributed by around 25,000 organisations to feed 15 million people, resulting in a cost of about US$ 2 billion to the national exchequer.

Legal Framework

The various laws enacted [16, 17] with regard to food security, in chronological order, are as follows:

1. Organic Law on Health (1990), which provides for the united health system.
2. Organic Law on Assistance (1993) which deals with the policy of social security and orients the building of the unified system of social assistance.
3. National Policy of Food and Nutrition (1999) which established the policy context of food security.
4. Law on Basic Income and Citizenship (2004) which established the minimum basic income needed to every person residing in the country to live with dignity, including feeding.
5. Law on Food and Nutrition Security (LOSAN) (2006) which established food security as a social right and formulated the SISAN (National System for Food and Nutrition Security) and the PNSAN (National Food and Nutrition Security Policy).
6. Law on Family Farming (2006) which establishes the parameters for the inclusion of farmers and the differentiated directives and policies for the sectors.
7. Law on Schools Meal Programme (PNAE) (2009) which included high school students, and youth and adult education programmes within the purview of the Alimentação Escolar.
8. Law on School Feeding (2009) which mandated that 30 percent of the food for schools must be acquired from family farms.

9. Law on Technical Assistance and Rural Extension (PNATER) (2010) which formulated the logistical aspects of the distribution of food.
10. Law on the Food and Nutrition Security Policy (PNSAN) (2010) which integrated the sectors involved in food security.

Bio-Fuels, Climate Change and Food Security

With the looming crisis of climate change, and the very real possibility of the exhaustion of conventional sources of energy, concepts such as sustainable development and alternative sources of energy have come to the fore. It has been stated that the growing sugarcane production business is resulting in excessive deforestation of the Amazon and an emission of greenhouse gases, in addition to reduced arable land for the production of essential produce such as rice, beans and maize.

Such issues have been taken up by the CONSEA, which has been urging the Brazilian government to invest in renewable agro-technology. The government has taken heed and is presently working on the development of such technology. As a result of proactive steps, Brazil became the first consumer of agro-chemicals, and the second largest producer of genetically-modified organisms (GMOs) in the world.

Meanwhile, in India, the Ninth Five Year Plan had allocated meagre amounts to the development of clean and green fertilizers and pesticides. However, the Tenth Five Year Plan expanded the scope of green technology in India to include international co-operation and the setting of international standards for organic produce. ₹ 100 crore were allotted for the purpose. An initiative called the 'National Project on Development and Use of Bio-Fertilizers' was also commenced, the objectives of which, according to an FAO report, are:

1. Production and distribution of bio-fertilizers.
2. Developing standards for different bio-fertilizers and quality control.

3. Releasing of grants for setting up bio-fertilizer units.
4. Training and publicity.

Further, the Agricultural and Processed Food Products Export Development Authority (APEDA) has been created under the aegis of the Ministry of Commerce and Industry, Government of India. This agency investigates into accreditation of organic products and their suitability as exports on the basis of how green the technology behind their production is. These measures have led to a remarkable increase in the domestic demand for organic food.

Civil Society in the Promotion of Food Security

The role of civil society organisations in world affairs cannot be emphasized upon enough. Governance, with all its connotations, is no longer fettered in the hands of the government. It goes above and beyond the government into the hands of the common man, who makes his own policy decisions, thereby shaping a nation's policy decisions. The infraction of the media into every aspect of our hitherto private lives has no small part to play in this. We see, or read of, anything that affects our interests; we want to be a part of the debate. This trait extends to matters of food security just as much as any other.

In Brazil, such involvement finds reflection in civilian representation at the municipal level. The erstwhile-Lula government specifically provided for civil society participation by making it mandatory for Schools Feeding Communities (or the CAEs, as mentioned earlier), to be formed before the government funds the School Meals Programme in question. This ensures that parents and local councilmen have a monetary incentive to be active members and monitor the efficient allocation and distribution of the government grants.

However, mere provision for civil society participation does not necessarily ensure it. A study of the momentum of the CAEs found that more than 20 percent of them had been formed only for purposes of legal compliance, with no active participation whatsoever. These were the results despite community participation being deemed the crucial catalyst for the success of the scheme.

However, lethargy was not the only reason for the inactivity. Some of the resources required to ensure the smooth functioning of the scheme simply were not available to the civil society. For example, the shortage of manpower of any aptitude, let alone skilled manpower, was a major dampener for civic spirit. It has been observed, that 'the issue of training of non-governmental councillors is considered, by the councillors themselves, to be one of the main obstacles to effective participation by civil society on the councils'. However, despite such shortcomings, as a whole, civic participation has been on the rise in Brazil and the CAEs are almost ubiquitous.

Characteristics of Brazil's Food Security Policy

Involvement of Multiple Sectors and Social Participation: A multi-dimensional approach is implicit in the implementation of food security policies in Brazil. [18] Such inter-sectoral involvement extends to individuals, social organisations, international allies and the Brazilian government. This approach only stands enhanced with the programme's dedication to civil society participation and the exaltedness of the common man as the main stockholder-cum-beneficiary of the programme.

Integration of Myriad Frameworks: The SAN in Brazil encompasses a gamut of organisations. The co-ordination between such organisations, such as the CONSEA and the CAISAN is a major determinant of the success of the nation's food security agenda. Other relevant groups include the Ministry of Agriculture, Livestock and Supply (MAPA), Ministry of Social Development and Fight Against Hunger (MDS), Program of Food Acquisition (PAA), National School Meal Program (PNAE), National Food and Nutrition Security Policy (PNSAN), and the National System for Food and Nutrition Security (SISAN). So far, due to their mutual dependence, these organisations have synchronised their initiatives rather remarkably.

Budgeting and Monitoring: The SAN's monetary policy has been bifurcated under two heads. One is the costs incurred in the maintenance of the hierarchy of the food security mechanism in the country. This mainly includes bureaucratic expenses, such as maintaining ministries and national organisations. The other is the cost of financing the government's initiatives.

The monitoring of the financing has been taken up by the CONSEA, and has been delegated to the SISAN. This prevents unnecessary out-flows from the government grants.

In recent years, the Brazilian government has concentrated efforts to ensure that civil society participation is not dependent on how resourceful and co-operative the local government is. True to former President Lula's commitment to social intervention, the present Rousseff government is promoting the idea of civic participation as an independent sector of food security, one that is crucial to the scheme. In this pursuit, not only has the right to food been adopted as an enforceable social right in the country's constitution, legal instruments are also being drafted to make the issue of food security a matter of human rights. Through such instruments, the government hopes to initiate social mobilization and generate public opinion on the issue.

As regards the integration between frameworks, as mentioned earlier, much progress has been seen on this front. According to the PNDS, 2006, Brazil has significantly reduced malnutrition. The percentage of underweight children below 5 years has reduced from 4.2 in 1996 to 1.5 in 2006. Further, food inaccessibility declined from 34.9 percent in 2004 to 30.2 percent in 2009, while poverty fell from 25.6 in 1990 to 4.8 in 2008. [19]

Brazil on the International Scene

The CONSEA has proposed the following guidelines [20] for international participation by the CONSEA and the

Brazilian government:

- Universality and equity in the access to adequate food.
- Social participation in inter-sectoral policies and transparency.
- Respect given to the food sovereignty, and assurance of the human right to adequate food and its claim.
- Countryside and family farming as essential components in the building of food and nutrition sovereignty and security.
- Solidarity, complementarily and cooperation among countries and social actors.

International Treaties: Accordingly, the Brazilian government has framed a foreign policy wherein it co-ordinates with its international allies in the war against hunger. Hence, apart from generally stressing on the importance of international co-operation for food security at various UN Summits, in 2002, it signed the International Treaty on Plant Genetic Resources for Food and Agriculture, at the World Food Summit in Rome. [21] The Treaty ensures the rights of farmers and creates a system for cross-border trade in genetic strains of important crops and forages. It was also a participant in the 2008 United Nations Task Force on the Global Food Crisis, and a member of the 2008 Global Partnership on Food and Agriculture, in Rome. [22]

Humanitarian Assistance: Since the country now has one of the world's most successful food security programmes, it has diverted some of its resources to helping other nations who are not as fortunate. Some state that its motives are hardly that philanthropic, and that Brazil hopes to gain geo-political prominence by humanitarian contributions. Either way, an Inter-Ministerial Working Group on International Humanitarian Assistance was formed in 2006, consisting of 15 government ministries under the general control of the Ministry of Foreign Relations. The Working Group mainly supervises the country's humanitarian contributions and drafts laws to make such contributions legal.

Brazil's humanitarian aid includes its participation in the

World Food Program, the Organization of American States and the 'White Helmets' initiative started by Argentina. It has also vowed to aid in the reconstruction of Lebanon and occupied Palestinian territories, and donated food, medicines etc. to the victims of floods in Guyana, Ecuador and Suriname.

South-South Co-operation: Several Latin American and African countries face severe problems with regard to ensuring food security. Venezuela, for example, is unable to fund food subsidies with domestic production. As a result, it uses earnings from petroleum export to finance its food security initiatives. Peru, on the other hand, faces an excess of illegal crop production. The government is now trying to incentivize these producers to cultivate bio-fuel crops. Suriname's civil struggle ruined most of its agricultural landholdings, due to which the government is seeking expertise in crop bio-technology to rehabilitate the sector. Uruguay and a few other Latin American countries have also invited international investment in their respective agricultural sectors. Brazil, being a major player in the region's food security, closely co-ordinates with these countries to ensure food security in South America.

Road Ahead: Main Challenges

In 2003, when the then-newly elected President LuizInácio Lula da Silva claimed that the Fome Zero programme would ensure three square meals a day to every person in Brazil, sceptics were abound. However, in the years since, the implementation of the programme has resulted in many converts. The movement has been especially popular because of its targeted beneficiaries. Those that lived on the fringes of the society were the main profiteers from the scheme. After Lula's tenure, the new President, Dilma Rousseff has kept up with the momentum of Fome Zero. This has raised hopes, that on the food security front, she will be as committed as her predecessor.

Rousseff, however, faces many challenges during her tenure. The CONSEA has delineated ten possible challenges for Brazil in its 2009 report. According to an Oxfam International case study, these delineations include the expansion of the right to food in the national and international context. In this pursuit, the right to food was included in the country's constitution as a social right. Further, the policy must ensure that more of the country's unorganised population is brought within the purview of the scheme.

Further, massive urbanisation has brought its own novel challenges. Now, the problems of obesity and overweight must also be tackled by the government. Among the children under 5 years, incidence of overweight increased from 6.4 percent to 9.7 percent during the period between 2003 and 2009. While obesity is still usually found in adults, it is a symptom of the much larger issue of the lack of awareness about food. Hence, the PNSAN has commenced new awareness programmes to inform communities about balanced diets and to promote nutritious food.

The climate change scare is also a very real one for Brazil's farmers, and the government must take measures to ward off these concerns. Uniformity in the government's implementation of the scheme at a local level would further promote the programme's objectives. Presently, such uniformity eludes the government, particularly in the north-eastern regions of Brazil, due to poor co-ordination.

Despite such major challenges, the Brazilian food security scheme is still touted as one of the best in the world, with many countries rushing to emulate its successes. The Brazilian government would do well to address the above glitches at the earliest to ensure the pace of progress of the food security sector.

The Indian Context

India and Brazil share a great many characteristics. Both are multi-party democracies, with flourishing, agrarian economics. While such similarities exist, there is a rather fundamental difference between the two. India's population is almost 50 times that of Brazil's. This means that to imitate Brazil's state of food security, for every policy that it implements, India has to implement policies taking an additional billion into consideration. This is no mean feat, especially since this population explosion has a major role to play in the sizes of farmlands.

India, with more than 53 percent of its population dependent on agriculture, necessarily has smaller farm sizes per capita. This small size has been blamed for the widespread farmer suicides in the country. However, many have decried the authenticity of such a statement. According to these sceptics, [23] India's domestic and export requirements can be more than met by the small landholdings. It is the productivity of the said land holdings which are suspect.

Brazil has an efficient mechanism in place to tackle this problem. Brazil has small and large farms, which are clearly segregated on the basis of the demand that they cater to. The large farms produce for commercial exports, while the small farms fuel domestic distribution. Two separate ministries regulate policies for commercial and domestic production; the Ministry of Agriculture, Livestock and Food Supply (MAPA) for commercial agriculture and the Ministry of Agricultural Development (MDA), which assists family farms. The budget for agriculture is also divided between these two ministries.

This bifurcation was supported by swift policy-making during changes in demographics. When the population statistics of Brazil started showing a rapid increase in the urban population, as was seen in India, the Brazilian Government immediately increased the public resources allotted for food security. This led to an expansion in the agro-market, 'both in terms of direct procurement and provision of resources to the beneficiaries'.

Due to such policies, Brazil, a country which was still a net importer till the 1970s, had a $2390 million trade surplus in 2013, of which 38 percent was through agricultural exports. In fact, agriculture has become the backbone of country's stability in terms of macroeconomic aggregates by virtue of an increased flow of funds in the market and the agricultural sector's contribution to the development of alternate fuels such as bioethanol. Further, despite occupying only 25 percent of the total agricultural land available, family farming is responsible for 70 percent of domestic production and the sector generates 77 percent of the country's rural workforce.

The Zero Hunger programme can be likened to the National Food Security Act, 2013 in India. As in India, food products are procured from domestic producers and supplied to people below the poverty line on a monthly basis. Further, parents are incentivised to send their children to school by setting it as a condition to receiving cash through the cash transfer scheme. Such measures are replicated in the Anganwadi (mid-day meal) scheme in India. Brazil also addresses maternal health though special programmes for pregnant and lactating mothers, and so does India.

However, in India, the public distribution system (PDS) is rather flawed. The government of the country has enough stockpiles of food to meet food security needs, but that stockpile hardly ever reaches the targeted consumer. [24] Food stocks rot in warehouses, while millions suffocate hunger pangs. Corruption among the middlemen is one of the reasons for this flawed distribution. Large-scale misappropriation of the resources is not uncommon. Another reason is distribution based on below poverty line (BPL) and above poverty line (APL) status. In a country like India, where such a massive population is employed in unorganised sectors, accurate identification of beneficiaries according to income is a near impossible task. Hence, most people who need the Government's aid most desperately, are usually not the ones who receive it.

Brazil's solution to this problem is a novel one. Instead of buying food and distributing it to the poor, the Government, under the Bolsa Familia scheme, just gives money to the poor. The coverage of the scheme since 2004 has increased to 12 million, and inequality has been reduced by 17 percent—figures unprecedented in the history of the developing world. India has enacted a similar scheme, called the Mahatma

Gandhi National Rural Employment Guarantee Act (MGNREGA), but the Brazilian programme is much more efficient in its implementation.

Further, Brazil has a virtually flawless mechanism in place to bring arable land into agricultural use, and it keeps introducing new land reforms which benefit the farmer population immensely. India desperately needs a similar scheme.

Endnotes

1. "Indian Organic Food Market Analysis", RNCOS Industry Research Solutions, accessed on March 14, 2013, available at: http://www.rncos.com/Report/IM365.htm.
2. "Farmers' Suicide Rates Soar Above the Rest", *The Hindu*, accessed on May 23, 2013, available at: http://www.thehindu.com/opinion/columns/sainath/farmers-suicide-rates-soar-above-the-rest/article4725101.ece.
3. "Brazil: Right to Food Now a Constitutional Right", Olivier De Schutter, United Nations Special Rapporteur on the Right to Food, accessed on March 22, 2012, available at: http://www.srfood.org/index.php/en/component/content/article/611-brazil-right-to-food-now-a-constitutional-right.
4. "Brazil Has Fastest Food Export Growth Rate," The Poultry Site, accessed on May 23, 2013, available at: http://www.thepoultrysite.com/poultrynews/23526/brazil-has-fastest-food-export-growth-rate.
5. "What is Food Insecurity?", Texas Food Bank Network, accessed on December 11, 2013, available at: http://tfbn.org/food-insecurity.
6. "Fighting Hunger in Brazil: Much Achieved, More to Do", Oxfam International, accessed on June 14, 2013, available at: http://www.oxfam.org/sites/www.oxfam.org/files/cs-fighting-hunger-brazil-090611-en.pdf.
7. "Building up the National Policy and System for Food and Nutrition Security: The Brazilian Experience", Food and Agriculture Organisation, accessed on February 02, 2013, available at: http://www2.planalto.gov.br/consea/biblioteca/publicacoes/copy_of_versao-em-ingles.
8. "Brazil's Lula Promises Change", The BBC News Corporation,

accessed on June 13, 2013, available at: http://news.bbc.co.uk/2/hi/americas/2621821.stm.

9. "Fighting Hunger in Brazil: Much Achieved, More to Do", Oxfam International, accessed on June 14, 2013, available at: http://www.oxfam.org/sites/www.oxfam.org/files/cs-fighting-hunger-brazil-090611-en.pdf.
10. "The Local Food Revolution in Brazil's Schools", Al Jazeera, accessed on June 4, 2013, available at: http://www.aljazeera.com/indepth/opinion/2013/02/201322853527633979.html.
11. "Brazil: How to Abolish Malnutrition", World Public Health and Nutrition Organisation, accessed on February 4, 2013, available at: http://www.wphna.org/2011_dec_hp2_consea.htm.
12. "Building up the National Policy and System for Food and Nutrition Security: The Brazilian Experience", Food and Agriculture Organisation, accessed on February 2, 2013, available at: http://www2.planalto.gov.br/consea/biblioteca/publicacoes/copy_of_versao-em-ingles.
13. "National Food and Nutrition Security System: SISAN", SlideShare, accessed on January 6, 2013, available at: http://www.slideshare.net/WFPCentre/national-food-and-nutrition-security-system-sisan.
14. "Implementing the Human Right to Food in Brazil", Hunger Notes, accessed on December 2, 2012, available at: http://www.worldhunger.org/articles/08/hrf/ananias.htm.
15. Laura Reynolds, "Feeding Mouths and Empowering Communities in Brazil", *Worldwatch Blogs*, March 10, 2012, available at: http://blogs.worldwatch.org/feeding-mouths-and-empowering-communities-in-brazil.
16. "Food Security Policy Context in Brazil", International Policy Centre for Inclusive Growth, accessed on May 5, 2013, available at: http://www.ipc-undp.org/pub/IPCCountryStudy22.pdf.
17. "Building up the National Policy and System for Food and Nutrition Security: The Brazilian Experience", Food and Agriculture Organisation, accessed on February 2, 2013, available at:

http://www2.planalto.gov.br/consea/biblioteca/publicacoes/copy_of_versao-em-ingles.

18. "Building up the National Policy and System for Food and Nutrition Security: The Brazilian Experience", Food and Agriculture Organisation, accessed on February 2, 2013, available at: http://www2.planalto.gov.br/consea/biblioteca/publicacoes/copy_of_versao-em-ingles.
19. "The Implementation of Brazil's Food Security Policies", Press Room, accessed on June 5, 2013, available at: http://pressroom.ipc-undp.org/the-food-security-policy-context-in-brazil/.
20. "Building up the National Policy and System for Food and Nutrition Security: The Brazilian Experience", Food and Agriculture Organisation, accessed on February 2, 2013, available at: http://www2.planalto.gov.br/consea/biblioteca/publicacoes/copy_of_versao-em-ingles.
21. "56 Countries Sign International Treaty Crucial to Food Security", Food and Agriculture Organisation, accessed on June 4, 2013, available at: http://www.fao.org/worldfoodsummit/english/newsroom/news/6460-en.html.
22. "Building up the National Policy and System for Food and Nutrition Security: The Brazilian Experience", Food and Agriculture Organisation, accessed on February 2, 2013, available at: http://www2.planalto.gov.br/consea/biblioteca/publicacoes/copy_of_versao-em-ingles.
23. "Food Security: Can India Learn from Brazil?", *The Financial Express*, accessed on January 18, 2013, available at: http://www.financialexpress.com/news/food-security-can-india-learn-from-brazil-/556083/0.
24. "A Further Attack on the PDS", *Frontline*, accessed on October 19, 2012, available at: http://www.frontline.in/navigation/?type=static&page=flonnet&rdurl=fl1802/18020280.htm.

4

Cuba: National Programme of Action for Nutrition

Aakanksha Mishra and Amrita Mohan

Socio-economic Profile

Cuba with a population of 11,254,700 is an archipelago island between the Caribbean Sea and the North Atlantic Ocean. Out of a total land area of 109,820 sq. km., 27.63 percent constitutes variable land, used for cultivating crops like wheat, rice and sugar and 6.54 percent for crops like citrus, coffee and rubber.

Cuba is a long but relatively narrow island. About two-thirds of its land surface is covered with fertile plains suitable for cultivation; three principal, heavily forested mountain ranges cover the rest of the country. In addition to arable land, Cuba's natural resource include chromium, cobalt, copper, iron ore, manganese, petroleum, salt silica, timber, natural gas and has world's second largest reserves of nickel.

Two-thirds of Cuba, or about 6,686,700 hectares, is covered with fertile plains suitable for cultivation; at least 3,701,400 hectares, and as much as 60 percent of the total arable land, is cultivated for agriculture. Agriculture and fisheries accounted for 5.2 percent of the gross domestic product (GDP) in 2006.

The health profile of the Cuban population is more like that of a developed country than a developing one, with low infant mortality, low fertility, low rates of infectious disease, and high cancer and cardiovascular disease rates. Despite Cuba's relatively meagre resources, the primary health care system is still able to provide almost universal coverage and to ensure the continuance of low mortality among those less than 65 years of age even in the face of rising health threats.

Cuba has a state-controlled economy since Fidel Castro seized power. Since he lost his power in the 1990s following the abrupt withdrawal of Soviet funding, the Cuban economy has been recovering slowly and remains feeble.

The sugar industry, the economic mainstay industry, is on decline, and the country now relies more on the nickel and tourism industries, as well as a barter arrangement with Venezuela under which Cuba supplies doctors and teachers in exchange for crude oil and petroleum products at a discounted rate. In the absence of large amounts of capital and access to markets and in the face of continued US trade sanctions, Cuba's economic situation was in shambles.

During 2005, however, the surge in the availability of foreign exchange, as a result of new financing from China, trade agreements with Venezuela, and the continued strong growth of international tourism—enabled the government to increase state investment in projects such as repairing the critically dilapidated infrastructure and to increase wages and benefits.

Food Security and Legislative Policies

Background: The collapse of USSR spelled over the chemical and machinery intensive model of agricultural production of Cuba. Cuba experienced an abysmal fall in food production as well as food imports. The crisis further deteriorated by the tightening of US embargo with the passage of Cuban Democracy Act, 1992 and the Helms Burton Act, 1996. Consequently, Cuba lost its major markets and primary source of foreign assistance. There was energy crisis due to the loss of cheap soviet oil. In the absence of substantial subsidies, Cuba felt the full consequences of 40 years of resource misallocation and heavily subsidized, inefficient production.

There was a huge fall in the economic output by one-third, severe shortages in all sectors, fall in foreign trade by about 73 percent, were some of the economic results due to the fall of USSR. Agriculture production fell by 54 percent, exports and imports in agricultural products fell by more than a half and one-third respectively. The crisis was so severe that the average calorie, protein and vitamin intake of the Cuban population in 1993 was 30 percent lower than the levels before 1989. [1] The collapse of the Soviet Union in 1990, led to a period of crisis in the Cuban economy known as the "Special Period in Peacetime".

Cuba heavily depended on the Soviet Union and the Council for Mutual Economic Assistance (CEMA) for over 80 percent of its foreign trade and also received substantial subsidies (preferential pricing for Cuba's exports) from the Soviet Union. There was a steep dip in the level of trade of Soviet Union with Cuba, fall in soviet oil deliveries and termination of soviet subsidies. [2] There were shortages in food, fuel, fertilizer, chemicals, spare parts, and other inputs needed for agricultural and industrial production.

Domestic food production was low because of fall in food imports from the Soviet Union. Average calorie, protein, and vitamin intake dropped by 30 percent from the levels achieved during the 1980s, and the first signs of malnutrition appeared. Factory closures, petroleum driven transportation coming to a standstill, lack of fuel and essential spare parts resulting in grounding of tractors, unavailability of agrochemicals etc. were some of the reasons for causing widespread crisis in Cuba.

To make matters worse, the US tightened its embargo. It banned ships that had been to Cuba from docking in the US. Simultaneously, it clamped several conditions on Russia and the newly independent states as they scrambled for US aid: one of these was to end all trade with Cuba. Food security had shown itself to be the 'Achilles heel' of the revolution. [3] To combat this, the Cuban government introduced significant changes in the organisation of agricultural production, agricultural markets and promoted organic and semi-organic farming techniques. [4] Rather than roll over and die, a new revolution began to foment in Cuba, an organic one. The main elements in this reorganisation are as below.

Cuban National Programme of Action for Nutrition, 1994: Food import substitution was aimed at changing production and consumption patterns to cover Cubans' food requirements without strategic imports from the Soviet Bloc. [5] In 1992, encouraged by the commitments that the International Nutrition Conference made in Rome, the Cuban government introduced the National Programme of Action for Nutrition (PNAN).

This programme aimed to shield the consequences of the crisis by advocating civil participation in agriculture to improve their own nutritional benefit. To deal with the precarious food shortage situation, the Cuban Action Program of Action for Nutrition (PNAN) was instituted. The objectives were to:

- Strengthen agrarian policy through widespread decentralization of land holdings and management, diversification of agricultural production and the transformation of land tenure of State lands.
- Encourage participation of the population in agricultural activities for their own nutritional improvement.
- Encourage the creation of autoconsumos or on-site farms/gardens to supply to dining halls of residential and educational establishments.
- Promote sustainable development compatible with the environment.
- Reduce post-harvest losses through improved methods, such as direct sale of food from producers to consumers in the cities (e.g. urban agriculture).
- Incorporate nutritional objectives in programs and plans of agricultural development.

Many of these measures taken by the State were key factors in the proliferation of sustainable Cuban agriculture.

Conversion of State Farms to Co-operatives:

On September 20, 1993, the Council of State enacted Decree Law No. 142 by establishing Basic Units of Cooperative Production (UBPC) on previous state farms to eliminate the state monopoly on 75 percent of Cuba's agricultural lands.

The Cuban Council of State enacted Decree Law No. 142, which converted the state farms into new units of agricultural production—the Unidades Básicas de Producción Cooperativa or the Basic Units of Cooperative Production. Although the land remained in state hands, it was given in usufruct to the tillers in the newly created cooperatives for an indefinite period of time. The other was the distribution of land in usufruct to thousands of small producers, state workers and pensioners. Decree Law No. 142 (1988) accordingly authorised the distribution in usufruct of small, dispersed parcels of land that could not be incorporated into UBPCs and also idle lands formerly used to farm tobacco.

The legislation aimed at replacing state farms with smaller, self-managing cooperatives in order to increase productivity by rewarding the UBPC members for their performance in meeting the production goals. Also the smaller farms were encouraged to adopt sustainable farming practices. [6] The families of the eastern province of Ciego De Aliva were given more than 268 hectare of idle land interested in growing tobacco in free usufruct and they were also given the right to self-consumption activities. Under this system, each family got on an average 4.5 hectare to cultivate non-traditional export crops like cacao, coffee, flowers or tropical fruits; most of them produced in a sustainable way.

Distribution of State Land in Usufruct to Small Producers: Pursuant to Resolution No. 356/93, the Ministry of Agriculture authorized the distribution in usufruct of small parcels of idle state land for self-provisioning. [8] By the end of 1998, 12,900 hectares had been distributed to 52,500 individuals. 308 successive resolutions authorized the distribution of state lands in usufruct to private farmers for the cultivation of tobacco, coffee, and cocoa.

By the end of 1998, 105,576 hectares had been distributed for the cultivation of these crops to just under 20,000 private farmers. The National Association of Small Farmers (ANAP) claimed that its membership increased by 35,000 as a result of these reforms, and now included retirees, urban workers with rural backgrounds, and college-educated urban dwellers that chose to leave the towns and cities in order to earn a living off the land.

- 357/93—authorising distribution of idle state lands in usufruct for tobacco cultivation.
- 419/94—authorising distribution of idle state lands in usufruct for cultivation of coffee and cocoa.
- 223/95—in usufruct to small farmers with specific production commitments.

Opening Agricultural Markets: During the 1990s, Cuba increasingly liberalised access to inputs, markets, technology and rural funding. The most important measure adopted in this regard was the reopening of the free market of agricultural activities. On September 19, 1994, the Council of Ministers enacted Decree No. 191 by virtue of which there was the establishment of free agricultural markets where farmers and cooperatives could sell their surplus production, after fulfilling their commitments to the state, at prices dictated by supply and demand. In 1994, there was a law which introduced more flexibility in commercialisation and price systems, methods to attract hard currency to boost non-traditional crops and a slightly relaxed and redesigned price system was also introduced to promote incentives for farmers. Financial mechanisms available for agriculture were also decentralised to give greater autonomy to small farmers while reducing state involvement in subsidies and other sources of funding.

The purpose of this legislation was to establish Mercados Agropecuarios (agricultural markets) where farmers could sell their products at prices determined by the market forces of supply and demand. Farmers were given incentives to produce more food for domestic consumption.

In expanding the horizon for the access to food outside the rationing system, the agricultural markets played an important role. Prices and sales were high conducted solely in US dollars prior to the opening of the agricultural markets. Cubans who did not have access to the US currency were excluded from executing transactions in the black markets to supplement their basic food requirements.

The opening of the agricultural markets enabled Cubans to purchase food with pesos, and also lowered black market prices by eliminating the "risk premium" associated with illegal activity. The increased availability of food was important from the perspective of food security given the inability of the state's food distribution system to fulfil the population's needs.

The Decree Law No. 259 enacted in 2008 was done to distribute idle lands in usufruct contracts for a 10 year period, representing an additional inclination to landholding decentralisation. Two parallel measures were announced within the new decree.

Firstly, idle, state-owned land would be redistributed in usufruct to 'anyone who wants to produce' (especially individuals, cooperatives, small farmers and even some UBPCs) making specific mention of tobacco and coffee. Yet, 51 percent of the land was idle or insufficiently subjugated and a great amount of this land was covered with mar abú bushes. Though it required a lot of work, this measure could raise farm production.

Secondly, the Decree proposed the creation of agricultural delegations in all municipalities to 'decentralise decision-making, with the ability to take responsibility and use appropriate marketing techniques'. This will enable UBPC and small farmers to directly commercialise their products in nearby communities and reduce Acopio control over production and commercialisation.

The National Office of Statistics conducted a survey in 2007 which exposed the underutilisation of Cuba's agricultural potential as the area under cultivation in the country had shrunk by 16.8 percent (6,03,000 hectares) and idle land had grown by 32.1 percent (12,30,000 hectares). In July 2008, Law Decree No. 259 was passed by the Raul Castro government. This decree provided for granting landless people up to 13.42 hectares in usufruct for a period of 10 years initially. People who already owned or who previously leased some land were able to increase their holdings to just over 40 hectares.

The usufruct is non-transferable, and may not be sold to a third party—but if the holder is unable to work on the land for reasons of age or illness, he or she may propose a successor from among the people who have worked on the farm. Usufructs granted under the new law can be terminated if the land is abandoned or not worked for six months.

Food Distribution and Rationing in Cuba: The vast majority of Cuban families rely, for their food intake, on the Libreta de Abastecimiento distribution system, instated on March 12, 1962. Most of these products are distributed at the local bodega, and in the case of meat, poultry or fish, at the local carnicería. The amount of rations and frequency of the supplies are fixed by this system for each person as per the age and gender. The system establishes the ration each person is allowed to buy through the system, and the frequency of supplies. A special government office, the OFICODA, has been set up which distributes a booklet which contains the family nucleus and their dietary details. The products sold through this mechanism are subsidised by the Cuban government. A detailed set of laws are laid down to govern and penalise any abuse of this system.

The reasons for the introduction of a system of food rationing in revolutionary Cuba just three years after the revolution, can be found in a combination of two factors. The first factor was the rising demand for food because of increasing purchasing power. The second factor was decreasing food production as a result of the drastic changes taking place in farm ownership and organization. The supply and demand imbalance, combined with the start of the US financial embargo in 1962, prompted the new Cuban government to seek some means of ensuring adequate access to food for a highly expectant population. The Cuban government states that this method of distribution serves to ensure each citizen, a minimum intake of food, regardless of the person's social and economic status.

While the government fully well understands that the sanctioned quantity might not be sufficient in all cases, however it finds that such a system is unavoidable and distributes foreign aid in a just manner. Detractors question the fairness of this method as well as its purpose, and stress upon its deficiencies, such as a historical decrement of the delivery frequency and quantities of goods distributed. [9] It is severely criticised that this method creates profound economical differences within the Cuban people, dividing the country in half—those that can afford the higher prices of goods in convertible pesos or in the mercadolibre, and those that simply cannot.

The Cuban government passed a motion to discontinue the decade old system which was voted down by the National Congress. The government planned to include cooperatives into the state monopoly of food distribution. The Cuban government is facing huge deficit in its budget due to massive subsidisation of food products. One option is to eliminate rationing of direct additional funds to social security pensions and social assistance payments, thereby increasing the purchasing power of the elderly and targeting the most vulnerable groups. [10]

Another option would be to keep the libreta but refining the eligibility criteria, such that only those below a certain income level could receive subsidized food rations. This method would not endanger those marginalised Cubans who would be affected because of complete elimination of this system. Certain areas are inhabited by people with low incomes or nutrient deficiencies—these areas could use the system rather than implementing it throughout the country. A target specific approach should be adopted by the government to achieve a balance between fiscal security and food security.

Labour Reforms: To increase the efficiency of labour,

provisions for incentives to workers and farmers have been made along with reorganization of the work process. The concerted effort to establish fair socialist norms of distribution in the area of cooperative or collective production in agriculture is based on the principle—"pagopor los resultades finales" i.e. pay according to the final results—the more you produce, the more you get paid. The break-up of state farms has made individuals or small work teams completely responsible for production on a given piece of land, thus making it feasible to tie their incomes to the amount actually produced on that area.

The question of appropriate material incentives still remains largely unanswered. Beginning in 1994, the prices of food sold to the population, outside of the ration-book channel, were liberalized with the establishment of markets where all suppliers—private farms, cooperatives, and state farms—could sell their produce at the market price under the given supply and demand conditions. Prices paid for deliveries to the state were increased for selected products, such as milk, beans, coffee, and tobacco. Tax policy was also being used to stimulate food production and urban marketing, including tax exemptions for small farmers. Other material incentives include access to goods, like bicycles, work clothes, and shoes, and various other goods that are otherwise only available in dollar-only stores. In-kind incentives, such as better housing and use of rest and recreation facilities, are also used to stimulate production.

Technological Shift: Cut off from favourable trade agreements with the Soviet Union and its allies a decade ago, and unable to afford buying in the international market, Cuba has been forced to change from conventional farming practices to organic farming in the absence of petroleum and petroleum derivatives that it earlier imported from the Soviet Union. From pest control to fertilization to soil preparation, the emphasis on chemistry has been replaced by biology.

Urban gardening was the first reaction of the Cuban people to feed their empty stomachs post the fall of the USSR. People organised themselves to cultivate vacant lots, backyards, rooftops etc. in the cities. From mid 1990s, urban agriculture was transformed into from subsistence production to a commercial activity. This movement grew rapidly in the Havana city and subsequently engulfed the entire country. The national system of urban agriculture was created to organise people involved in this movement.

The Crop Protection Institute operates over 220 centres that provide cheap and plentiful beneficial insects and micro organisms that attack plant pests. At hundreds of vermin-compost centres, one million tons of natural compost per year is produced. The Ministry of Agriculture has supported this process with a network of extension agents and supply stores called the 'seed houses'. In Havana, the TCAs i.e. agricultural consulting stores, offer technical advice along with seeds, soil improvers, biological products, and technical literature. The extension agent plays the key role as disseminator of information about services offered by the TCA and communicator of scientific-technical advice and information to the urban agriculturalists. Across Cuba, urban agriculture employs the services of close to ten thousand professionals and over forty thousand technicians.

The general turn to organic agriculture and the renewed use of animal traction power has produced the tremendous savings of imported energy and other products derived from petroleum. In 2003, the Ministry of Agriculture was using less than 50 percent of the diesel fuel it used in 1989, less than 10 percent of the chemical fertilizers, and less than 7 percent of the synthetic insecticides. In fact, all aspects of food production are daily battlegrounds in the fight to save energy.

The basic principles of urban agricultural practice in Cuba are as under:

1. Uniform distribution throughout the country (i.e. in every area of the country with an urban population, urban agriculture should be developed).
2. Local consumption by the urban population of local production in each region.

3. Crop-animal integration with maximum synergy (i.e. internal cycling of nutrients) to boost production.
4. Intensive use of organic matter to increase and conserve soil fertility.
5. Employment of biological pest controls.
6. Use of all available land to produce food, guaranteeing intensive but not import-dependent high yields of crops and livestock.
7. Multidisciplinary integration and intensive application of science and technology.
8. A fresh supply of good quality products offered directly to the population, guaranteeing a balanced production of not less than 300 gms. of vegetables daily per capita and an adequate variety of animal protein.
9. Maximum use of the food production potential, such as the available labour force and the recycling of wastes and by-products for plant nutrients and animal feed.

Rice is the staple diet of the Cubans. On the onset of the crisis in the1990s, the production was unsustainable and more than 40 percent of rice was imported. The popular production of rice was a grass-root movement towards self-provisioning wherein people cultivated this cereal in abandoned areas, small plots between sugar cane fields, in road ditches etc. This system of rice intensification (SRI) is promoted world-wide by, among others, the Cornell International Institute for Food, Agriculture and Development. This system has doubled or even tripled rice yields in Cuba, as elsewhere in the third world, while reducing seed, water, and petroleum requirements. Optimistic rice experts are claiming that Cuba is potentially on its way to self-sufficiency in rice. This form of self-organisation and lower input agriculture had a positive impact on national food self-sufficiency.

Urban agriculture movement was started as a temporary solution to the food crisis. Today, it ought to look for more integrated approach which emphasises on the preservation of urban environment in the permanent management of resources in urban settings, avoiding pollution and creating a culture of nature conservation. The input substitution strategy which emphasises on ecological management of soil, biological control, animal traction, poly cropping, mixed farming and crop rotation etc. are the moves towards enhanced sustainability.

Cuban Food Security: International Aid

European Union-Cuba Relations: The European Union (EU) has created a very extensive network of cooperation agreements with the Caribbean countries covered by the Cotonou Agreement. The EU policy towards Cuba is based on a Common Position of the 27 EU Member States of December 1996. This is the founding document. The EU's main aims with this position are to encourage the transition towards pluralist democracy and the respect of human rights and fundamental freedoms in Cuba, as well as to improve the standard of living of the Cuban people.

Regarding economic relations, the latest trade data shows that Spain, which was traditionally Cuba's main trading partner, has seen its position progressively eroded. In the last few years, trade with Spain has been eclipsed by the growth of trade with Venezuela and China. The Commission expects this trend to continue. Among EU countries, the Netherlands and Germany follow Spain, although with a less diversified export base. Overall, the EU remains Cuba's main trading partner with 3 billion dollars worth of exchanges. Cuban imports are mostly comprised of tobacco, fisheries products, sugar and rum. In 2006, EU exports amounted to US$ 2.1 billion and imports to US$ 900 million. This corresponds to 28 percent growth of exports but only a 2 percent growth of imports.

Following the official re-launch of cooperation in October 2008, emergency assistance of € 4 million was made available to cover the most important humanitarian needs of the population affected by hurricanes Gustav, Ike and Paloma. An additional amount of € 36 million was committed in 2009 for cooperation in the fields of post-hurricane reconstruction and rehabilitation, food security, environment and climate change, business management and culture.

On May 12, 2010, the Commission adopted the first Country Strategy Paper for the Republic of Cuba. An indicative allocation of € 20 million was earmarked for Cuba for the period 2011-2013 under the EU Development Cooperation Instrument (DCI). Three priority sectors were identified for this Country Strategy Paper, namely food security; environment and adaptation to climate change and expertise exchanges, training and studies.

Cuba and the United Nations: Three new international cooperation agreements channelled through the United Nations system in Cuba are aimed at strengthening food security, especially in the poorest parts of the country with an emphasis on the easternmost provinces that cover one-third of the island. A study by the National Statistics Office (ONE) on progress towards the MDGs in eastern Cuba made it possible for U.N. agencies and local authorities to identify which areas should be especially targeted in development efforts, including maternal health programmes, promoting greater access to food, and defence of the environment. The three programmes are aimed at:

- **Fighting Anaemia:** This programme involving 8.5 million dollars in aid, is focused on support for the fight against anaemia in disadvantaged groups in Cuba. It will provide financing for a dairy company in Pinar del Río to expand production, in order to make an iron-fortified porridge which includes milk, to be provided to children between the ages of six months and five years, pregnant women, and other people facing a risk of anaemia.
- **Boosting Decentralisation in the Countryside:** The project will support new decentralisation initiatives and production stimulation in Cuba which will include seven million dollars in aid to bolster the participation of the small private sector as a dynamic agent in local development. Individual producers and cooperatives from five municipalities in five different provinces will be the beneficiaries. Both initiatives will be

partly financed by the MDG Achievement Fund (MDG-F), whose main donor is Spain. The MDG-F is a U.N. instrument that backs up national efforts to meet the MDGs, fight inequality and increase active participation by civil society in social and economic development.

- **Diversification of Agriculture:** The third agreement mentioned by the U.N. involves 20 million dollars in aid from the European Commission, channelled through the UNDP, up to September 30, 2011, with the aim of diversifying agriculture. The plan is to strengthen local food production capacity, while improving farm management and the availability of local produce in 27 selected municipalities. In addition, efforts will be made to improve quality and quantity of skilled farmers in another 10 municipalities.

PALMA (Programa de Apoyo Local a la Modernización del sector Agropecuario en Cuba): To support farmers and to contribute to Cuba's ambition to be able to rely on domestic production of food, UNDP and EU work in close partnership with the Cuban Ministry of Agriculture through the UNDP-EU programme PALMA (Programa de Apoyo Local a la Modernización del sector Agropecuario en Cuba). The partnership has, since its start in 2009, supported the modernization of local agriculture in 37 pilot municipalities in Cuba.

PALMA has provided seeds, fertilizers, farming tools and machines to farmers and cooperatives, and trained them on modern and sustainable farming, including training on issues such as running a cooperative; and finance and accounting.

With the help of the UNDP-EU supported PALMA:

- More than 13,200 new farmers (14 percent women) and 366 cooperatives (6 percent of total) in different parts of Cuba have received agricultural equipment and inputs.
- The beneficiaries have also been trained sustainable agriculture and business and cooperative management, which has empowered the farmers and helped them to increase their production.

- The cooperatives have been able to increase their production levels of basic food products—such as milk, grains (rice and beans), fruits and tubers—from 25 percent to up to 80 percent.
- In 2011 alone, this increased food production substituted food imports for more than US$ 15 million.

Cuba-Brazil Relations: Recently, Cuba's Ministry of International Trade and Foreign Investment signed a US$ 200 million MoU with the Ministry of Development, Industry and Foreign Trade of Brazil. This would serve as a loan to implement the 'More Food for Cuba' program to ensure food security in Cuba.

Coordinated by the Ministry of Agrarian Development (MDA), the 'More Food Program' is a financing facility for family farming, established in Brazil in 2008.

The funds will be released in three instalments—the first in 2012 and the next two in 2013—and will serve to finance exports of Brazilian agricultural machinery and equipment. With this project, the Brazilian government will assist existing Cuban programs to achieve food security targets, increase levels of mechanization in family farming and, accordingly increase productivity.

The Hunger Free Latin America and the Caribbean Initiative is a commitment from the countries of the region to eradicate hunger within the term of a generation. The monitoring and follow-up of this initiative is done through the Group of Latin America and the Caribbean in the United Nations (GRULAC), the Working Group 2025 (GT2025) and the Committee on World Food Security (CFS).

The objective of this initiative is to eradicate hunger within one generation and ensure food and nutritional security for all inhabitants within the framework of the Millennium Development Goals (MDGs) of cutting in half, hunger and poverty rates by 2015; it sets out to reduce child malnutrition below 2.5 percent by 2025.

Lessons from Cuba for India

India is reeling under a high rate of inflation in the food prices. In adverse conditions such as this, where there is increasing demand in the market but lack of production in the supply side of the market, promoting urban agriculture, carried out in a scientific manner, would definitely reduce the food insecurity crisis.

In India, low per capita consumption of food and increasing urbanisation lend greater urgency for promoting urban agriculture. [11] India's urbanisation rate is accelerating by the year—in 2008, a majority of the global population was classified as urban. The share of urban population was 30 percent in 2010 and the United Nations Development Program (UNDP) estimates that this would rise to 40 percent in 2030 and over 50 percent by 2045. By 2012, India's population residing in the cities will increase by 15.5 percent. When such large proportion does not practice agricultural activities it applies stress on the supply side of the food production which can only be supplemented by advocating the practice of urban agriculture. There are a significant number of people who migrate from the rural areas to the urban cities in search of better opportunities and lifestyle, these people would profess the knowledge and skill of farming, which could be put to use in the urban setting.

This urban agriculture is definitely not a substitute for rural agriculture or for improving productivity and sustainability of the agricultural sector; however, it would certainly reduce the stress on the supply chain. Compared to 2010, the FAO's 2011 food price index was 37 percent higher. The G20 nations in their annual meeting launched an agriculture market information system (AIMS) in order to improve the data sharing on global production and stocks on food production in order to reduce volatility in the price market.

Urban farming yields direct income through sales and employment, or indirect income through reduction of expenditure on food. As India develops new townships and as the concept of sustainable cities becomes increasingly acceptable, there are opportunities to build environmentally and economically sound urban agriculture systems, involving waste and water management that can be incorporated from the beginning.

Space constraint cannot be said to be a major constraint as the vertical spaces in the cities like open spaces of instructions or municipal lots or areas of housing societies, household kitchens, schools, colleges, terrace gardens could be put to use for urban agriculture.

India has the scope to expand its microfinance in the urban areas along with the others financial institutions like cooperative banks and finance agricultural activities in the urban areas through self-help groups. A facilitative environment, including clarity of property rights of urban open spaces, and co-ordination among multi-stakeholders are needed.

The mindset of the urbanites, particularly the upper income groups who regard food security as simply being able to buy food from the market and regard farming as a loco status and less skilled activity, needs to undergo a change in order to recognise the importance of urban agriculture.

Viability of Urban Agricultural Programme in India

Community economic development approach is a method worth trying—for it improves local food security needs because it provides employment opportunities, incentives and long-term life skills. It aims to achieve community independence and empowerment, and most significantly, it exists so that future food security needs can be met because these urban farms focus on long-term solutions. City dwellers and urban planners need to approach entrepreneurial gardens supportively and critically in order to generate sustainable gardens that encourage community economic development.

Community economic development can bring food insecurity to a level of reality through practicing entrepreneurial urban agriculture; a reality where communities are participating in increasing their safety net to reduce their chances of becoming food insecure. Hence, it is important for urban planners to be well informed about the costs and feasibility of incorporating entrepreneurial gardens as viable land uses in the city so that they can contribute to this activity as part of the urban reality. [12]

At the city level, the aggregate income and employment effects of urban agriculture must be weighed against the costs of the assistance supplied to the urban farmers in form of extension and training, quality control, etc. Further, the indirect costs and benefits of urban agriculture for the city, the positive and negative effects on the social, health and environmental situation of the urban population, must also be considered while assessing the economic viability of an urban agricultural project. In order to enhance the positive impacts and to mitigate the negative impacts, it is essential that adequate policies, legislations and support be available in the city. These positive impacts can be quantified and economically assessed.

The contribution of urban agriculture to urban food security and healthy nutrition is its most important asset. Food production in the city is generally a response of the urban poor to inadequate, unreliable and irregular access to quality food worsened by their meagre purchasing power. Most cities in developing countries are not able to generate sufficient income opportunities in urban areas. Lack of income translates into lower quantity or poor quality of food intake.

Urban agriculture in Cuba helped stimulate the development of related micro and larger agro-enterprises, such as those related to agricultural inputs like production of compost from urban organic wastes, vermin-composting, bio-pesticides, small-scale irrigation equipment, product processing, packaging and marketing, street vending, of outputs and other services like transport etc. It also helped the rise of employment and income levels of people residing in Havana.

There is less transport, cold storage, losses, processing and packaging, leading to direct economic savings for urban residents. There is improved access to food for the urban poor because of lower prices, accessible location and distribution. Self-production of food in backyard gardens, roof top etc. reduces the monthly household expenditures on food, leaving more cash available for other basic household needs. Urban agriculture eliminates the monetary and ecological costs of transportation. It is estimated that half the produce that comes into Mumbai is lost in transit. Urban agriculture in Mumbai can eliminate this wastage. Furthermore, when people grow food where they live, they have ready access to produce, and they can harvest when it is ripest and most nutritious. Growing smaller quantities of food in diverse locations assures that food is available in sufficient quantity.

In the major cities of India, the percentage of rural immigrants amongst the urban poor is high. Farming in and near cities helps in the integration of these immigrants and it complements their livelihood strategies by acting as a source of income. Many of these immigrants are already well trained in farming activities as they have shifted from the villages and hence there is no extra expenditure in training them.

An economic evaluation of the impacts of urban and semi-urban agriculture on food security must take into account the eventual negative impacts on health of the urban population and the costs to prevent such negative impacts. The health risks linked with urban agriculture include harmful impact of polluted irrigation water, pesticide use, soil nutrient depletion etc.

Urban agriculture provides a good buffer against political or economic shocks and thus is an effective social safety net—a well-known example being Havana (and other cities in Cuba) under the economic blockade in the nineties. In times of crisis, urban households can start this activity and secure food or income for the household. With the advent of techniques such as organoponics, hydroponics, tyre and cage farming, vertical farming techniques, roof top farming, etc., even access to land is no longer a hurdle to engage in farming when the need arises.

Many city governments have realized that urban agriculture

aids the social inclusion of vulnerable and hence can prove to be an important strategy for poverty alleviation. They have therefore started UA projects, including the provision of access to municipal land, training, technical assistance and investment and marketing support for agricultural production and processing enterprises. The Community Patio project in Havana, Cuba, encourages the practice of UA, utilizing permaculture techniques in home gardens to produce food, medicinal plants, spices and ornamental plants. It further includes environmental education and capacity building for neighbours, schools and hospitals for the elderly.

Urban agriculture is knowledge-intensive and involves scientific management of solid waste and scarce water resource. It has potential opportunities for socially-oriented enterprises to specialise in this area. As India develops new townships and as the concept of sustainable cities becomes increasingly popular, there are opportunities to build economically sound urban agriculture systems. The role of government should be limited to that of a facilitator, as any uniform regulation for heterogeneous needs and capacities will be counter-productive. This is especially true in India where urban governments still struggle to perform the basic municipal functions with reasonable degree of technical competency and economic efficiency.

Conclusion

Following the collapse of Soviet Union in early 1990s, the Cuban economy fell to abysmal depths. Cuba lost all of its fuels and agricultural imports which led to widespread hunger and breakdown of their agricultural system that was heavily dependent on sugar. As a response to this catastrophe, Cuba underwent dramatic shift towards low input, ecologically sustainable agriculture, encouraging its citizens to grow food in the urban centres like Havana etc. This Cuban experiment has produced prolific results and countries all over the globe are inspired by Cuba's experience to deal with food insecurity in their own nations. In general, there are very encouraging signs of increased production and efficiency. In 1999, there were gains in yields for sixteen of eighteen major crops, including not only vegetables, tubers, and plantains, but also corn, beans, rice, fruits, and coffee. Potato, cabbage, malanga, bean, and pepper yields were superior to those of Central America and above the average yields in the world. By mid-2000, vegetable and fresh herb sales nationwide had reached a level of 469 grams per day per capita, well above the FAO recommended amount of 300 grams per day.

In the midst of all these transformations, it is pertinent to note, that, in contrast to the shrinking role of the state in many third world countries in the current neo-liberal era, in Cuba, the state and other collective forms of economic organization continue to play a major role, both in production and in facilitation and support. The bottom line is that, by the end of 2000, food availability in Cuba reached daily per capita figures of 2,600 calories and more than 68 grams of protein. The UN's Food and Agriculture Organization considers 2,400 calories per day and 72 grams protein per day to be an adequate diet. Despite the remaining problem areas, the acute food shortage crisis is essentially over. Cuban society has successfully made, while under considerable duress, heroic efforts to construct its own version of food security for its population, and has perhaps shown the way for other societies.

India ranks among the 15 hungriest countries of the world says the Global hunger Index—indeed a grim statistic. With increasing pressure from an ever-growing population, the country is faced with the challenge of building an agricultural economy that not only produces enough nutritious food for all its citizens but also provides good work to both the urban poor as well as rural farmers. The cities are expanding and more and more villagers are migrating in search of better livelihood opportunities. The pressure on rural agricultural production is enormous. Transport losses and inadequate storage facilities have further diminished the economic worth of such produce. Food prices in urban dwellings have sky-rocketed. In times such as this, any practice that would alleviate the burden shouldered by the poor farmers residing in the villages of India is a welcome step.

Urban agriculture seems to be a viable option, for it promises to reduce some of the burden shouldered by the rural farmers. It will in fact encourage the city dwellers to produce for themselves and achieve self-sufficiency. Scalability of such a project, however, remains a concern. Growing crops on terraces and roof tops and backyard definitely cannot satiate the hunger of a mammoth Indian population, but it is one positive step towards holistic growth.

Endnotes

1. Julio A. Diaz Vazquez, "Consumo Y Distribución Normada De Alimentos Y OtrosBienes En Cuba", in La Última Reforma Agraria Del Siglo: La Agricultura Cubana Entre El Cambio Y El Estancamiento 33, 50, Hans-Jürgen Burchardt (ed.), 2000.
2. Carmelo Mesa-Lago, "Market, Socialist and Mixed Economies", 2000, p. 289.
3. Carmen G. Gonzalez, "Seasons of Resistance: Sustainable Agriculture and Food Security in Cuba", *Tulane Environmental Law Journal*, 16 Tulane Envtl. L.J. 685, 2003.
4. HéctorSáez, "Resource Degradation, Agricultural Policies, and Conservation in Cuba", 27 Cuban Stud. 40, 49-50, 1997.
5. Companioni, N. et al., "The Growth of Urban Agriculture", in Funes , F., García, L., Bourque, M., Pérez, N. and Rosset, P. (eds.), Sustainable Agriculture and Resistance: Transforming Food Production in Cuba, Oakland: Food First Books, 2002.
6. Carmen G. Gonzalez, "Seasons of Resistance: Sustainable Agriculture and Food security in Cuba", 16, *Tulane Environmental Law Journal*, 2003, 24.
7. Julio A. Díaz Vázquez", Consumo y distribuciónnormada de alimentos y otrosbienes en Cuba", in La Última Reforma Agraria Del Siglo: La Agricultura Cubana Entreel Cambio Y El Estancamiento 33, 50, Hans-Jürgen Burchardt (ed.), 2000.
8. Andrea Carter, "Cuba's Food-Rationing System and Alternatives", Cornell University Press, New York.
9. Cuba American National Foundation, accessed on 31-07-13, available at:

http://www.canf.org/2005/1es/desde-Cuba/2005-ene-13-con-solo-tres-productos.htm.

10. Andrea Carter, "Cuba's Food-Rationing System and Alternatives", Cornell University Press, New York.
11. Mukul G. Asher, "Promote Urban Agriculture for Food Security", June 23, 2011.
12. Tara D. Johnson, "Enterpreneurial Urban Agriculture", *City Farmer*, April 2005.

5

France: Programme National Nutrition Sante (PNNS)

Garima Gothwal and Taruna Dhingra

Socio-economic Profile

In France, the growing concern has been the rising obesity. Obesity has grown quickly in France, especially since the beginning of the year 1990; [1] but especially, it appeared at an increasingly early age (16 percent of the children being overweight in 2006 against 5 percent in 1980) [2] and strikes especially the underprivileged population (25 percent of the underprivileged children).

Pathologies associated with a bad nutrition resulted in 170,000 deaths per annum related to cardiovascular diseases and the "fatty" diabetes touching 2 million people along with cancer, osteoporosis, anorexia etc. have weighed very heavily on health care expenditure.

To answer these challenges, France had set up in 2001, the National Program Nutrition Health (PNNS), and had thus become the first European country to have such an overall strategy.

The first PNNS (2001-2006) established a base of nutritional reference marks which constitute from now on the official French reference. [3] In conformity with the French food culture, they associate the objective of public health and the concepts of taste, pleasure and user-friendliness. Indeed, France is very attentive with the promotion of its geographical indications and "terroirs". The National Institute of the Origin and Quality (INAO) [4], created in 1935 to defend the classified wines, have extended its field of activity since 1979 to other products (for example, butter of Charente-Poitou or the Abondance cheese).

By "terroirs", as this word does not exist in English language, it is necessary to hear a conjunction of factors which gives an inimitable taste to a natural product, obtained starting from a ground and from a particular climate and thanks to know-how of our ancestors. This concept is also shared by other Southern Member States such as Spain and Italy. [5] The concept of "terroirs" and the importance of the taste are anchored in the spirit of the French and this plays a part in a certain reserve with globalisation and fast food.

These results are corroborated by those of the annual barometer of the perception of the food, which makes it possible to better know the state of mind of the consumers, their food practices (preferred purchases, consumption, dishes), their perception of the bond between food and health and their perception of food quality. Results of 2006 [6] were reassuring:

- "Concerning the practices, it should be stressed that quality is the prevalent criterion of purchase, even if the price remains determining since appearing in second place.
- The concept of pleasure remains paramount, the time taken for the meals, the research of the variety in the food let us think that the French food model still exists, this is reassuring. We must endeavour to maintain this model, because it takes part in the fight against obesity".

It thus seems necessary to reinforce the links between agriculture and the consumers. Indeed, the consumers, by their way of life, are increasingly far away from the fields and do not know much about agriculture. This is why the French Agency of Information and Agricultural and Rural Communication (AFICAR) was created. This publicly-owned establishment aims at improving knowledge of the public of the agricultural and rural world, promoting the image of agriculture near the consumers and at developing the trade and the products originating from the rural territories. It is necessary to familiarize general public with the realities of agriculture and to restore near the consumers, the bond between food and raw materials. The agency put on the rails in 2007, a "Train of the Earth" which tours France for one month. This "train exposure" shows how much the products resulting from agriculture are present in our daily life.

In addition, the Ministry continues to promote the network of "form in farm", [7] network of a score of farms created by women of farmers where the urban ones can rediscover the rural world, taste the products of the farm and receive the guides of the PNNS.

Lastly, the Ministry supports an association "The Senses of the Taste" located in the North of France which aims to make it possible to the individuals to feel itself well in their environment, to be an actor of their life and to be open on the world which surrounds them. For that, the Association develops programs of sensory education based on the culinary inheritance. For that purpose, the Association is pressed on the products of quality and the emotional products, which are factors of the maintenance and development of the territories. These same products have a history—they have sense and offer sense. They constitute the cultural inheritance. They support the feeling of membership of a ground, the awakening of its roots and its identity. They are pledges of a variety and a food richness, guarantors of good physical and moral health. To educate with the taste, it is to bring people to an acceptance of the difference. The taste is a factor of communication, initiator of culture and user-friendliness.

Concerning nutritional labelling, one could note a different approach between the French and the British. The latter developed a labelling system of "traffic lights" which fires a tricolour aimed at alerting the consumer on "nutritional quality". [8] Such a system, which puts forth an external judgment and extremely prescribes on the product, is rejected in a massive way by the French consumer, as depicted in a joint study conducted by Direction générale de l'alimentation

(DGAL) and the Association nationale de défense des consommateurs et usagers (CLCV) on nearly 1,200 consumers in 2006. French consumer does not wish to see their Camembert cheese, Roquefort or marked foiegras of a red pastille like that—it would be to disavow a whole inheritance which makes the cultural identity of France.

Export and Imports: According to a recent survey, [9] France is the world's second largest agricultural exporter, world's sixth-largest agricultural producer and European Union's leading agricultural power, accounting for about one-third of all agricultural land within the EU.

Northern France is characterized by large wheat farms. Dairy products, pork, poultry, and apple production are concentrated in the western region. Beef production is located in central France, while the production of fruits, vegetables, and wine ranges from central to southern France. France is a large producer of many agricultural products and is currently expanding its forestry and fishery industries. The implementations of the Common Agricultural Policy (CAP) and the Uruguay Round of the General Agreement on Tariffs and Trade (GATT) have resulted in reforms in the agricultural sector of the economy.

As the world's second-largest agricultural exporter, France ranks just after the United States. The destination of 70 percent of its exports is other EU member states. France also provides agricultural exports to many poor African countries (including its former colonies) which face serious food shortage. Wheat, beef, pork, poultry, and dairy products are the principal exports.

The United States faces stiff competition from domestic production, other EU member states, and third world countries. US agricultural exports to France, totalling some $600 million annually, consist primarily of soybeans and soybean products, feeds and fodders, seafood, and consumer products, especially snack foods and nuts. French exports to the United States are much more high value products such as cheese, processed products and wine.

Legislative Framework

National Health and Nutrition Programme i.e. PNNS (Programme National Nutrition Sante): This project basically focuses on a specific policy of the Government of France and how it has been quite successful in enhancing the health of the people.

Launched in January 2001 and driven by the Ministry of Health, the National Health and Nutrition Program (Programme National Nutrition Santé-PNNS) aims to improve the health of the entire French population by acting on one of its major determinants, nutrition. The programme was extended in 2006 and in 2011. The PNNS involves not only the Ministries of Health and Agriculture but also the Ministries of Education, Sports, Consumption and Research. This strong inter-ministerial dimension shows the complexity of this issue.

This plan provides a reference framework and many incentive tools, used as supports for different actions. It allows the mobilization of many actors (ministries, local representatives, health and education professionals, volunteers etc.).

National Food Plan: A new public policy for food was defined by a legislation known as loi n°874-2010 du 27 juillet 2010 de modernisation.

Its strategic objective is to eat better. It is a comprehensive vision of food, covering all related themes (culture, social issues, health, environment, economy etc.). The aim of this national food policy is to assure access for all to affordable food that is safe, diverse, in sufficient quantity, of good nutritional quality, tasty and obtained in sustainable conditions.

School Meals Law: On December 6, 2011, the Telegraph reported [10] that, "the French government has stated that all students will have to eat meat if they want lunch at school. The regulations state that each meal has to include: a main dish, a side dish, a dairy product and either a starter or a dessert. The menu has to vary every day over 20 days. The main meal has to be based on 'meat, fish, eggs, offal or cheese'. The number of meals with more than 15 grams saturated fat or more than 20 grams sugar per serving is limited over the 20 day cycle.

Agencies Working for Food Security

French National Institute for Agricultural Research (INRA): Ranked the number one agricultural institute in Europe and number two in the world, INRA carries out mission-oriented research for high-quality and healthy foods, competitive and sustainable agriculture and a preserved and valorized environment. It is a mission-oriented research institute that addresses core development issues, from the local to the international level. Their research is guided by developments in scientific fields and focuses on worldwide challenges related to food and nutrition, the environment and land use facing the world of agriculture and agronomics today.

Challenges such as climate change, human nutrition, competition between food and non-food crops, the exhaustion of fossil resources and appropriate land management has put agronomists in a position to generate compatible economic, social and environmental development. INRA produces fundamental knowledge that leads to innovation and know-how for society. INRA lends its expertise to public decision-making. [11]

- INRA initiates research projects in France and Europe that it knows are relevant for society, because it is attentive to society's needs. That is why it carries out forward-planning research with a strategic vision in concert with representatives of the society (strategy partners).
- INRA commits to contributing to society through contracts that set out specific objectives, together with the French government.
- It lends its expertise to public decision-making.
- It helps in generating knowledge, innovation and know-how for the society.
- INRA assists the development of industries and regions of France—it actively participates in a transfer partnership while seeking the public good.

- INRA is ranked 2nd in the world and 1st in Europe for publications in agricultural sciences, and plant and animal sciences.
- It maintains scientific partnerships with major scientific research institutes worldwide, universities, and agronomy and veterinary schools, and is committed to helping build the European Research Area.
- INRA encourages a multi-disciplinary approach to research.
- It has received a number of prestigious awards for its researchers and their work.

Committee on Climate Change, Agriculture and Food Security (CCAFS): The changing global climate threatens food security, livelihoods and the environment worldwide but particularly those who are already most vulnerable—the millions of rural poor in developing countries.

The CGIAR Research Programme on Climate Change, Agriculture and Food Security (CCAFS) explores new ways of helping farmers to adjust to global changes in climate and helping decision-makers to weigh up the pros and cons of different policies. Inevitably, both at grass-roots levels and in the corridors of power, adjusting to climate change will mean making complex tradeoffs between food security, livelihoods and the environment. This important research will help policymakers, farmers and others affected by climate change understand the implications of their decisions when making difficult compromises.

Position with Regard to International Treaties

International Treaty on Plant Genetic Resources for Food and Agriculture: The International Treaty on Plant Genetic Resources for Food and Agriculture (ITPGRFA), popularly known as the International Seed Treaty, is a comprehensive international agreement in harmony with the Convention on Biological Diversity, which aims at guaranteeing food security through the conservation, exchange and sustainable use of the world's plant genetic resources for food and agriculture

(PGRFA), as well as the fair and equitable benefit sharing arising from its use. [12] It also recognizes farmers' rights: to freely access genetic resources, unrestricted by intellectual property rights; to be involved in relevant policy discussions and decision-making; and to use, save, sell and exchange seeds, subject to national laws.

International Portal on Food safety, Animal and Plant Health: The International Portal on Food Safety, Animal and Plant Health facilitates trade in food and agriculture products and supports the implementation of the Sanitary and Phytosanitary (SPS) Agreement by providing a single access point for authorized official international and national information across the sectors of food safety, animal and plant health. [13] It was launched on May 25, 2004 to enable a speedy and authoritative search for current food safety and food quality standards, regulations and other relevant official materials from a single search tool. [14]

Analysis

Hypothesis: France has been successful in improving the health of the entire French population with the help of the National Health and Nutrition Programme i.e. PNNS (Programme National Nutrition Sante).

Research Questions: For the last few years, the establishment of a French nutritional policy has become a public health priority. Nutrition has been recognized as a key element for the prevention and the protection against non-communicable diseases, like cancer, obesity or heart diseases. Indeed, the inadequacy of nutritional intake, linked to the lack of physical activity, contributes to the spread of these diseases, which represents more than 55 percent of annual deaths in France currently.

The public health nutrition goals set by the High Council of Public Health structure the strategic baseline and constitute the basis for defining the actions planned for the PNNS. These objectives have been grouped into four main categories:

1. To reduce obesity among the French population by stabilizing the prevalence of obesity among adults and decreasing it among children and teenagers.
2. To increase physical activity and decrease physical inactivity, regardless of age.
3. To improve eating habits and the nutrient intake: by increasing the consumption of fruits and vegetables, reducing the sodium consumption, increasing calcium intakes and supplementing iron deficiency among women experiencing poverty.
4. To reduce the prevalence of nutritional disorders viz., malnutrition and eating disorders.

To achieve these objectives, the PNNS uses the resources and the skills of different sectors, plans and programs implemented by other ministries, especially the one implemented by the Ministry of Agriculture and Food, i.e. the National Plan for Food (Programme National pour l'Alimentation-PNA).

At the national level, the PNNS ensures the coordination and the monitoring of the implementation of actions and provides scientific support, essential to the development of actions. At the regional level, the regional health agencies implement the public health actions defined in the PNNS, in partnership with all the stakeholders.

The PNNS is led by several general principles:

- The word "nutrition" includes issues related to food (nutrients, the social, cultural, economic, sensory and cognitive determinants of eating behaviours) and physical activity.
- This plan takes into account the biological, social and symbolic act of eating and of physical activity.
- The goals and messages promoted through the PNNS are based on a scientific expertise, coordinated by public authorities.
- The plan aims to promote certain diet and lifestyle habits to protect health and reduce the risk of chronic diseases.

All these actions include in their design and development the issue of social inequalities in health.

- The nutritional guidelines of the PNNS are designed to promote diet and physical activity in favour of an optimal health. No specific product is forbidden but some food groups are promoted, and some others are subject to recommendations as to their limitation.
- Given that living conditions and food environment determine behaviour, the PNNS must help to build global dietary environment and to facilitate positive choice for consumers' health.
- The PNNS promotes and organizes real dialogue between the different stakeholders of the plan at the national, regional and local level.
- The PNNS regularly assesses its progress (using efficiency indicators or process evaluation).

Several initial goals have been partially or fully achieved, such as reducing the prevalence of obesity among children, reducing the sodium and sugar consumption or increasing the consumption of fruits. However, these improvements have not uniformly affected all segments of the population and health inequalities have become more pronounced in the field of nutrition.

In France, there is an authority of dialog and discussion upstream of the PNNS, which tackles all the questions relating to the quality of food. This force of proposal, called National Council of Food (CNA), gathers all the actors of the food chain. The subjects of study are proposed by the ministers in charge of agriculture, of consumption or of health. The treatment of subjects such as "nutritional claims and health relating to the foodstuffs", "practical proposals for the implementation of a national strategy of prevention of infantile obesity" or "proposal for the installation of an observatory of the food", help the authorities.

The PNNS is also an alive tool—a committee of people which meets every month comprising experts like public health practitioners, sociologists, nutritionists etc., the association of the mayors of France, professionals concerned, the CNA, the French Agency of Sanitary Safety (AFSSA) and the INPES (National Institute of Prevention and Education to Health). It constitutes a small parliament which discusses various nutritional aspects and the related initiatives.

Only the subjects making consensus within the administration are put on the agenda of the meetings of the PNNS. The divergences between administrations are treated within the framework of the National Council of Public Health [15] or lastly in meetings organized by services of the Prime Minister.

The PNNS has made a massive effort to make known with the consumers, the nutritional recommendations, in particular by means of guides (more than 5 million copies) and through communication campaigns of great width.

How does PNNS ensure health of the French population? The French Ministry of Agriculture consistently works on the nutritional quality of the raw products and the manufactured goods.

First of all, with regard to the raw products, one realizes that the consumption of the fruits dropped by 16 percent, that of vegetables of 15 percent and that of the meat by 13 percent between 1999 and 2003. The interest of the consumers for the raw products must be preserved—this food has all the place in a varied and balanced mode.

With regard to the fresh fruits, the disinterest of the consumers seems to be before a whole problem of generation. According to a study of the CREDOC [16] carried out in 2005, "the generation which is today between 20 and 30 years, consumes twice less fresh fruits than the generation between 40 and 50 years and four times less than the generation between 60 and 70 years. It is thus advisable to target the actions on the younger generations".

In order to realise the objectives of the PNNS, the Ministry for Agriculture carries out various types of actions.

This includes supporting projects and works concentrating on the distribution of fruits in the schools and the ones focussing on food and nutritional education.

To supplement its action in the field of fruit and vegetables, the Ministry of Agriculture decided to establish a National Institute of Agronomic Research (INRA)—a collective scientific expertise, on the stakes and determinants of the consumption of fruit and vegetables. [17] This expertise asked for 15 months of work and requested for a score of experts on a broad range of disciplines, namely epidemiology, toxicology, nutrition, agronomy, genetics, sociology and marketing. The corpus of the studied text included 2,400 references.

It can be asserted here that the PNNS aims at reinforcing the consumption of fruit and vegetables, by targeting the 'weak consuming population' of such products.

More generally, the Ministry of Agriculture, in association with the INRA has created places for more discussions between researchers and producers or manufacturers regarding the nutritional aspects. [18] A conscious effort, dedicated towards the transfer of knowledge arising out of research, to the companies has been made so that the companies can gauge the requirements desired for innovations in the area of nutrition. Interestingly, professionals working in the meat industry showed a certain enthusiasm to work in the nutritional field. Professionals in the fruit, vegetable and cereal sectors were also brought closer to the INRA. In the sector of cereals, a working group gathered all the partners, viz. farmers, collectors of cereals, professionals in flour-milling etc. for discussions focused on taste, fibrous content and the mycotoxins in diets.

With regard to the manufactured goods, the approach of the authorities is to act as partners with the actors of the food supply chain (producers, manufacturers and retailers) and to privilege the voluntary approach with a coercive approach.

Thus, the DGAL established a working group of the PNNS

to improve the glucid levels in the food products. The objective of the PNNS is to increase the complex glucid consumption level so that it contributes to 50 percent of the daily energy contribution, by encouraging the starchy food consumption, thereby reducing the simple sugar contribution to 25 percent and increase the fibre contribution by 50 percent.

An important exchange between the partners (producers of sugar, agro-alimentary manufacturers, associations of consumers, retailers, AFSSA, [19] various experts, administrations) was completed between September 2005 and February 2007. It outlined the following:

- An assessment of the existing data to establish shared references, in particular the respective contribution of each type of food for its simple glucids contribution;
- An inventory of the actions already carried out and in progress by the economic actors, in particular, the modification of the receipts, the size of conditioning or publicity;
- An analysis of the benefits/risks of the modification of the nutrient content (simple glucids, complex glucids, fibres), taking into consideration the impact of technological and medical constraint on the behaviours of the consumers (transfer of consumption, acceptability);
- An impact study on the beet sugar producers.

In the second phase, tracks of engagement were worked out by each agro-alimentary sector concerned.

In order to more quickly achieve the objectives of the PNNS, the State invited the economic actors of food industry to sign, on in individual or collective mode, engagements relating to the nutritional composition of food, their presentation and promotion.

A schedule of conditions was written by a committee of experts in 2007 and is used as a reference frame with these engagements. In the same way, the companies of collective restoration were invited to sign similar engagements. Finally, a nutritional reference frame for the school restoration was defined in the regulation.

A working group on the lipids, controlled by the DGAL, constituted under similar conditions, was set up in September 2007. The objectives laid down in the PNNS were to reduce the proportion of lipids to less than 35 percent of the daily energy intake and to reduce the average consumption of saturated fatty acids by 25 percent.

An analysis of the food policies of France, in particular, of its National Health and Nutrition Programme, makes it quite clear that it has been successful in combating health problems and enhancing the nutritional intake of people. The government has ensured proper implementation of its scheme with major achievements that have been clearly highlighted. The health of the French population has shown a positive change because of the excellence of the National Nutrition Policy.

On the other hand, the picture of India in this regard is deplorable. India's malnutrition figures are not coming down despite a number of government programmes, as per a new report released by World Food Programme. [20] The research points out the need for a revamped public distribution system and greater public investment to address the wants of rural population.

"High economic growth rates have failed to improve food security in India, leaving the country facing a crisis in its rural economy", warns the latest report released by the World Food Programme and the M.S. Swaminathan Research Foundation (MSSRF). The report clearly states that the number of undernourished people is rising, reversing gains made in the 1990s. Slow growth in food production, rising unemployment and declining purchasing power of the poor in India has resulted in weakening of the rural economy.

While famines and starvation deaths remain the popular representation of the contemporary problem of hunger, one of the most significant yet understated and perhaps less visible area of concern today is that of chronic or persistent food and nutrition insecurity. It is indeed commendable how France has placed special emphasis on this particular problem and has undoubtedly succeeded in dwindling the rate of such health related issues.

India being afflicted to such major problems relating to the health of the people, should definitely learn from French policies so that we have can develop a stable economy in terms of food security.

Endnotes

1. "Congress on Global Hunger and Sustainable Food Security", Caritas, accessed on April 2, 2013, available at: http://www.zukunft-ohne-hunger.at/download/Congress_Future_Without_Hunger_Program.pdf.
2. "Agriculture and Food Security", France Diplomatie, accessed on June 2, 2012, available at: http://www.diplomatie.gouv.fr/en/global-issues/development-assistance/agriculture-food-security.
3. "A Reinforced Inspection Plan to Ensure Food Safety during Christmas Holidays", French Food in the US, accessed on June 13, 2013, available at: http://www.frenchfoodintheus.org/spip.php?article4557.
4. "Ministry of Social Affairs", Government of France, accessed on March 3, 2012, available at: www.inao.gouv.fr.
5. "How do Food Traceability and Labelling Guarantee Food Safety for Consumers?", French Food in the US, accessed on June 28, 2013, available at: http://www.frenchfoodintheus.org/spip.php?article4411.
6. "Antibiotic Resistance: Recap of French Plan", French Food in the US, accessed on November 19, 2012, available at: http://www.frenchfoodintheus.org/spip.php?article4218.
7. "Forms in Farm", Government of France, accessed on March 5, 2012, available at: www.formeenferme.com
8. "G20 and G8 Agriculture and Food Security Outreach", French Food in the US, accessed on March 28, 2013, available at: http://www.frenchfoodintheus.org/spip.php?article3585.

9. "The French Republic", FAO Country Profiles, accessed on June 17, 2013, available at: http://www.fao.org/countryprofiles/index/en/?iso3=FRA.
10. FAO, "France Vows Partnership for Food Security", International Service for the Acquisition of Agro-Biotech Applications, accessed on June 17, 2013, available at: http://www.isaaa.org/kc/cropbiotechupdate/article/default.asp?ID=10170.
11. "Agriculture/Food Security", France in the United States, accessed on December 23, 2013, available at: http://ambafrance-us.org/spip.php?article2677.
12. "Action Plan G20 France", Food Security Portal, accessed on June 19, 2013, available at: http://www.foodsecurityportal.org.
13. "France Earmarks €400m for Sub-Saharan Africa Food Security", StarAfrica.com, accessed on June 17, 2013, available at: http://en.starafrica.com/news/france-earmarks-e400m-for-sub-saharan-africa-food-security.html.
14. "Food Security: A Timely Political Issue", Mouvement pour une Organisation Mondiale de l'Agriculture, accessed on March 18, 2013, available at: http://www.momagri.org/UK/focus-on-issues/Food-Security-A-Timely-Political-Issue_471.html.
15. "L'Aquila Food Security Initiative: France", Integrated Implementation Framework, accessed on January 2, 2013, available at: http://iif.un.org/content/laquila-food-security-initiative-france.
16. "CREDOC", Research Centre for the Study and the Observation of the Living Conditions, accessed on March, 9, 2012, available at: www.credoc.fr.
17. "The International Responses to Global Food Security", The Global Mechanism, accessed on February 22, 2013, available at: http://www.globalmechanism.org/dynamic/documents/document_file/food_security_paper.april2011.final.pdf.
18. "Gabon Will Implement GIS Dedicated to Food Security Issues", IGN France International, accessed on August 24, 2012, available at: http://www.ignfi.fr/en/content/securite-alimentaire-le-gabon-se-dote-dun-sig.

19. AFSSA (French Food Sanitary Agency), Government of France, accessed on March 10, 2012, available at: www.afssa.fr.
20. "Food Security: Dampened Prospects", Financial Times, accessed on June 4, 2013, available at: http://www.ft.com/cms/s/0/6ed52738-4746-11e1-b646-00144feabdc0.html#axzz2ZnOIet12.

6

Germany: Food Security Policies

Laboni Bhakta and Pallavi Lakshmi Lakra

Socio-economic Profile

The German economy is heavily export-oriented. In fact, exports account for more than one-third of national output. As a result, exports traditionally have been a key element in German macroeconomic expansion, accounting for over half of the economic growth in recent years. Germany is a strong advocate of closer European economic integration, and its economic and commercial policies are increasingly determined within the European Union (EU). With globalisation at its peak, the global markets have seen an international flow of goods and the ever changing production and consumption patterns harbour not just opportunities but risks also. This calls for new strategies to ensure food safety.

Household Compositions: Food security is achieved when households have sufficient means and resources to obtain appropriate foods for a nutritious diet. Poverty and food insecurity may force indigenous people to overburden the environmental resources and destroy their basis for survival. Therefore, within the development policy of the German government, programmes are supported that reduce poverty, improve the food and nutrition security situation, and maintain the ecological environment and natural resources. [1]

The ratio of people going for a single household is altered by the number of young people who want to leave their parents' house and the number of elderly who want to live with their children. [2]

Single-person households constitute at least 35 percent of

households in Denmark, Finland, Germany, Norway and Switzerland. By contrast, this proportion is less than 20 percent in Greece and Portugal.

Given rising uncertainties, policymakers are faced with a multitude of challenges. In the short-run, a marked deterioration of the cyclical situation requires letting automatic stabilisers operate fully around the structural consolidation path, as allowed by the fiscal rule. In addition, attention should continue to focus on raising the medium-term growth potential, which remains low at around 1½ percent and is set to decline to below 1 percent after 2020 on account of significant population ageing. Ageing will also have a bearing on living standards as the labour force declines as a share of total population and thus fewer contributors face a growing share of benefit recipients.

Changes in the distribution of household types have a potential effect on overall income distribution. This in turn affects the food distribution pattern. Consumers are affected with the economic situation. There was an increase in deposits with the state associated and co-operative banks, which in turn affected the spending habits of German consumers. The most affected were earners and the elderly. In terms of demographic characteristic, bigger households tend to experience hunger compared to smaller households. [3]

The German government should ensure that the most vulnerable group are addressed and should improve and secure nutritional situation of malnutrition groups at lowest costs. Poverty may increase a lot of chance of over-utilization of natural resources. Therefore, the German government has commenced development policy programmes which help in poverty reduction and improvements in food security situation while maintaining ecological environment and natural resources.

Unemployment barely increased during the recession. This is due to a decline in structural unemployment as well as a significant increase in flexibility in working hours, demonstrating the beneficial effect of past labour market reforms. [4] There was also a good performance in labour market in Germany.

According to a study by the European Commission (2007), employment patterns in rural and urban areas generally became more similar. This holds true for Germany, wherein a majority of the people were employed in the tertiary sector followed by the secondary sector. Average agricultural employment in Germany accounted for only 2.2 percent in 2005.

However, while looking at the different district types, agriculture and forestry were more important for employment in rural districts and surroundings. Its share in employment amounted to about 4.5 percent.

On an average, employment in agriculture and forestry was of little importance in comparison to other employment opportunities. While agricultural employment in cities was negligible, the highest share of persons employed in agriculture and forestry (4.7 percent) [5] was observed in rural surroundings of West Germany.

In rural districts and surroundings, relatively more persons worked in agriculture and forestry in West Germany where generally more and smaller farms/family farms are located. Family members engaged in agricultural activities were included in the database.

With regard to Germany as a whole, about 61 percent of farm family members worked on farms in 2005. However, the number of family members has been decreasing, more than the number of other persons employed.

The main cause of slow investment and consumption spending is the weak trade growth. The future prospect of domestic demand is high—so for both households and non-financial companies, there is no need for de-leveraging.

In addition, domestic demand benefits from monetary stimulus, notably if the divergence of growth rates across euro area countries continues and monetary conditions remain supportive for Germany. Such easy conditions will support investment in particular, including residential investment and keep the financing costs for government debt low. [6]

Inequality in Access to Food and Income: Food security is achieved if adequate food is available and accessible for and satisfactorily utilized by all individuals at all times to live a healthy and happy life. [7]

Lack of addressing power to food due to deficient purchasing power is the prime cause of food insecurity. With economic growth, labour shifts focus to higher growth sectors and higher wage sectors. Consumption is highly touchy to the changes in income. With changes in income patterns one witnesses difficulty in accessing food. The income elasticity for food will be higher for population with lower income.

From 2000 to 2006, Germany experienced an unprecedented rise in net income inequality and poverty. At the same time, unemployment rose to record levels and there was evidence for a widening distribution of labour market returns, as well as that of other market incomes. [8]

Poverty is one of the primary global problems and it has not been dealt with till now. Therefore, the government of Germany has installed development policies. Germany has witnessed a stable environment with reference to the income. There is less inequality of income. In fact, the situation prevalent there is that the poor remains poor for a fewer time period.

With increase in household income, the rate of demand for food increases and there is a downfall in malnutrition and poverty. There is a fundamental relationship between income distribution and food demand. With an income increase, more households' disposable income is available for food consumption. With an increase in population, there can be increase in the food demand.

Health: Health is one of the influential factors of consumer behaviour. Total health spending accounted for 10.5 percent of GDP in Germany in 2008. Smoking rates among adults in Germany have decreased from 28.5 percent in 1978 to 23.2 percent in 2005, a rate that is roughly equal to the current OECD average. [9]

German respondents in a research carried by Datamonitor (Recession and Recovery: Retail and Consumer Goods Industry, Germany, June 2009) indicated that health has gained importance during the period April 2007 to April 2009. This rise in health awareness has stimulated consumer interest in healthy foods and related products for both people and pets, leading companies to look at marketing food and drinks on a health platform as a means of differentiation.

The life expectancy has risen in Germany in the recent decades. The main reason for this rise is the better standard of living. But this better standard of living has bought a threat with it—the threat of poor eating habits and sedentary lifestyle.

The Germany's obesity statistics are not staggering. The Germans are below average for obesity rates but are heading towards that path. They spend approximately € 100 million on slimming aids which is adversely affecting their health. A combination of fast food chains adapting to the wellness trend, and the food and catering sectors demonstrating improvements in the health of their products makes obesity a less urgent problem in Germany.

They are becoming more conscious about their well-being. This has opened doors for health orientated agro-food suppliers.

Germany is ranked 5th in the world for cases of diabetes. This major concern has shifted suppliers to focus more on healthier options which deal with specific health matters. As the topic of health consciousness is rising, mothers are becoming more concerned about meeting their children's dietary needs.

The busy lifestyles of parents have repositioned their attraction towards healthier options for their babies. Various actions were taken by the government to improve the children's health as children are the future of the country.

The National Action Plan focuses on the daily structures, social environment, income and education. Health is an important economic factor and a driver behind participation in society and social equity.

In the key issues paper approved by the Cabinet on May 9, 2007, [10] the Federal Government stressed the need to draw together and further develop these diverse initiatives for the first time in a national strategy seeking to strengthen and establish health-promoting daily structures in the areas of nutrition and physical activity.

They pointed out that the Länder have already taken a series of steps to promote a healthy lifestyle with sufficient physical activity and a balanced diet.

Continuing on from these projects, nationwide structures are to be proactively encouraged and established in the Länder and communes to improve health promotion and disease prevention. One major precondition is deemed to be the forging of lasting co-operation between all the stakeholders.

In Germany, besides the state, the business community and the family, civil society is another pillar in all social developments. Civil society encompasses the totality of civic engagement and the actions of non-governmental organisations beyond state decision-making processes.

When it comes to promoting a healthy lifestyle and physical activity, Germany boasts a wealth of non-governmental activities. They range from parents preparing healthy food in day-care centres for children over membership of sports clubs down to major research and intervention programmes of private foundations.

€5 million was earmarked in the budgets of the lead federal ministries every year, initially for the period 2008-2010 for the implementation of the National Action Plan and the necessary instruments. Furthermore, the funds were made available by other federal ministries, the Länder, civil society and industry through their respective activities and measures to support the National Action Plan.

The German children and adolescents are affected by eating disorders. There has been a rise in issues of diabetes in older generations. Therefore, the government has put in a whole lot of real initiatives for healthy living. The health insurance funds have become aware of statutory prevention remit.

Macroeconomic Aggregates: The food crisis has affected the demand and supply of the food systems. However, economic and agricultural growth can offset the damage (of higher food prices), but this will require more determined efforts to boost food production.

Weather directly and indirectly affects production and consumption decision-making in every economic sector. The private sector is very sensitive to weather variability.

Weather affects the economy by affecting both supply and demand for the products and services of an industry. We particularly note the consumption (i.e., demand) side of this discussion because the consideration of weather impacts is usually focused primarily on the production (i.e., supply) side.

The quality of demanded food is the relationship between price of that food commodity and the quantity demanded. Germany has witnessed changes in tastes and preferences. They have shifted their focus on healthier options available to them in the market. The German population is a mixture of high income generated households. Weather forecasting accuracy is an aspect of consumer demand held constant in the demand function.

The economic theory indicates that the price which is to be given for additional unit of good is the benefit received by the consumer. Here, the height of demand curve shows the marginal consumption at each quantity. On the supply side, the higher the price of the food product, the more quantity is provided by the profit-maximizing firms.

While there may be negative or positive quantity impacts from weather-related shifts in demand and supply, if these are offset by price changes, the impacts from an economic perspective will not be as apparent.

There can be mitigation by investments in production

methods to reduce weather impacts and some may be improved by weather forecasts. There can be a decrease in weather sensitiveness after advancements in technologies and investment in capital. Improved forecasting reduces the negative economic impacts. The weather changes shift activities either in production or consumption. In the long-run there can be a little effect of weather on the German economy.

Production: Germany, a wealthy country known as one of Europe's economic powerhouses, occupies a central position in Western Europe.

Over the past few years, German imports of agri-food and seafood products have increased from US$ 62 billion in 2005 to US$ 97 billion in 2008, an increase of 56 percent. Of the US$ 97 billion imported in 2008, US$ 22 billion came from countries outside the European Union (EU). [11]

There were many organisational changes to ensure that consumer protection is accorded precedence over pure economic interests in agricultural and food policies. At the same time, this increased the need for a coordination of other legitimate interests at national, European as well as international levels. The new players in the stage of food policy are health insurance companies, doctors and therapists. There has been a rise in the awareness about quality of life and food.

The food industry is also pro-actively engaged in food policy through the large sums spent on advertising. In 2004, the food industry accounted for an advertising budget of € 2.6 billion. Due to the criticism voiced by consumer protection groups, the report issued by the German Advertising Industry Federation opposed the restrictions on advertising of children's products under discussion in the EU and Germany and the planned nutrition and health claims made on food.

Despite the synergy of multiple factors relating to the economy, health concerns and environmental initiatives, Germany is world's largest agri-food importer with imports totalling US$ 92 billion in 2008. [12] Statistics show that most of the areas which are affected by rising prices are milk, egg, oils and fats, sugar and confectionary, and meat. Consumption has increased in areas of bread and fruit.

Germans have always focused on products on the basis of value or cost. Private label products have been very popular with the German masses. This has greatly influenced the different categories of retail such as pharmacies, drugstores and supermarkets.

In this era of high paced lifestyles, the Germans have shifted their focus to healthier options available to them in the market. This has led to an increase in demand of convenient options like ready to eat meals or at home consumption coupled with health benefits. They are looking for more natural ways of losing weight.

With Germans favouring sustainable consumption, it is estimated that it will bring potential opportunities for the Canadian suppliers in eco-nutrition. With environment concerns on a high, manufacturers are shifting focus to organic ingredients, ethical packaging and healthy features. With fierce competition in Germany, very few foreign competitors are expected to enter the market in the coming years. However, some large players in the market may create new areas of opportunity as they spin off some of their less profitable operations in order to better cope within a challenging market.

Germany's market is the most dynamic market for organic products. Over the years, there has been a rise in the sale of organic products. According to reports from ZentraleMarkt- und Preisberichtstelle (ZMP), the official German agricultural research company, the recent economic crisis with the accompanying inflation slowed growth in the organic sector to 4 percent in the first half of 2008, compared to 20 percent in the previous half year.

But with global increase in food market the organic products sector is also affected. Increased meat prices have reduced the meat consumption. The trend towards a healthier lifestyle has influenced vitamin and dietary supplement sales patterns. Increased health awareness has brought new chances to this sector. Consumers are turning towards functional foods and herbal options present in the market. Personalised products are gaining new heights as consumers are becoming inclined towards nutritional content. Manufacturers are focusing on personalization. Personalization trend offers a significant growth. Personalization of foods is an important component of future focused food and beverage branding.

Manufacturers' have responded to the needs of the consumers including allergies and intolerances as well as tastes and flavours. With advancement in the nutri-genomics sector, various studies have started which will lead to formation of food products to provide health benefits based on a person's genes.

Studies indicate that the food industry will actively support the reduction of greenhouse gases associated with climate change. The chairman of the Federation of German Food and Drink Industries stated that the percentage of greenhouse gas emissions occurring during food production is already relatively low. However, all areas involved in the overall life cycle of food products, such as agriculture, food processing and packaging industries, wholesale, retail, transport and consumer consumption should be examined in order to identify a viable emission reduction potential.

Organic options still remain important in the ready meals sector as the health effects of pesticides and genetic modifications on food are heavily discussed and important to German consumers. Moreover, products with low fat and sugar content, no additives and, ideally, 100 percent organic ingredients are expected to grow to take on a significant share of the ready meals sector in Germany.

Consumers are eating at home now—this is increasing the sale in supermarkets and hypermarkets. Consumers are concentrating buying more ethical products and paying attention to environment friendly packages. The agrarian sector has been facing low productivity and inefficiency. Poor harvests have exacerbated the recent economic difficulties.

A summary of investigation of the estimated contributions of existing climate change or climate variability to crop performance shows that in Germany, the warmer winter temperature and an associated earlier start to the growing season probably had an influence on the yield during the period 1987-96. [13]

Many analysis show that change in temperature has led to phonological changes. Variation in climate leads to a short-term effect on crop production. The agriculture production is sensitive to climate fluctuations. The after-effects of climate change will be negative in Germany as it is water limited.

However, crop production alone cannot ensure food security and other factors related to availability, plus components of access and utilization, are essential contributors to robust food systems. Food crisis has brought back the issue of food security on national and international agenda.

Population: Faced with a low birth rate and insufficient immigration, Germany's population continues to age and shrink. The effects of this will include increased value growth in organic foods as well as vitamins and supplements typically not found in food. [14]

Germany's population is aging and, like other western countries, is struggling with a number of related health issues like rising obesity rates. As a result, health and wellness is at the forefront of the German consciousness and is an important trend affecting the German diet and food choices.

As is the case with all EU countries, the proportion of the elderly in Germany will continue to increase well into 2020. A study shows that the number of people over 65 years is predicted to increase from 16 million today to 22 million in 2030, rising to about 23 million by 2050; this implies that one in three people living in Germany would be over 65 and that only one in six would be under 20, compared to 2007 when there were equal numbers in both generations. Moreover, the overall size of the population in Germany will continue to decline, even as the ranks of the older generations increase.

History of the Country's Food Policy: The Roman trade routes were famous even after the Romans left. The trade routes brought artefacts into the Viking settlements. The food consumption suffered a shift after the meat exchange started. It was challenging for the rural farmers to cope up with the supply of enough food for the population. This was followed by food crisis which forced the peasants to rely on imported food items such as spices etc.

This change was precipitated by an extensive construction of railways that linked the countryside with the cities. With the new foodstuffs, came grocers to the villages. They were called "Kolonialwarenhändler" in the German language, which means "colonial produce merchants". Yet only exotic food imports were sold in the grocery shops, whereas the most important constituents of the diet were provided by the farmers themselves.

The dietary habits in the Federal Republic of Germany result from changing living conditions. Dynamics in the food sector as a sphere of action should be perceived within the context of social changes—the rising demand for so-called functional foods and for organically produced foods. In 2004, the BMVEL started a new program called the "Diet and the Physical Activity" which drew attention of many organisations.

A scheme was started to allow preventive health care through adequate diet and physical activity among the German population. It was funded with € 15 million and had to run for 3 years. The programme was called "Eat better...Move around more, the competition". The BMVEL is conducting measures to ensure that the overweight problem is minimised among the adolescents and the children.

Changes have also been done in day-care centres for children and schools within the scope of the campaign "Eat better". In Germany, the measures to ensure food safety currently not only comprises food control and inspection and food monitoring, but also instruments of communication such as food labelling.

The Federal Länder handles the official food control. They examine the functional capacity of the system through own tests performed by food operators (cross-checks). However, joint action is required by the Federal Government for uniform execution of the various programmes. The food policy strategy is continuously witnessing a system of medium- to long-term targets that is to be acted on.

Food policy goals have come up at a national level in Germany (e.g. in the Coalition Agreement) and steps towards a restructuring of the organisational setup in food sector have been taken by the Ministry. A strategy has not come up since long keeping in view the increasingly dominant EU policy which is aimed at complete harmonisation.

The Community Action Programme, "Healthier, Safer, More Confident Citizens: A Health and Consumer Protection Strategy", [15] formulated the following targets for health and consumer protection for the period 2007-2013: (a) protection of citizens against risks and dangers on which individuals cannot exert any influence (e.g. health hazards, unsafe products, unfair commercial practices), (b) strengthening the decision-making ability of citizens with regard to their health and consumer interests, (c) incorporating all targets of health and consumer policy into all policy fields addressed by the community so as to mainstream health and consumer issues in policy formulation, and (d) an executive agency to be established to support the new programme.

With the potential recognition of a healthy diet as a way of improving the health situation and of cutting costs in the health care sector, the Federal Government took the EU Action Programme on Health Promotion, Education, Information and Training within the Action Plan on Public Health [16] as well as the document on the integration of health care requirements into community policies, into account. The panel of experts on sustainable development was set up by the Federal Government to help develop the sustainability strategy further by making proposals on targets and indicators as well as to suggest projects to implement this strategy (e.g. sustainable basket of goods).

With regard to food policy, it is the role model of sustainable production and consumption included in the guiding principle of sustainable development that manifests itself in striving for a health-sustaining, low-risk diet adapted to persons or groups of people, whilst conserving the natural resources such as soil, water air and biodiversity, fostering social systems in farming, processing and trade and contributing to the value-adding process.

Role models are generally values nurtured by humans that provide orientation and guidance for conduct and decision-making. They frequently manifest themselves in subjective principles of action.

Farmer Markets: Farm households may take up a variety of alternative activities as an additional income source. For example, organic production is often combined with direct marketing and farm tourism. While some combination of additional income generating activities go together, others seem to conflict or may even hinder each other. However, resource availability obviously limits the uptake of additional income-generating activities.

While larger farms commonly have capital and land resources, labour can be considered as the surplus factor for smaller farms, and alternative income-generating activities tend to be chosen accordingly. [17] In the present context, we would not specifically consider alternative income combinations and would mainly focus on activities (on-farm non-agricultural and off-farm activities) that do not involve primary agricultural production.

Agriculture is closely integrated with other sectors of the economy. On the one hand, agricultural holdings demand inputs (production inputs, investment goods, and services) for their farming activities, and on the other hand they supply their output either to consumers or to further processing, both commercial and craftsmanship. Through these linkages agriculture affects income and employment in upstream and downstream sectors. These effects in the upstream and downstream sectors are indirect and are in addition to the direct effects on farm households. If income generated by either direct or indirect effects is spent within the region, further economic effects are induced. Due to these multiplier effects, agriculture is often claimed to be a motor for economic development in rural areas, and the possible multiplier effects should be ideally included when analysing the importance of agriculture in rural areas.

In 2004, more than half of the entire land territory (53 percent) was under agricultural cultivation. Only 30 percent of the German land territory was covered by woodland. While these rather large shares indicate the general importance of agriculture and forestry in land use for Germany as a whole, the following paragraphs focus on land use patterns by matching the available district data with the classification of districts.

Agricultural land use was not significant in rural districts. In urbanised districts, surprisingly high shares of land were in agricultural use. In urbanised districts in East Germany, for example, about 61 percent of the area was under agricultural cultivation, the overall highest share. While certainly resulting from the rather broad definition of agriculture land in the statistics, the high proportion of agricultural land use may point out two potentially important functions of agriculture there. First, despite advanced logistics, agriculture in urbanised districts (as well as rural surroundings) may still supply people living in adjacent centres of cities or towns with food products, mainly fresh and perishable products. Secondly, agriculture creates landscapes, and may therefore contribute to the environmental quality as well as recreational possibilities in the vicinity of cities and town. With respectively 30 percent and 40 percent in West and East Germany, the share of agricultural land use was considerably lower in cities.

While the area of agricultural land only marginally

changed over time, the number of farms significantly decreased. The change in the number of farms between 1999 and 2003 was evident—it was distinguished between the different district types as well as part-time and full-time agricultural holdings. Both the number of part-time and full-time agricultural holdings fell in all district types, except for rural surroundings and districts in East Germany. Here, the number of full-time agricultural holdings rose, whereby the increase in rural districts (6.3 percent) was larger than in rural surroundings (1.2 percent), and the number of part-time farmers decreased. [18]

Possibly due to the relatively high proportion of smaller family farms, the decline in the number of farms was more pronounced in West Germany than in East Germany, in relative and absolute terms. The number of part-time farms fell particularly sharply. Given that part-time farmers more frequently engage in off-farm activities to sustain their income, this observation could indicate that farmers find the step between part-time farming and ceasing production generally easier to take. [19]

Germans are looking for healthy, tasty, and nutritious products that are safely grown and processed. Demand for fresh and organic food is particularly strong with Germany's ageing population, but is found throughout all generations of the population.

Sales of fruits and vegetables are growing, while sugar and confectionary sales have declined. Fish and seafood is also growing in popularity due to perceived health benefits. Ethically sourced and fair trade products are also gaining in popularity among German consumers, particularly those in their thirties. German consumers are turning towards easy to prepare foods, but are unwilling to sacrifice taste and quality for convenience. Demand for convenience is helping to drive pre-packaged foods, ready-meals and take-away foods. Healthier food options are also appearing in the pre-packaged food industry with significant success.

More frequently, Germans are replacing home cooked meals with snacks and foods that can be consumed on the go. It is not uncommon for one or two meals a day to be missed and replaced by snack type foods.

Vegetarians are also increasing in prominence in Germany, as is the popularity of ethnic/foreign cuisines such as Indian and Asian dishes.

While the German food market is quite competitive and EU members are close trade partners with Germany, opportunities may lie with Canadian exporters who can provide innovative, quality products to a market of discerning and health conscious consumers leading busy lifestyles. Germany is considered a 'mature market' because of its advanced development. Therefore, exporters are encouraged to seek out established importers with unique and originally labelled products, as these products have the most success in the consumer market. Goods such as maple syrup products, pet foods, fruit and vegetable juice, fruit and edible nuts as well as organic products, among others will likely have the most appeal to German importers and consumers.

Agriculture and Agri-Food Canada (AAFC) has identified Germany as a secondary priority market for increasing Canadian food brand awareness through sponsored marketing and promotional activities. AAFC also manages the Canadian presence at the ANUGA food and beverage trade show held in Germany, with an official Canada pavilion that provides a variety of services to Canadian exhibitors.

The German retail food sector is dominated by five large retailers that claim more than half of the market. In 2010, the overall market share of discounters offering a limited selection of mainly private labelled goods at low prices remained stable at 41.6 percent. As mentioned above, all these retailers rely on specialized distributors/wholesalers for their 'Promoted by Federal Ministry of Economics and Technology, and Federal Government Commissioner for the New Federal States in accordance with a German Parliament Resolution' products.

However, some supermarkets will sometimes contract directly with a foreign supplier and appoint an importing company of their choice to bring the products into Germany accordingly. [20]

Exports and Imports: The German food and beverage industry is highly fragmented and competitive. Food imports from other countries within the European Union fall under the 'free movement of goods' principle. This means that products that are imported by other EU-countries may be brought into Germany even if they violate German food laws. If this is the case, importers must obtain a permit from the Federal Office for Consumer Protection and Food Safety (BVL) in order to sell the product in Germany. The duties to be paid for food brought from outside the European Union are subject to European legislation as well. The tariffs for different food products are published in TARIC, the Online Customs Tariff Database.

According to the Department of Foreign Affairs and International Trade, Canada (DFAIT), the German food market can be characterized through a combination of four factors: retail is dominated by a small number of large chains; discounters hold a very strong presence in the market; consumers are very price sensitive, compared to other European markets; and lastly, Germany represents a rapidly growing organic market and a consumer base that is aware of and resistant to GMO food products.

Legislative Framework

LMBG: This law is also known as Food and Commodities Act. It contains a set of fundamental facts and definitions. The main purpose of this law is protection of consumers against health hazards deceptions regarding food, tobacco products, cosmetics and other necessaries. With the age of globalisation coming in, there is a need for legal food provisions. Regulations were laid down in the German Legislation which defined the packaging of foodstuff. Foodstuffs which are harmless to health are imported.

German Food Code: The German Food Code is an assemblage of guidelines, which are described in the production, composition or other characteristics of foods that are responsible for the marketability. The guidelines are adopted by the German Food Code Commission, taking into account the ones recognized by the Federal government for international food standards. The guidelines are published by the Ministry in consultation with the Federal Ministry of Economics and Technology.

German Food Code Commission: The German Food Code Commission is formed at the Federal Ministry. The Ministry, in agreement with the Federal Ministry of Economics and Technology, appoints the members of the Commission from the scientific community, the food control department, consumer organizations and food industry in terms of numbers and ratio. The Ministry appoints the chairman of the Commission and his deputy after consultation with the Commission's Rules of Procedure. The Commission shall decide on the guidelines in principle unanimously. Decisions in which no more than three quarters of the members of the Commission agree, are ineffective. The arrangements made by the Rules of Procedure are as follows. [21]

Article 8 of the LMBG refers to food definitely harmful to health. A violation of the latter provision can be pursued and punished as a criminal offence. At the same time, Article 8 of the LMBG prohibits the marketing of objects and substances which, due to their external appearance, can be confused with food by consumers, in particular by children. Article 17 of the Act prohibits the marketing of degraded or deceptively labelled food.

The German government is very conscious about the health of its inhabitants. Most of the food laws are made for consumer protection. With time, the need for a better law emerged as LMBG was very concise.

LFGB German Food Commodity and Feed Law: The food, consumer goods and feed Code is a federal law. It largely replaces the Food and Commodities Act (LMBG).This law was developed in 2005 and provides basic definitions, procedural rules and goals of the German food Law.

They define the general food safety and health protection rules, address labelling requirements, regulate inspection, detention and seizure rules of suspect food. There has been uniform legal framework as food crisis is the main issue of modern world.

The LFGB on September 7, 2005 came into force and replaced the hitherto applicable Food and Commodities Act. The new Food and Feed Code includes all production and processing stages from field to plate and is applicable for food and consumer products for animal feed and cosmetics.

It was approved by the Federal Council of Germany in September 2006. The marketing standards were replaced by the respective EU regulations. It includes product-specific law and regulations (milk and margarine law, wine law, regulation cheese), cross-product regulations (MRL regulation, food labelling regulations, product liability law), neighbouring rights law (law regulating prices, Infection Protection Act), implementing regulation, guidelines and court rulings.

The German food law consists of about 230 different ordinances, including the Food Labelling Ordinance, Packaging Ordinance, Dietetic Foods Ordinance, various hygienic and veterinary requirements, as well as numerous other special product or product group rules and regulations. The provisions of the food law are voluminous, frequently quite complicated and often subject to interpretation. Ultimately, the German importer has final responsibility for the marketability of any imported products into Germany. The German law enforcement agencies hold the German importer solely responsible for any violations of the food law since they cannot take action against foreign producers including those in other EU countries. Violations of the food law by the importer constitute a punishable offence.

The protection of health and the protection of consumers against deception are the two basic concerns of the food law. An EU based regulation plays an important role in the sense that it lays down the general principles and requirements for the manufacture and handling of food and feed. The basic regulation is equilibrated by a series of regulations that also apply directly in all states of the community. These include the European hygiene regulations. There are also European directives, which must be implemented by individual states or in national legislations, for example, the food supplements directive. In the German food law, the task of the European guidelines—if they are not directly applicable—are incorporated in national legislations and supplements, if necessary.

The food law is influenced by the requirements of Germans. Establishment of laws provide a crucial step in framing the legislation. There is a conjugation with a multitude of special laws and ordinances, providing the basic regulations of the food law. The LFGB and German Food and Feed Law are combined to form one code. It is the purpose of LFGB to protect consumer health by preventative measures. It provides a legal framework for circulations of food. It also discusses about health of consumers.

The Food and Feed Law had new provisions for legislation and administration in conformity with the EU regulations. The policies focus mainly on consumer interests and consumer protection which includes food safety and public health. The principles used are same as compared to EU. On many instances, findings suggest that the German Food and Feed Law have stricter provisions.

Many provisions are made which discuss about prohibition of food items for the purpose of health protection. According to Article 14 of the framework regulations, in determining whether or not a food is potentially injurious to health, not only the probable immediate or short-term effects of that food on the heath of a person consuming it, but also the effects on subsequent generations have to be considered. It is prohibited to place into the stream of commerce, any food if consumed, can cause health hazards.

Nutritional value of the food product plays an important role in the lives of Germans as they have shifted their focus to healthier options. There is an urgent need of regulations to be implemented. The NKV provides information about the nutritional value. The aim of the NKV is to protect the individual from having an unbalanced diet.

Food supplements have reached to the houses of Germans. The Code stipulates that the food must be safe. They are registered with the Federal Office of Consumer Protection and Food Safety (BVL) and do not require marketing authorisation. They act as a supplement in a diet. Misleading advertisements are prohibited in Germany.

Formal responsibility lies with the public authorities of the federal state in which the product is in the market or in which the manufacturer, importer, seller or distributor has its head office. The virtually incalculable number of food supplements on the market wrongly give the consumer, an impression that sufficient nutrient intake is not possible solely from a diet with traditional foods. In principle, a balanced, diverse diet supplies a healthy body with all the essential substances. In most cases supplements are, therefore, superfluous.

Food control does not work in Germany. The meat scandal opened eyes of the people. The main problem is with the German federal structure. No inspections are done by the government to investigate into food chains. The law has many loopholes and exceptions. The laws are not implemented efficiently. There is a need for an entire food monitoring system.

German Dietetic Food Law: The German Dietetic Food Law defines the properties foods must have in order for the manufacturer to label them as dietetic. It requires that foods and beverages labelled as dietetic must differ substantially from other regular foods. A simple listing of the nutrient content, bread units, and/or caloric value on the label is not sufficient to allow the use of the term "dietetic". Health-related statements are strictly limited. It is strongly recommended that US exporters consult with a German food laboratory before making any dietary claims for products to be marketed in Germany.

Agencies that Work for Food Security

Federal Ministry of Food, Agriculture and Consumer Protection (BMELV): The Federal Ministry of Food, Agriculture and Consumer Protection (BMELV) is Germany's food safety communications centre. This is where things come together: reports on public food and feed monitoring, scientific opinions, the minutes of parliamentary debates, EU-level hearings and talks, information from industry associations, and, of course, media reports and press releases. Given that somewhere between 80 and 90 percent of Germany's food law is based on EU legislations, one of the ministry's main tasks is to maintain close contact with Brussels and represent German interests there. BMELV delegates certain risk management activities to the Federal Office of Consumer Protection and Food Safety (BVL).

According to the Federal Ministry of Food, Agriculture and Consumer Protection (BMELV), regulators have, "for many years, been collecting data on the levels of dioxins and dioxin-like compounds in foods and animal feed", but now this information and industry's internal controls are "to be brought together in a joint data pool at the Federal Office of Consumer Protection and Food Safety (Bundesamtfür Verbraucherschutz und Lebensmittelsicherheit) in Berlin". The office will evaluate this data each quarter in an effort to "instigate counter-measures more quickly".

Agriculture and nutrition research are the basis for a safe, healthy and balanced diet. The Federal Ministry of Food, Agriculture and Consumer Protection (BMELV) allocates € 250 million to its research institutes every year. BMELV has announced plans to revise the statutory orders governing the approval of feed businesses and the separation of feed fats and industrial fats during production. Cabinet ministers are still debating, whether "an infringement of the Food and Feed

Code should be classified as either a criminal or a regulatory offence or whether the current range of penalties is appropriate".

In 2009, the production of agricultural produce from organic farming received around € 137 million in public funds in Germany. Under the 2010 to 2013 framework plan of GAK, the promotion of organic cultivation methods takes the following shape under the principles governing the promotion of market- and site-adapted land management (MSL).

Germany has by far the greatest demand for organic products in the EU and is second only to the US at global level. The share of sales of organic foods in the total turnover of foods in Germany increased from € 1.48 billion in 1997 to approximately € 5.9 billion in 2010 (excluding beverages, tobacco and away-from-home catering). This accounted for 3.4 percent of the food market. Experts believe that organic farming still has considerable growth potential.

Organic production and regional products from welfare-oriented animal husbandry play an important role in the agricultural policy. Organic farming is an essential component of Germany's national sustainability strategy. The organic products and transparent production processes truly shine on the hopes of many consumers. The development of organic farming is upto the consumers. They are the ones who must be prepared to pay higher prices for organic produce and, in this way, to reward the special ecological contribution and quality features of organic farmers.

The departmental research of the BMELV was newly structured in 2008 taking greater consideration of the subject of climate protection and the topic of "climate protection and adaptation to climate change" was adopted in the BMELV 2008 research plan as one of the seven main objectives of the departmental research.

Climate adaptation is a social task to which all actors in industry, science, research, administration, education and politics must contribute. The public authorities have the task of modifying the requirements for efficient adaptation and preventive planning so that the holdings can make intelligent decisions for successful adaptation.

Climate change has hardly any effects on processing. Changes occur in particular for the basic products. BMELV works on the subject of climate protection and the topic complex “climate protection and adaptation to climate change”.

Agriculture and forestry are the main areas affected by climate change and must adapt to this development. Carbon dioxide is stored in forests, the soil, wood and agricultural products but is also comprised in greenhouse gas emissions in agriculture. That is why active climate policy is an important element of agricultural policy.

In Germany, the farming industry contributes to conserving our cultivated landscapes. The Federal Government, the Länder and the EU encourage the farming industry to protect the climate, soil, waters and biodiversity by means of special agri-environmental measures. Environmental protection, nature conservation, biodiversity and climate change likewise play a major role for forests and fishing.

German/EU politicians claim that German/EU consumers oppose foods derived from genetically engineered plants. Whether or not such a statement is true cannot be verified since there are very few products labelled as “genetically modified” in the market. Since 1998, a de facto moratorium for further approvals of genetically engineered events has been in place in the EU, restricting the importation of bulk corn and other products. In April 2004, the new EU legislation for labelling food and feed products derived from genetically engineered plants, and for implementing a tracing system became effective.

Under the EU labelling regulations, processed products produced from biotech crops, such as soybean oil, must have a “GMO” label even though no “GMOs” are present in the final processed product. The new regulations require that an adventitious presence of more than 0.9 percent genetically engineered material in one single ingredient has to be labelled on the final product. The relevant authority for the approval of new biotech events and for monitoring the trade of products derived from biotechnology is the Federal Ministry of Food, Agriculture and Consumer Protection.

Food and Agriculture Organization of the United Nations (FAO): The Food and Agriculture Organization of the United Nations (FAO) is a specialised agency of the United Nations that leads international efforts to defeat hunger. Serving both developed and developing countries, FAO acts as a neutral forum where all nations meet as equals to negotiate agreements and debate policy. The donation, from Germany's food security trust fund with FAO, will finance a global project as well as inter-regional projects and a number of smaller initiatives in sub-Saharan Africa. They will be implemented between 2010 and 2012 and countries already targeted include Sierra Leone, Uganda, Tanzania and Kenya. The aim of the global project is to improve the abilities of regional organizations to develop, implement and monitor food security training programmes. German funding will also be provided for a project aimed at improving the design and planning of smallholder systems that integrate food and bio-energy production.

World Bank: The World Bank is an international financial institution that provides financial and technical assistance to developing countries for development programs (e.g. bridges, roads, schools, etc.) with the stated goal of reducing poverty.

The Heavily Indebted Poor Countries (HIPC) Initiative was launched by the World Bank and the IMF in 1996, and endorsed by some 180 governments around the world as an effective and welcome approach to help poor and severely indebted countries, reduce their debt as part of an overall poverty reduction strategy. In September 1999, at the annual meeting of the World Bank and IMF, the HIPC Initiative was significantly expanded to provide deeper, broader and faster debt relief to some three dozen countries. This enhancement, and a redesigned strategy to link debt relief to poverty reduction, will help to eliminate debt as an obstacle to development and allow countries to invest more in their future. The Initiative was designed to reduce debts to sustainable levels for poor countries that pursue economic and social policy reforms, and is used specifically in cases where traditional debt relief mechanisms will not be enough to help countries exit from the rescheduling process.

European Union (EU): It is an economic and political union or confederation [22] of 27 member states which are located primarily in Europe. The EU traces its origins from the European Coal and Steel Community (ECSC) and the European Economic Community (EEC), formed by six countries in 1958. In the intervening years, the EU has grown in size by the accession of new member states, and in power by the addition of policy areas to its remit. The Maastricht Treaty established the European Union under its current name in 1993.

The latest amendment to the constitutional basis of the EU, the Treaty of Lisbon, came into force in 2009. The EU has developed a single market through a standardised system of laws which apply to all member states. Within the Schengen Area (which includes EU and non-EU states) passport controls have been abolished. EU policies aim to ensure the free movement of people, goods, services, and capital, [23] enact legislation in justice and home affairs, and maintain common policies on trade, [24] agriculture, [25] fisheries and regional development. [26] A monetary union, the euro zone, was established in 1999 and, as of June 2015, is composed of 19 member states. Through the Common Foreign and Security Policy, the EU has developed a limited role in external relations and defence. Permanent diplomatic missions have been established around the world and the EU is represented at the United Nations, the WTO, the G8 and the G-20.

With a combined population of over 500 million inhabitants,

[27] or 7.3 percent of the woıld's population, [28] the EU generated a nominal GDP of 18,451 billion US dollars in 2014, which represents an estimated 20 percent of global GDP when measured in terms of purchasing power parity.

Position with Regard to International Treaties

ASEAN: As of 2015, ASEAN (Association of Southeast Asian Nations) has 10 member states, one candidate member state, and one observer state. The ASEAN is an organization on the Southeast Asian region that aims to accelerate economic growth, social progress, and cultural development among its members and to promote regional peace.

The ASEAN Regional Forum is an informal multilateral dialogue of 27 members that seeks to address security issues in the Asia-Pacific region. [29]

International Treaty on Plant Genetic Resources for Food and Agriculture (ITPGRFA): ITPGRFA recognises the enormous contributions—past, present, future—of the world's farmers in conserving, improving and making available plant genetic resources for food and agriculture as the basis of Farmers' Rights Project. The Farmers' Rights Project is an international project set up at the Fridtj of Nansen Institute in Norway with support from the Norwegian Ministry of Agriculture and Food, the Royal Norwegian Ministry of Foreign Affairs and the German GTZ, with affiliated experts in Peru, India and Ethiopia, to facilitate such a common understanding and develop a basis for proposals to the governing body of the ITPGRFA on specific measures to be taken.

Recognizing that the responsibility for realizing farmers' rights rests with national governments, Article 9 of the ITPGRFA calls on contracting parties to take appropriate measures to protect and promote farmers' rights. A number of resolutions were adopted by FAO conference on farmer's right. However, in 1993, the FAO conference recognized the need for further steps to realize farmers' rights and adopted

Resolution 7/93 to request the director general of the FAO to provide a forum for negotiations among governments on, *inter alia*, the issue of the realization of farmer's right. The negotiation on the realization of farmer's rights was long and difficult. Discussions began during the process of adopting GPA (Global Plan of Action) for the conservation and sustainable utilization of plant genetic resources for food and agriculture.

However, it was at the final hour that the Fourth International Conference on Plant Genetic Resources which was held in Leipzig, Germany from June 17 to 23, 1996, adopted a text stipulating that one of the main aims of the GPA is to recognize the desirability of sharing equitable benefits arising from the use of traditional knowledge. Non-Annex 1 PGRFAs or those that are not under the control of the contracting parties or in the public domain may be voluntary included in the international common pool. Consequently, Netherlands and Germany have already taken some steps to put non-Annex 1 materials in the multilateral system.

Major Challenges Faced by Germany

Business expectations of German enterprises are improving from the entire spectrum of the economy. The recovery is domestically driven and—more than expected—driven by exports. For the first time, Germany is ranked as the world's best logistics location. All in all, entrepreneurs have confidence in the economic revival; they are investing and hiring. Besides creating new jobs, companies also need to increase their productivity and operate closer to full capacity. But despite the current euphoria, companies are aware of the future challenges.

Firstly, according to the report from Deustche Bank research in December 2010, which states that cyclical risks in major economies could have an impact on Germany. In US, for instance, there is an economic slowdown given the continuing dire labour market situation.

Secondly, if there is a major setback or downfall in the real estate markets, then interest rates could be hiked further, leading to slowdown in the growth. Moreover, Germany is the third largest exporting country and due to its strategic geographical location and due to present 'currency war' it might include political risk of increasing protectionism, which could result in another setback for the global trade.

A review of the various subsidies used to stimulate environmental protection may also be needed, particularly with regard to the environmental and economic effectiveness. The use of economic instruments (e.g. fees, charges and deposit-refund systems) could be expanded in Germany in combination with regulatory instruments to achieve environmental objectives more cost effectively. Experience with waste water charges provides a precedent concerning water management. Other areas, such as air and waste management, could also benefit from a wider use of economic instruments to address, for instance, the challenges posed by CO_2 emission targets. Hence, on the one hand when Germany is focussing in providing for agricultural benefit for increasing the standard of the farmers, especially the small land holding farmers, at the same time they should keep focus on the agricultural degradation. As a result, the environmental degradation cost as well as the maintenance cost gets included in the food cost.

We must also look into the environmental hazards which might indirectly cause a major harm to the society as well as the other endangered species which in turn will result in disequilibrium in the maintenance of balance in the environment as well as meeting future disasters. So, keeping in mind all these things, the environmental scientists, policy makers, economists and legal experts in their opinions have suggested long-term solutions to the problems of food security, thereby keeping balance in all the issues.

Food security is a prerequisite for development. In most cases it is caused by structural factors such as poverty, food production not keeping pace with the population growth, natural resource degradation, the HIV/AIDS pandemic, and the neglect of rural areas in infrastructure and public service provision. Weather risks destabilise households and countries and create food insecurity. Germany focuses on sustainable use of natural resources, biodiversity and poverty alleviation. Food security, agriculture and rural development are the main focus areas of German development cooperation with its partner countries. In addition, the government uses aid to deal with short-term food shortages.

In future, as far as Germany is concerned, food security is to be integrated into policies and projects in fields such as rural development, health, education and social development.

Germany needs to make financial commitments in compensation for the damage caused by climate change. This should happen through international funds governed under the UN umbrella—especially the UN Adaptation Fund—and also new instruments such as insurance schemes. National governments need to mainstream adaptation into all government policies.

They also need to make sure that the most vulnerable groups within their country are identified and supported in their adaptation. Guiding principles for new climate treaty should be focused on. It would partly shift the focus of adaptation policies from national states to the individual people who are threatened by climate change in a way that might become existential.

National governments need to mainstream adaptation into all government policies. They also need to make sure that the most vulnerable groups within their country are identified and supported in their adaptation. Rights based adaptation policies are one good tool to ensure that money earmarked for adaptation is spent reasonably. The office of BMELV and Food and Agriculture Organisation should work together and develop guidelines which help governments to design adaptation policies accordingly.

Endnotes

1. "Food and Nutrition Security in Poverty Alleviation: Concepts, Strategies, and Experiences", German Agency for Technical Cooperation, Review Article, accessed on March 23, 2012, available at: http://apjcn.nhri.org.tw/server/apjcn/Volume11/vol11sup4/Gross.pdf.
2. "The New Generations, the Family and Society", *Population Issues,* 1999, accessed on March 23, 2012, available at: http://www.unfpa.org/6billion/populationissues/generation.htm.
3. "Germany Health and Environmental Trends", Agriculture and Agro-food Canada, accessed on March 23, 2012, available at: http://www.gov.mb.ca/agriculture/statistics/agri-food/germany_health_environment_en.pdf.
4. OECD, "Economic Survey: Germany", February 2012.
5. "Development Cooperation", DAAD, accessed on March 16, 2013, available at: https://www.daad.de/entwicklung/exceed/projekte/11604.en.htm
6. OECD, "Economic Survey: Germany", February 2012.
7. "Food and Nutrition Security in Poverty Alleviation: Concepts, Strategies, and Experiences", German Agency for Technical Cooperation, Review Article, accessed on March 23, 2012, available at: http://apjcn.nhri.org.tw/server/apjcn/Volume11/vol11sup4/Gross.pdf.
8. "Understanding Rising Income Inequality in Germany", Discussion Paper Series, accessed on March 24, 2012, available at: http://www.lsw.wiso.unierlangen.de/VfS/Vortr__ge/Biewen_dp5062.pdf.
9. "Germany", OECD Better Life Index, accessed on March 23, 2012, available at: http://oecdbetterlifeindex.org/countries/Germany/.
10. "Transatlantic Experts Group on Food Security", The German Mashall Fund of the United States, accessed on June 2, 2013, available at: http://www.gmfus.org/programs/sustainable-development/transatlantic-experts-group.

11. "Germany Health and Environmental Trends", Agriculture and Agro-Food Canada, accessed on March 23, 2012, available at: http://www.gov.mb.ca/agriculture/statistics/agri-food/Germany_health_environment_en.pdf.
12. "Germany Health and Environmental Trends", Agriculture and Agro-Food Canada, accessed on March 23, 2012, available at: http://www.gov.mb.ca/agriculture/statistics/agri-food/Germany_health_environment_en.pdf.
13. "Review Climate Change and the Current Food Crisis", CAB Reviews: Perspectives in Agriculture, Veterinary Science, Nutrition and Natural Resources, accessed on March 23, 2012, available at: http://www.gecafs.org/publications/Publications/Gregory_&_Ingram_CC_and_the_current_food_crisis.pdf.
14. "The German International Green Week", International Food Policy Research Institute, accessed on February 17, 2013, available at: http://dgcorner.ifpri.info/2013/01/24/the-german-international-green-week-to-advance-the-global-agricultural-development-and-food-security-agenda.
15. Commission communication to the European Parliament, the Council, the European Economic and Social Committee (EESC) and the Committee of the Regions about a community action programme with regard to health and consumer protection (2007-2013) of April 6, 2005.
16. CEC, Commission of the European Union, Programmed' áctioncommunautaire de promotion, d'ínformation, d'éducation et de formation en matière santé, conformement au cadre de l´actiondans le domaine de la santé publique, COM (94) 202 Final, Brussels.
17. "Plant Technology", Research in Germany, accessed on June 16, 2013, available at: http://www.research-in-germany.de/dachportal/en/Research-Areas-A-Z/Plants.html.
18. "Scientists to Reach Out to Farmers to Ensure Food Security", *Business Recorder*, accessed on May 21, 2013, available at: http://www.brecorder.com/agriculture-a-allied/183/1206307.
19. "German Academics Unite to Deliver Urban Food Security", *Pacpard*, accessed on May 16, 2013, available at: http://paepard.blogspot.in/2013/05/german-academics-unite-to-

deliver-urban.html.

20. "Food and Beverage: A Large Potential Market for Foreign Exporters", IXPOS, accessed on October 10, 2012, available at: http://www.ixpos.de/IXPOS/Navigation/EN/Your-business-in-germany/Business-sectors/Consumer-goods/food-and-beverage.html?view=renderpdf.
21. "German Food Code Commission" Bundesministerium der Justiz, accessed on March 24, 2012, available at: http://www.gesetze-im-internet.de/lfgb/__16.html.
22. Catherine Barnard, "The Substantive Law of the EU: The Four Freedoms", New York: Oxford University Press, 2007, p. 447.
23. "The EU Single Market: Fewer Barriers, More Opportunities", European Commission, accessed on March 30, 2012, available at: http://ec.europa.eu/internal_market/index_en.htm.
24. "Common Commercial Policy", *Europa*, accessed on September 6, 2012, available at: http://europa.eu/pol/agr/index_en.htm.
25. "Agriculture and Fisheries Council", The Council of the European Union, accessed on September 3, 2012, available at: http://europa.eu/pol/agr/index_en.htm.
26. "Overview of the European Union Activities: Regional Policy", *Europa*, accessed on September 9, 2012, available at: http://europa.eu/pol/agr/index_en.htm.
27. "First Demographic Estimates for 2009", *Eurostat*, accessed on December 11, 2012, available at: http://epp.eurostat.ec.europa.eu/cache/ity_offpub/ks-qa-09-047/en/ks-qa-09-047-en.pdf.
28. "European Union Reaches 500 Million through Combination of Accessions, Migration and Natural Growth", Vienna Institute of Demography, accessed on June 13, 2013, available at: http://ec.europa.eu/ewsi/UDRW/images/items/news_14979_370303423.pdf.
29. "Association of South East Nations", ASEAN Security Community, accessed on March 23, 2012, available at: http://www.asean.org/3839.htm.

7

Indonesia: Yayasan Bahan Makanan (Food Stuff Handling Foundation)

Sharngan Arvindakshan and Kaustubh Rastogi

Economic Overview

History and Upheavals: In the 1960s, the Indonesian economy deteriorated drastically as a result of political instability, a young and inexperienced government, and economic nationalism, which resulted in severe poverty and hunger. By the time of Soekarno's downfall in the mid-1960s, the economy was in chaos with 1,000 percent annual inflation, shrinking export revenues, crumbling infrastructure, factories operating at minimal capacity, and negligible investment. Following President Soekarno's downfall in the mid-1960s, the 'New Order' administration brought a degree of discipline to economic policy that quickly brought inflation down, stabilized the currency, rescheduled foreign debt, and attracted foreign aid and investment.

Indonesia was until recently Southeast Asia's only member of OPEC, and the 1970s oil price rise provided an export revenue windfall that contributed to sustained high economic growth rates, averaging over 7 percent from 1968 to 1981. High levels of regulation and a dependence on declining oil prices resulted in slow growth rate of an average of 4.3 percent per annum between 1981 and 1988. A range of economic reforms were introduced in the late 1980s including a managed devaluation of the rupiah to improve export competitiveness and de-regulation of the financial sector. [1] Foreign investment flowed into Indonesia, particularly into the rapidly developing export-oriented manufacturing sector, and from 1989 to 1997, the Indonesian economy grew by an average of over 7 percent.

The Asian Financial Crisis that began to affect Indonesia in mid-1997 became an economic and political crisis. Indonesia's initial response was to float the rupiah, raise key domestic interest rates, and tighten fiscal policy. In October 1997, Indonesia and the International Monetary Fund (IMF) reached agreement on an economic reform program aimed at macroeconomic stabilization and elimination of some of the country's most damaging economic policies, such as the national car program and the clove monopoly, both involving family members of President Soeharto. The rupiah remained weak, however, and President Soeharto was forced to resign in May 1998. In August 1998, Indonesia and the IMF agreed on an extended fund facility (EFF) under President B.J. Habibie that included significant structural reform targets. President Abdurrahman Wahid took office in October 1999, and Indonesia and the IMF signed another EFF in January 2000. The new program also had a range of economic and structural reforms and governance targets.

The effects of the financial and economic crisis were severe. By November 1997, rapid currency depreciation had seen public debt reach US$ 60 billion, imposing severe strains on the government's budget. In 1998, real GDP contracted by 13.7 percent. The economy reached its low point in mid-1999 and the real GDP growth for the year was 0.3 percent. Inflation reached 77 percent in 1998 but slowed to 2 percent in 1999.

Green Revolution: The 'Green Revolution' was initially hailed as a cure-all for underproduction in the impoverished countries of Southeast Asia and the Third World in general. Recent critics, however, looking beyond gross national product, have indicated that these programs result in various forms of environmental degradation and increased economic polarization. Uprgradation in technology has improved production and helped the impoverished, but has also led to the reduction in employment opportunities. [2]

The fact that the 'Green Revolution' has encouraged new forms of labour recruitment in harvesting, does not explain their acceptance at this particular time, nor does it explain the social consequences for rural society. The concept of Focault's governmentality was introduced and was accompanied by training camps. They promoted the concept of working together as a group, away from their villages.

Foreign Relations: While Indonesia's foreign policy has gained new significance because policies no longer focus on the West, the United States remains the largest benefactor of Indonesia and is the only major economic power, other than ASEAN perhaps, that Indonesia has strong ties with.

Suharto in his tenure, followed a moderate foreign policy and this was followed by all his successors so far. The separation from East Timor aside, Indonesia has and maintains relatively cordial relations with the other countries in the area. Economic development is the driving force behind all the foreign policies of Indonesia.

An example of the above statement is its participation in the Association of Southeast Asian Nations (ASEAN), of which it was a founding member in 1967 along with Thailand, Malaysia, Singapore, and the Philippines.

US-Indonesian Relations: The United States has been a staunch supporter of Indonesia and has been the highest benefactor in terms of monetary contributions to the development of the Indonesian economy. With US support, 43 billion US dollars was sent to Indonesia from the International Monetary Fund (IMF) in the year 2004. US aid to the country has primarily focused on programs for improving the policy environment for rapid, inclusive and sustainable economic growth and on the production and marketing of high value crops, particularly coffee, cocoa, and horticulture, including related agribusiness. The resulting increase in production and economic growth has generated substantial employment to increase incomes and reduce poverty.

On November 19, 2011, Secretary Clinton signed a five-year, $600 million Millennium Challenge Corporation (MCC) compact with the Government of Indonesia on the sidelines of the East Asia Summit in Bali. The MCC compact with the Republic of Indonesia was designed to reduce poverty through economic growth. The compact's three projects were expected to increase household income in project areas through increased productivity, reduced energy costs, and improved provision of public sector growth—enhancing goods and services.

The U.S. Agency for International Development (USAID) and its predecessor agencies have provided development assistance to Indonesia since 1950. Initial assistance focused on the most urgent needs, including food aid, infrastructure rehabilitation, health care and training. Throughout the 1970s and 1980s—a time of great economic growth in Indonesia—USAID played a major role in helping the country achieve self-sufficiency in rice production and in reducing the fertility rate.

Legislative and Administrative Framework

In the past, the agrarian policy of Indonesia has centred on rice production due to its central role in the Indonesian economy. [3] Since the 1950s, various methods have been employed by the government to stabilize rice prices. The most important being "Yayasan Bahan Makanan", later known as Food Stuff Handling Foundation—whose main aim was price stabilisation—was unsuccessful due to low rice productivity and poor infrastructure.

New Order Reforms: During this period, not only the output of products such as steel, aluminium, and cement increased quickly, but also of the products such as food, textiles and cigarettes. From the 1970s onward, the increased oil price in the world market provided Indonesia with a massive income from oil and gas exports. Wood exports shifted from logs to plywood, pulp, and paper, at the cost of large stretches of environmentally valuable rainforest.

Soeharto managed to apply part of these revenues towards the development of technologically advanced manufacturing industry. Referring to this period of stable economic growth, the World Bank Report of 1993 speaks of an 'East Asian Miracle' emphasizing the macroeconomic stability and the investments in human capital (World Bank, 1993: vi).

In the New Order period there was a very interesting system of food security. A logistic agency was set up, known as the BULOG (Badan Urusan Logistik) with the aim of stabilising the prices. The price stabilisation mechanism that it employed was two-fold. There was a price flooring with respect to the price at which this organisation procured rice from the farmers and also a price ceiling with respect to retail prices. This made sure that the farmers got a minimum price for their product and also that the consumers did not have to pay huge sums for the rice.

Under this scheme, BULOG has been quite successful in minimising the fluctuation of rice price through stock management mechanism. [4] The ability of BULOG to control its stock effectively has been enabled by various factors among others—wide distribution and storage networks as well as close cooperation with local farmer cooperatives and rice traders. As for the successful implementation of price stabilisation, the availability of special credit scheme from Bank Indonesia (The Central Bank) called liquidity credit has played a critical role. Under this scheme, BULOG was provided inexpensive credits for its procurement activity to reduce the excess supply of rice during the harvest season.

Post the Suharto era, Indonesia witnessed a more liberal political system called the Reformasi. This period which marked ten years in 2008, was bent more towards a democratic set up with civil liberties being given more importance. However, some people look back at the authoritarian rule of Suharto, with fondness, as there was ample economic growth and improved living conditions. On a more positive note, civil liberties and steady economic recovery have been the upsides of this system.

As noted in Law No. 25/2000, poverty eradication is articulated by three programs: equitable fulfilment of basic needs, such as essential food, basic health, education and housing services for poor families and communities; the development of entrepreneurial skills among the poor to enable them to be more productive economically and self-reliant; and the development of social security systems to protect vulnerable groups.

Food and Nutrition Surveillance System (FNSS): In approaching the food insecurity situation, Indonesia had developed a Food and Nutrition Surveillance System (FNSS) which was initially only introduced in areas facing acute hunger. [5] Since 1994, the system has been adopted as a part of improving the effectiveness of food insecurity monitoring system. This system basically consists of three sub-systems, namely:

1. Production and availability surveillance sub-system (MOA).
2. Distribution surveillance subsystem (BULOG).
3. Consumption and nutrition sub-system (MOH).

This team was coordinated by Ministry of Food and Horticulture (MOFH). It was able to identify the food insecure areas on the basis of a number of parameters. However, this approach does not provide any information concerning the list of households facing the famine threat.

Food Act: In 1996, Indonesia for the first time promulgated the food law for food related matter. The law basically outlined the basic regulation on food safety and food security issues. The formal definition of food security that has been adopted by Indonesia is the condition that food should be sufficient for all households as indicated by the availability of food supply sufficiently in terms of quantity and quality, that food is safe, equitably available and affordable. The Food Act was enacted on November 4, 1996 prior to the holding of the World Food Summit in Rome. This law provided the legal basis for food security regulation in the future.

One of the most important legislations in Indonesia has been the Food Act, 1996. It entails various methods and requirements to provide for better and cleaner agricultural products coupled with better distribution techniques. Certain health and nutrition labelling requirements make it easier for the consumers to identify the products, thus creating a brand name with respect to quality products. The year of 1997 was recorded as the worst food crisis in the history of Indonesia's economic development in post-Independence. The first half of the year 1997 was dominated by optimism on the stability of food production as experienced in the previous year of 1996. That achievement resulted in the domestic rice surplus being available in domestic market where the domestic purchase of rice by government exceeded 2 million tons.

The increase during the 1979-1990 period was mainly due to productivity jump initially. However, later it was due to the expansion of harvested area. [6] Entering the second half of the year, Indonesia faced double disasters. The prolonged drought had serious effects on food production and the monetary crisis started since the end of July 1997. The long drought persisted until early 1998 which caused delay of rice planting for the main crop season and harvesting in the consecutive year. Therefore, rice production was below the target for two consecutive years in 1997 and 1998. [7]

Food Security Crisis in Indonesia: The drought situation in Indonesia prior to the crisis, was caused by the El Nino effect. It caused a decline in the production of food and its availability, between 1997 and 1998. Rice production fell by 8.8 percent which was the highest in a single year since the last 20 years. Urban households, were the first to experience the brunt of the crisis, in the form of soaring food prices. Rice virtually disappeared from the market and hence was specially affected.

The breakdown of the food distribution system was the primary cause for the threat to food security. Riots in cities like Jakarta caused the collapse of transport systems which blocked areas with surplus produce to transport it to areas that needed it.

Food Security Monitoring: In response to the need for the crisis centre, the government also formed a National Team for Food Security Monitoring with the main task to coordinate three aspects in handling the food crisis. These were: (i) identification of food insecure areas and targets group; (ii) identification of sources of food assistance; and (iii) coordination and monitoring of distribution of food aids provided by all parties including the distribution by NGOs using the local and domestic sources of assistance. The team was led by the Minister of Food and Horticulture and reported to the Cabinet on the food indicators on a monthly basis. This intense involvement of the government in the food security measures taken in the country has helped in self-sustainability.

Tax Exemptions: Other measures have been taken as well. On January 8, 2007, the Indonesian Government issued the third amendment to Government of Indonesia Regulation No. 12/2001 on imports and/or delivery of certain strategic taxable goods on which value added tax are exempted. This regulation stated that in order to accelerate the improvement and to increase the competitiveness of the domestic agricultural business industry, the Government is eliminating the 10 percent VAT on the import and delivery of certain strategic taxable goods.

NGOs: Among others, is the relaxation of the institutional support to increase the absorption of financial facilities and the participation of NGOs in confronting the issue. This in turn will affect the design of future programs that should be well targeted and food security oriented. Therefore, the community based food reserve should be promoted and strengthened by giving more attention on assisting them to organize the local food security arrangement. This idea is also pursuant to the mandate of the Food Law. Therefore, other than government reforms, help from NGOs has led to a better situation in the country.

Role of International Agencies

Food and Agricultural Organization: Indonesia became a member of the FAO in 1948, and an FAO representative office was opened in Jakarta in 1978. Since then, more than 500 projects have been implemented throughout Indonesia, generating over US$ 700 million worth of external and domestic investments in agriculture, fisheries and forestry. Indonesia and FAO has been in partnership for over 37 years and significant achievements have been made during these years. [8] Indonesia has also benefited from a number of FAO regional and global programmes, including integrated pest management (IPM) programme and the special programme for food security (SPFS). Although there is not much development in the country, international organisations such as FAO have helped in improving production, thus leading to a self-sustainable food structure.

The Indonesian government and international agencies have implemented a series of complementary programmes during the past 17 years aimed at reaching the poorest and hungriest. These include the FAO-assisted special programme for food security. Another project supported by the International Fund for Agricultural Development helped foster self-reliance amongst poor families living in dry lands through participatory integrated development.

FAO supported the Indonesian government's goal of rice self- sufficiency in many ways, but the integrated pest management and farmers field schools which were introduced by the Organization, are recognized as the two most important contributors to the success of this policy. IPM was launched in 1979 and became an official government policy. IPM is a dynamic process that faced a variety of problems in implementation. Since 1989, the government has been undertaking a large scale IPM programme that works directly with frontline agricultural extension workers and a large number of farmer's groups across the country. The IPM programme's emphasis on developing human resources and increasing knowledge brings about tremendous changes in behaviour and field practice, enabling farmers to change their approach and resist persuasive advertising campaigns by companies producing chemical pesticides. IPM in Indonesia has honed the skills of fieldworkers and farmers in ecology-based methods.

World Bank: Rural PNPM Mandiri is a core part of PNPM Mandiri and is developed from the Kecamatan Development Program (KDP) launched in 1998. PNPM Mandiri, Indonesia's largest community-driven poverty reduction program, works nationwide to provide funds to poor rural and urban communities so they can invest in their own development priorities. This loan will help the Indonesian government provide block grants and implementation support to almost 5,000 rural sub-districts. The Rural PNPM Mandiri's overall objective is to reduce poverty and improve local level governance in rural areas of Indonesia through the provision of investment resources to support productive proposals developed by communities, using a participatory planning process.

In the wake of the tsunami and earthquakes, Indonesia received multiple pledges for relief, rehabilitation and reconstruction of Aceh and Nias (estimated at US$ 8.5 billion). The government requested the World Bank to set up a Multi Donor Fund as one of the mechanisms to ensure an efficient and coordinated delivery of financial support.

- It currently pools US$ 704.06 million, making it one of the Bank's largest trust funds.
- The Multi Donor Fund has a close working relationship with BRR–BRR co-chair and identifies priority areas for funding and receives technical assistance from the Fund.

United States Agency for International Development (USAID): USAID and its predecessors have provided development assistance to Indonesia since 1950. Initial assistance focused on the most urgent needs of the new republic, including food aid, infrastructure rehabilitation, health care, and training. Through the 1970s—a time of great economic growth in Indonesia—USAID played a major role in helping the country achieve self-sufficiency in rice production and in reducing the birth rate. USAID assistance programs focus on basic education, democratic governance, rebuilding after the tsunami, economic growth, health, water, food, and the environment. While improving the nutritional status of the Indonesians, the USAID food assistance program targets poor communities.

These activities directly impact women and children through targeted supplemental feeding and nutritional education activities. The food assistance program works with villages to construct public latrines, washing facilities, protected water stations, and to organize solid waste disposal efforts to better protect community health. Over one million people have been the direct recipients of the food security policy of the USAID in Indonesia.

In a real and important sense, USAID's entire portfolio contributes to food security. USAID's strategic priorities—economic growth, health and population, the environment, democracy, and humanitarian assistance—each supports improved food security. Helping countries to achieve sustainable development is the surest way to eliminate the chronic poverty, which is the root cause of food insecurity. USAID will continue this integrated approach, drawing on development assistance resources to target critical problems in needy countries.

USAID investments in agriculture have played a leading role in this effort. The International Agricultural Research Centre provided key technological breakthroughs, which led directly to this 'Green Revolution' in the early 1970s. [9] USAID bilateral assistance programs provided policy counsel, coordination with other donors and international institutions such as the World Bank and direct investments in agriculture. Food aid was used to improve access to food and provide balance of payments support. In some cases, direct feeding was used to improve household nutrition. The United States has prepared a program worth US$ 15 million or equivalent to Rp. 135 billion to increase Indonesia's food production commodities. The program will run for five years.

The programme titled, 'Agribusiness Market and Support

Activity' (AMARTA I) from 2006-2011 was initiated by the U.S. Agency for International Development (USAID). According to U.S. Ambassador to Indonesia, Scot Marciel, the program focuses on increasing the production of high value commodities such as cocoa, coffee, and horticultural crops, expanding access to credit for rural areas, and support for regulatory reforms of the farmers.

The AMARTA II program will further expand activities and cooperation between the U.S. and Indonesia in agriculture and food security", he said in a press release on February 8, 2012. Besides AMARTA II programme, the U.S. Government also supports agricultural production and sustainable fisheries and pushes for private sector investment while preserving natural resources. These efforts are a core component in the U.S.-Indonesia Comprehensive Partnership", he said. United States is also working with Indonesia to address food security through aquaculture. Sea plays an important role in Indonesian food security. The U.S. is partnering with the Indonesian government and private sector companies to develop and expand the business model and the management of natural resources which are certainly sustainable.

USAID's Agricultural Biotechnology Program valued at US$ 1.5 million over three years is aimed to build partnerships between U.S. institutions and Indonesia to introduce new technologies such as beta-carotene enriched rice varieties of potatoes and tomatoes and made them virus resistant. The program also promotes integrated pest management techniques to improve the low-cost agricultural production and rural livelihoods. With Cochran and Borlaug Fellowship Program, the U.S. Department of Agriculture plans to support human resource development in Indonesia in the field of food and agriculture by selecting the best person to go to the U.S. for short-term education and research.

He said that agricultural trade is a very important component in food security. Indonesia and the U.S. has set a target of Rp. 10 billion or equivalent to Rp. 90 trillion of trade in agriculture, fisheries and forestry products by 2014.

Association of Southeast Asian Nations (ASEAN): It is a geo-political and economic organization of ten countries located in Southeast Asia, which was formed on August 8, 1967 by Indonesia, Malaysia, the Philippines, Singapore and Thailand. Since then, membership has expanded to include Brunei, Burma (Myanmar), Cambodia, Laos, and Vietnam. Its aims include accelerating economic growth, social progress, cultural development among its members, protection of regional peace and stability, and opportunities for member countries to discuss differences peacefully. [10] It is also important to note that trade among the member nations is the primary concern of ASEAN.

Trade matters for food security. Increasingly, trade and trade policies do not only influence the availability of food at the global level, but also production and food imports, including food aid, at the national level. Many developing countries, particularly those where food production is often constrained by natural and other factors, are now keen to use the world market as an important source of food. The same is happening in Indonesia.

The food security policy of a country is normally defined in terms of either food self-sufficiency or food self-reliance. While the former emphasizes the production of various food items for domestic consumption, the latter focuses more on the availability of food for domestic consumption. Consequently, countries that pursue food self-sufficiency generally support small-scale enterprises to ensure local food production and are reluctant to rely on the international marketplace as the source of their food supplies. In other words, these countries rule out imports as a component of their food security policy. On the other hand, countries who apply the food self-reliance principle are generally keen to promote market liberalization and export-oriented agriculture, supported by a strong local market achieved through improvements in physical infrastructure and credit facilities.

Many countries in Southeast Asia still attempt to apply the

philosophy of food self-sufficiency, for at least three reasons. Firstly, rice dominates the region's diets and the extreme instability in the price of this staple commodity has prompted some Southeast Asian governments to insulate the domestic price of rice from the international price (normally through the exclusion of rice from their countries' tariff systems). Secondly, many Southeast Asian countries seek to ensure that short run fluctuations in prices do not make the poor even more vulnerable to malnutrition. Finally, weak domestic infrastructure in some countries in the region has made imports expensive and difficult, and so governments have opted instead for policies that ensure sufficient domestic production and thus manage the stability of food prices accordingly.

Food security has three dimensions:

- **Availability** of sufficient quantities of food of appropriate quality, supplied through domestic production or imports;
- **Access** by households and individuals to adequate resources to acquire appropriate foods for a nutritious diet; and
- **Utilization** of food through adequate diet, water, sanitation, and health care.

Both elements of the Asian strategic approach to food security—rapid economic growth and food price stability—address the 'macro' dimensions of food security, not the 'micro' dimensions found at and within the household. Governments can do many things to improve food security at the household and individual level, and most countries in East and Southeast Asia have programs to do so. Rural education accessible to females and the poor, family planning and child-care clinics in rural areas, nutrition education, and extension specialists helping to improve home gardens are just a few of the possibilities. Most of the literature on food security deals with approaches at this level, but problems of definition, measurement, project design, and management vastly complicate strategies that rely on household interventions.

Without dismissing the potential effectiveness of these

approaches to enhance food security in particular circumstances, it is still important to realize the scale of the problem. Hundreds of millions of people still do not have food security in Asia, and programs directed at households will not bring it. Only food security at the macro level can provide the appropriate facilitative environment for households to ensure their own food security.

ASEAN Free Trade Area (AFTA) [11]: It is a trade bloc agreement by the Association of Southeast Asian Nations supporting local manufacturing in all ASEAN countries. The AFTA agreement was signed on January 28, 1992 in Singapore.

The primary goals of AFTA seek to:

- Increase ASEAN's competitive edge as a production base in the world market through the elimination, within ASEAN, on tariffs and non-tariff barriers; and
- Attract more foreign direct investment to ASEAN.

The primary mechanism for achieving the goals given above is the common effective preferential tariff (CEPT) scheme, which established a schedule for phased initiative in 1992 with the self-described goal to increase the "region's competitive advantage as a production base geared for the world market". It has been seen that the implementation of the ASEAN Free Trade Area has been one of the definite factors for Indonesia's development and emergence as a primary player in the ASEAN. Moving beyond self-sustainability, AFTA has allowed open economic reforms to allow growth in the economy which has led to the high GDP.

It is important to understand, however, how the ASEAN Free Trade Area is able to bring in more trade among the Southeast Asian nations. Unlike the EU, AFTA does not apply a common external tariff on imported goods. Each ASEAN member may impose tariffs on goods entering from outside ASEAN, based on its national schedules. However, for goods originating within ASEAN, ASEAN members are to apply a tariff rate of 0 to 5 percent (the more recent members of

Cambodia, Laos, Myanmar and Vietnam, also known as CMLV countries, were given additional time to implement the reduced tariff rates). This is known as the common effective preferential tariff (CEPT) scheme.

By rigidly following the common effective preferential tariff scheme, Indonesia has been able to increase its GDP and also provide monetary benefit to the other nations of ASEAN.

ASEAN members have the option of excluding products from the CEPT in three cases: (a) temporary exclusions; (b) sensitive agricultural products; and (c) general exceptions. Temporary exclusions refer to products for which tariffs will ultimately be lowered to 0-5 percent, but which are being protected temporarily by a delay in tariff reductions.

Sensitive agricultural products include commodities such as rice. ASEAN members had until 2010 to reduce the tariff levels to 0-5 percent.

General exceptions refer to products which an ASEAN member deems necessary for the protection of national security, public morals, the protection of human, animal or plant life and health, and protection of articles of artistic, historic, or archaeological value.

ASEAN members have agreed to enact zero tariff rates on virtually all imports by 2010 for the original signatories.

The CEPT, however, only applies with the rule of origin. According to the rule of origin, only those products and commodities originating from within the ASEAN can be taxed according to the CEPT rates.

This ensures that while trade among the ASEAN members is robust, the member nations can use their normal schedules for commodities during trade with nations from outside ASEAN.

It must be admitted that while the CEPT may have helped increase trade among the member nations of ASEAN, the administration and implementation of the rules of CEPT are faulty. Unlike the EU or NAFTA, ASEAN is not employing joint teams to ensure compliance and investigate non-compliance of the rules and regulations. ASEAN nationals must rely instead, on the reports and analysis of other ASEAN ministers in matters relating to dumping, etc. Also, the dispute resolution mechanism of ASEAN needs reform. The ASEAN Secretariat has no legal authority to resolve disputes, so such disputes are resolved bilaterally or through informal means. [12]

Dispute resolving mechanisms exist in the form of the ASEAN Protocol on Enhanced Dispute Settlement Mechanism, which governs formal dispute resolution. Members of ASEAN may also seek SEOM or senior economic officials meetings in order to resolve their disputes. But this protocol has almost never been invoked because the SEOM require consensus and since the disputing countries are members of the SEOM, resolution is practically impossible through the protocol.

The World Bank, as part of its Trade Costs and Facilitation Project, published a report in 2008 stating that the member nations of the ASEAN have the potential to reap benefits from further reforms, since the reforms by the ASEAN Free Trade Area have already started taking effect. It suggested that the member nations could look at the port facilities and competitiveness in the internet sector. Also, cutting down the tariff rates to the regional average would increase trade by about 2 percent.

Asia-Pacific Economic Cooperation (APEC): It is a forum of 21 Pacific Rim countries (formally member economies) that seeks to promote free trade and economic cooperation throughout the Asia-Pacific region. Established in 1989 in response to the growing interdependence of Asia-Pacific economies and the advent of regional economic blocs (such as the European Union) in other parts of the world, APEC works to raise living standards and education levels through sustainable economic growth and to foster a sense of community and an appreciation of shared interests among Asia-Pacific countries. Members account for approximately 40 percent of the world's population, approximately 54 percent of the world's gross domestic product and about 44 percent of world trade.

Countries of the Association of Southeast Asian Nations (ASEAN) opposed the initial proposal, instead proposing the East Asia Economic Caucus which would exclude non-Asian countries such as the United States, Canada, Australia, and New Zealand. This plan was opposed and strongly criticized by Japan and the United States.

The first APEC Economic Leaders' Meeting occurred in 1993 when U.S. President Bill Clinton, after discussions with Australian Prime Minister Paul Keating, invited the heads of government from member economies to a summit on Blake Island. He believed it would help bring the stalled Uruguay Round of trade talks back on track. At the meeting, some leaders called for continued reduction of barriers to trade and investment, envisioning a community in the Asia-Pacific region that might promote prosperity through cooperation. The APEC Secretariat, based in Singapore, was established to coordinate the activities of the organization.

During the meeting in 1994 in Bogor, Indonesia, APEC leaders adopted the Bogor Goals that aimed for free and open trade and investment in the Asia-Pacific by 2010 for industrialized economies and by 2020 for developing economies. In 1995, APEC established a business advisory body named the APEC Business Advisory Council (ABAC), composed of three business executives from each member economy.

To meet the Bogor Goals, APEC carries out work in three main areas:

1. Trade and investment liberalisation.
2. Business facilitation.
3. Economic and technical cooperation.

According to the organization itself, when APEC was established in 1989, average trade barriers in the region stood at 16.9 percent, but had been reduced to 5.5 percent in 2004.

APEC has long been at the forefront of reform efforts in

the area of business facilitation. Between 2002-2006, the costs of business transactions across the region were reduced by 6 percent, thanks to the APEC Trade Facilitation Action Plan (TFAPI). Between 2007 and 2010, APEC hopes to achieve an additional 5 percent reduction in business transaction costs. To this end, a new Trade Facilitation Action Plan was been endorsed. According to a 2008 research brief published by the World Bank as part of its Trade Costs and Facilitation Project, increasing transparency in the region's trading system is critical if APEC is to meet its Bogor Goal targets.

International Treaty on Plant Genetic Resources for Food and Agriculture (ITPGRFA): Popularly known as the International Seed Treaty, it is a comprehensive international agreement in harmony with the Convention on Biological Diversity, which aims at guaranteeing food security through the conservation, exchange and sustainable use of the world's plant genetic resources for food and agriculture (PGRFA), as well as the fair and equitable benefit sharing arising from its use. It also recognises Farmers' Rights: to freely access genetic resources, unrestricted by intellectual property rights; to be involved in relevant policy discussions and decision-making; and to use, save, sell and exchange seeds, subject to national laws.

The treaty has implemented a multilateral system (MLS) of access and benefit sharing, among those countries that ratify the treaty, for a list of 64 of some of the most important food and forage crops essential for food security and interdependence. The genera and species are listed in Annex 1 to the treaty. The treaty was negotiated by the Food and Agriculture Organization (FAO) of the United Nations Commission on Genetic Resources for Food and Agriculture (CGRFA) and since 2006 has its own governing body under the aegis of the FAO. Such a treaty allows uninhibited access to the genetically modified resources, which leads to a furtherance of self-sustainability goal.

Its objectives are the conservation and sustainable use of plant genetic resources for food and agriculture and the fair and equitable sharing of benefits derived from their use, in harmony with the Convention on Biological Diversity, for sustainable agriculture and food security.

Through the Treaty, countries agree to establish an efficient, effective and transparent multilateral system to facilitate access to plant genetic resources for food and agriculture, and to share the benefits in a fair and equitable way. The multilateral system applies to over 64 major crops and forages. The governing body of the Treaty, which will be composed of the countries that have ratified it, will set out the conditions for access and benefit-sharing in a 'material transfer agreement'.

Resources may be obtained from the multilateral system for utilization and conservation in research, breeding and training. When a commercial product is developed using these resources, the Treaty provides for payment of an equitable share of the resulting monetary benefits—if this product may not be used without restriction by others for further research and breeding, or if others may use it, payment is voluntary.

The Treaty provides for sharing the benefits of using plant genetic resources for food and agriculture through information-exchange, access to and the transfer of technology, and capacity-building. It also foresees a funding strategy to mobilize funds for activities, plans and programmes to help, above all, small farmers in developing countries. This funding strategy also includes the share of the monetary benefits paid under the multilateral system.

The Treaty recognizes the enormous contribution that farmers and their communities have made and continue to make to the conservation and development of plant genetic resources. This is the basis for Farmers' Rights, which include the protection of traditional knowledge, and the right to participate equitably in benefit-sharing and in national decision-making about plant genetic resources. It gives governments the responsibility for implementing these rights. The Treaty has longstanding benefits for Indonesia as it facilitates the continued open exchange of food crops and genetic materials.

Conclusion

The condition of food security in Indonesia is of primary importance mainly because Indonesia is the main producer of rice in Southeast Asia and one of the largest producers of rice in the world. Rice is the staple food of about 45 percent of the world's population. The food security policies of Indonesia affect not only itself, but the other countries of Southeast Asia as well, especially ASEAN. This paper has focussed on that perspective.

Clearly, it can now be seen that the food security of Indonesia depends almost singularly on rice. Hence, any fluctuations in rice production or processing or export could result in drastic changes in the country's economy. That said, the services sector has also been booming under the current regime. Education is gaining significance, leading to more employment in the service sector. Today, employment in the service sector is higher than any other, including agriculture.

Indonesia may have suffered much in the Asian financial crisis and in recent times, but the mitigation policies used with admirable speed by their Government has lessened the effects. Indonesia also escaped unscathed from the recession which left many developed countries such as the United States crippled. U.S. aid has had an excellent effect on the agriculture sector especially since Indonesia has been able to rapidly phase out the use of outdated farming techniques and improve its rice production.

So what lies ahead for Indonesia? It is indeed hard to say with the price of rice fluctuating but it can be said that if Indonesia moves ahead with its current policies, it will certainly lead to gradual development and progress. A little slow perhaps, but progress nonetheless.

Endnotes

1. Following a slowing of growth in the 1980s, due to over regulation and dependence on declining oil prices, growth slowed to an average of 4.3 percent per annum between 1981 and 1988. A range of economic reforms were introduced in the late 1980s. Reforms included a managed devaluation of the

rupiah to improve export competitiveness, and de-regulation of the financial sector. *Schwarz* (1994), pp. 52-57, "Indonesia: Country Brief", Indonesia: Key Development Data and Statistics, The World Bank, September 2006.

2. Ann L. Stoler, "Rice Harvesting In Kali Loro: A Study of Class and Labour Relations in Rural Java", Blackwell Publication.
3. H.S. Dillion and Marcellus Rantetana, "Food Security in Indonesia", p. 57.
4. H.S. Dillion and Marcellus Rantetana, "Food Security in Indonesia", p. 59.
5. Noer Soetrisno, "Food Security in Indonesia: Short-run and the Long-run Issues", available at: http://www.scribd.com/doc/106974061/Food-Security-in-Indonesia.
6. H.S. Dillion and Marcellus Rantetana, "Food Security in Indonesia".
7. Robert F. Emery, *Far Eastern Survey*, Vol. 29, No. 8 (August 1960), pp. 113-120, available at: http://www.jstor.org/stable/3024617.
8. FAO Representation in Indonesia and FAO Achievements and Success Stories, June 2011.
9. "Forty Years After the Green Revolution", last accessed on September 22, 2012, available at: http://www.thejakartapost.com/news/2009/06/30/forty-years-after-green-revolution039.html.
10. Asean.org, *Overview*, ASEAN Secretariat official website, retrieved June 12, 2006.
11. AFTA and FTAs, ASEAN Secretariat.
12. Edmund W. Sim, "Improving Governance in the ASEAN Economic Community". The ASEAN Secretariat has no legal authority to resolve disputes, so such disputes are resolved bilaterally or through informal means, 2009.

8

Kenya: Food and Nutrition Security Policy (FNSP)

Nuhar Bansal and Shubhangi Roy

Socio-economic Profile

Kenya is a country in East Africa that lies on the equator. With the Indian Ocean to its south-east, it is bordered by Tanzania to the south, Uganda to the west, South Sudan to the north-west, Ethiopia to the north and Somalia to the north-east. Kenya has a land area of 580,000 km^2 and a population of nearly 41 million, representing 42 different people and cultures. [1] The country is named after Mount Kenya, a significant landmark and second among Africa's highest mountain peaks.

Following a referendum and adoption of a new constitution in August 2010, Kenya is now divided into 47 counties that are semi-autonomous units of governance. These units are expected to be fully implemented by August 2012—in time for the first general election under the new constitution. The counties will be governed by elected governors and will operate independent of the central government in Nairobi.

The country's geography is as diverse as its multi-ethnic population. It has a warm and humid climate along its coastline on the Indian Ocean which changes to wildlife-rich savannah grasslands moving inland towards the capital Nairobi. As a part of East Africa, Kenya has seen human habitation since the Lower Paleolithic period. The Bantu expansion reached the area by the first millennium AD, and the borders of the modern state comprise the crossroads of the Niger-Congo, Nilo-Saharan, and Afro-Asiatic linguistic areas of Africa, making Kenya a truly multi-cultural state. European and Arab presence in Mombasa dates to the Early Modern period, but European exploration of the interior began only in the 19th century. The British Empire established the East Africa Protectorate in 1895, known from 1920 as the Kenya Colony. The independent Republic of Kenya was founded in December 1963.

The capital, Nairobi, is a regional commercial hub. The economy of Kenya is the largest by GDP in East and Central Africa. [2] Agriculture is a major employer and the country traditionally exports tea and coffee, and more recently fresh flowers to Europe. The service industry is a major economic driver, mostly the telecommunications sector, and contributes 62 percent of the GDP.

Kenya, like other developing countries is faced with hunger and poverty and these problems are getting worse by the day. A number of factors contribute to this situation but poor agriculture performance lies at the heart of the problem.

Despite the importance of the agriculture sector in its contribution towards employment, government revenue, GDP and raw materials for the industrial sector, its performance has been poor owing to misallocation and under investment in the sector, disengagement of the government support to agriculture, poor infrastructure, limited access to credit, high cost of farm inputs, lack of land policy and framework among others. The governments have been accused of under-investing in agriculture and food production especially after the advent of the liberalization.

An often conflicting set of policy objectives, coupled with confusion in policy and regulatory implementation, hinders the sector's progress. Kenya's long-term goal of food self-sufficiency (producing everything consumed in the country) remains unmet. Frequent droughts precipitate requests for donor-provided food aid to mitigate the ravages of famine, especially in the arid and semi-arid regions populated largely by livestock-based pastoral tribes.

The intensity and prevalence of poverty in Kenya varies across different regions with 56 percent of the total population living below the poverty line. The poverty levels are in both urban and rural areas and are closely connected to agriculture and land and its dependence on means of generating income. The ASAL areas in Coast, North Eastern and Eastern Provinces and the densely populated areas of Western, Nyanza, Rift Valley and Central Provinces have the highest levels of poverty. The contributing factors to poverty include unemployment and low wages, low agricultural productivity and poor marketing, inaccessibility to productive assets, particularly land, poor infrastructure, high cost of social services, bad governance and HIV/AIDS among others.

There has also been food insecurity occasioned by lack of proper food distribution where areas neighbouring food surplus districts have had people starving and even dying for lack of food. The food insecurity also occurs in high potential areas due to the combination of lack of information and failed infrastructure. Food insecurity has also been caused by poor food distribution and marketing within the country. Lack of information on the areas with surplus/deficit makes people to starve while food is available in some other parts of the country.

Food security is basically defined as, "when all people at all times have physical, social and economic access to sufficient, safe and nutritious food which meets their dietary needs and food preferences for an active and healthy life". [3]

The Kenya Food Security Meeting (KFSM) is the main coordinating body that brings together food security actors in a forum where information is exchanged, options debated and decisions on activities formulated for referral to the Government of Kenya and donors. It is an open forum of high level presentation of a broad grouping of organizations at the national level with interest in food security.

KFSM is responsible for addressing food security issues, building trust, shared purpose and understanding, as well as maintaining institutional memory of the key national actors. It provides the mechanism to channel decisions upwards to the appropriate government bodies and donors, and is a mechanism for advising, accountability and legitimacy.

Legislative and Policy Framework

Article 43(c) of the Constitution of Kenya provides that everyone has the right to be free from hunger, and to have adequate food of acceptable quality. In pursuance of achieving this objective, Kenyan governments over time have struggled with policy making. In fact, the flawed policy making of the government over the years is partly responsible for the difficult food situation in the region.

Historically, the policy on agriculture has been to pursue the goal of attaining self-sufficiency in key food commodities that include maize, wheat, rice, milk and meat. While this has been the objective, it has not been attained except in the 1970s when maize production was so high to the extent that some was exported. In 1986, there was a shift from a food sufficiency goal to an outward strategy which identified seven commodities that form the core of the current food and agricultural policy: maize, wheat, meat, milk and horticulture crops for both home consumption and export and coffee and tea for raising farm income and earning foreign exchange.

The government of Kenya came up with the vision 2030 in the year 2008. It is the new long-term development plan for Kenya which aims to make it "a newly industrializing, middle income country providing a high quality of life to all its citizens in a clean and secure environment".

Agriculture has been the backbone of the Kenyan economy with a direct contribution of 24 percent to the gross domestic product and employing nearly 80 percent of the population. The food availability has been declining largely because maize production was down by 44 percent on per capita basis in 2000 compared to 30 years before. The per capita food decline has been because local staple food production has been outstripped by a relatively high rate of population growth and increased life expectancy. Chronic under-nutrition is the most common form of malnutrition and is mainly associated with insufficient dietary intake because households lack enough income to secure their basic food requirements.

However, the Government has over the years aimed at improving the condition of its citizen by liberalising the food market of the country along with focussing on agricultural innovation.

Food and Nutrition Security Policy (FNSP): The new Food and Nutrition Security Policy (FNSP) provides an overarching framework covering the multiple dimensions of food security and nutrition improvement. It has been purposefully developed to add value and create synergy to existing sectoral and other initiatives of government and partners. It recognizes the need for multi-public and private sector involvement, and that hunger eradication and nutrition improvement is a shared responsibility of all Kenyans. The policy and associated actions will remain dynamic to address contextual changes and changing conditions over time. This policy is framed in the context of basic human rights, child rights and women's rights, including the universal right to food.

"Kenya's policy response to food and nutrition security can be grouped into three approaches. First, consumer-oriented responses that provide direct support to consumers and vulnerable groups in the form of food subsidies, social safety nets, tax reductions and price controls among others. Secondly, producer-oriented responses intended to support farmers to increase production, using measures such as input supply. Thirdly, trade-oriented responses that use policy instruments, such as reducing tariffs and restricting exports to stabilise prices and/or increase domestic supply".

Promotion of Urban and Peri-Urban Agriculture: An approach that would fall within their producer-oriented responses is the promotion of urban and peri-urban agriculture. Approximately, 34 percent of 33 million Kenyans were estimated to be living in cities and towns in 1999, with their numbers projected to grow to 16 million by 2005, representing about half the population. Although most of the migrants search for jobs to support their immediate families and dependants, most end up unemployed or are casually hired in low-earning engagements with no job security. At least 60 percent of Nairobi's residents live in very low-income neighbourhoods, with headcount poverty ranging between 60 to 78 percent in the various city suburbs. Recent surveys in low-income areas of Nairobi showed malnutrition of children to be quite common, with the prevalence of wasting, a condition characterized by chronic diarrhoea and dangerous deficiencies of protein, among children aged 6-60 months ranging from 5 to 13 percent and stunting from 10 to 57 percent.

The link between hunger, malnutrition and HIV-AIDS in both adults and children is established, and the pivotal role urban agriculture can play to alleviate this, as a survival strategy for the urban poor, the urban unemployed and those unable to engage in other useful income generating activities.

Thus, the government aims to promote urban and peri-urban agriculture to absorb the urban unemployed and also provide better food security. A recent report of the International Livestock Research Institute (ILRI), shows high correlation between cattle and human populations, meaning that the density of livestock increases around towns. Figures from Nairobi from the 1980s show a total of 23,000 head of cattle in the city back then, confirmed by recent figures presented by the Director of Agriculture. These figures also indicated similarly high volumes and values of urban crop production. Twenty nine percent of Kenyan urbanites grow crops in town, 20 percent in Nairobi, while Kenyan urban farmers, mostly female, were using mainly organic inputs.

These statistics are very encouraging since it has multi-level advantages. It provides employment, promotes easier access, reduced cost of transportation and promotes environmental friendly agricultural practices. This is a unique solution to ensure that, unlike other countries, the phenomenon of urbanisation is not followed with a shift of focus from agriculture to manufacturing or service sector. A country with such food insecurity cannot afford such a shift presently.

Strategic Grain Reserve: Over the years, it has also liberalised agriculture to ensure wider availability and access of essential food commodities at competitive prices. Another means to improve accessibility is by maintaining a Strategic Grain Reserve. "The Strategic Grain Reserve (SGR) was established through the Exchequer and Audit Act Cap. 412 (Strategic Grain Reserve Fund) Regulations, 2002 vide Legal Notice No. 55 of April 15, 2002 through a special issue of Kenya Gazette Supplement No. 34. The Fund is expected to purchase and maintain up to 8 million bags of grains for National Food Security. The stock is maintained by the Department through the National Cereal and Produce Board under an agency agreement. The stocks are supposed to cushion the nation against severe food shortage as well as to assist in stabilization of local prices of grain". [4]

Kilimo Biashro Programme: Perhaps the most effective partnership of international and national level organisations in improving the economic condition of the Kenyan population is the Kilimo Biashro Programme. It is a partnership of The Alliance for a Green Revolution in Africa (AGRA), International Fund for Agricultural Development (IFAD), the Government of Kenya and Amiran Kenya. In the words of its official website, the program aims the following:

"To open up credit facilities to farmers and agro-businesses at an affordable interest rate (10 percent). With these loans, farmers can purchase farming supplies and cover immediate costs when awaiting payment for their crops, and agro-businesses can invest in improving and expanding their capabilities.

Under the programme, farmers also receive training on improved farming techniques and business management, in addition to government vouchers that enable them to purchase new farming inputs.

Equity Bank and Alliance for a Green Revolution in Africa partnered with others to create an investment climate that meets the needs of farmers and agro-businesses in Kenya while also reducing lending risk to any single organisation. Additionally, the programme relies on the extensive expertise, both financial and agricultural, of various project partners to deliver training in areas such as crop development, improved farming techniques and business management". [5]

Thus, the government is trying to structure a holistic economic policy which not only approached the problem of food security as a consumer issue (where all are not being able to afford or access enough food) but also a producer issue (where the farmers are not able to achieve their full potential) as well as a trade issue (where countries with excess food production are not considering Kenya as a competitive market destination).

Role of International Organizations

Right to food is fundamental to most international covenants and each of its member states is obliged to attempt to achieve a situation where no one is deprived of this sacrosanct right. "Article 25 of the UDHR [6] and Article 11 of the ICESCR [7] enshrine the right of everyone to an adequate standard of living, including food. Article 11 of the ICESCR also recognizes the fundamental right of everyone to be free from hunger and obliges the state parties to adopt concrete measures and programs to achieve this goal".

"At the African level, the right to food can be found in the African Charter on Human and Peoples Rights (ACHPR), its Protocol on the Rights of Women and in the African Charter on the Rights and Welfare of the Child (ACRWC). Although the ACHPR does not include specific reference to the right to food, it was derived in SERAC vs. Nigeria by the African

Commission on Human Rights, which is mandated with the interpretation of the ACHPR from the right to life (Article 4), the right to dignity (Article 5) and the right to health (Article 16). Further, Article 60 stipulates that all state parties should implement the rights enshrined in international human rights treaties they have ratified such as the ICESCR. State parties to the ACHPR and the ICESCR such as Kenya thus have an obligation to implement the right to food.

Moreover, the protocol to the ACHPR on the Rights of Women in Africa stipulates in Article 15 (Right to Food Security) the state's obligations to provide women with access to clean drinking water, sources of domestic fuel, land, and the means of producing nutritious food; and to obligation to establish adequate systems of supply and storage to ensure food security.

The African Charter on the Rights and Welfare of the Child, to which Kenya is a party, specifically recognises the right to food under the right to health. According to Article 14, state parties must "ensure the provision of adequate food and safe drinking water". According to Article 20(2) they must also take all appropriate measures to assist parents or other persons responsible for the child and, where needed, should provide material assistance and support, specifically in relation to nutrition".

Thus, there exists not only a national obligation that the government of Kenya owes to its people but also an international obligation to ensure that Kenyans achieve the standard of life envisioned in these covenants and treatise. Failure of a member state also creates a responsibility on the international organisation as well as the better endowed member states to extend a helping hand to the failing state.

"Since Kenya's independence in 1963, and indeed even before then, the United Nations family has contributed to the country's socio-economic development, touching virtually every aspect of the lives of its people.

United Nations has more than twenty five of its agencies

working in Kenya with two agencies, namely United Nations Environment Programme and United Nations Human Settlements Programme (UN-HABITAT) having their global headquarters located in Kenya at the United Nations Office in Nairobi".

Kenya hosts nearly a quarter of a million refugees who have fled from conflict in neighbouring countries. The United Nations is helping to house and feed them. The United Nations is also helping the Government of Kenya to feed the neediest of its own people. Every day the United Nations provides food for a million school children. At the same time, all across Kenya, the United Nations is working with communities so they can feed themselves better and raise their standards of living. By sharing local innovations and spreading existing knowledge, the United Nations is improving livelihoods for the rural and urban poor. The United Nations is also helping to create jobs and alleviate poverty by supporting small enterprise and sustainable industrial development.

MDG-7: Ensure Environmental Sustainability: Kenya's environmental resources are the foundation for its future. The United Nations is helping the government to respond to natural disasters, such as floods and drought. It is helping the Kenya Wildlife Service to monitor the country's precious mountain forests, and supporting communities who want to conserve biological diversity. The United Nations is also helping to preserve Lake Victoria's environment by promoting community-based management of fisheries. Upgrading slums in Nairobi and elsewhere is essential if Kenya is to meet its development goals. The United Nations is supporting projects to improve living conditions for the country's poorest inhabitants. [8]

Both these goals, aimed to be achieved till 2015, are in fact a step towards greater food security and sustainability.

"More than a million school children in Kenya have benefited from the WFP School Feeding Programme. The programme is part of the WFP's food aid in Kenya, which is aimed at improving the nutrition and quality of life of the most vulnerable people at critical times in their lives. It uses food aid to support economic and social development and to promote food security. In Kenya, the need for the programme was brought home by the 1979 drought that seriously affected arid and semi-arid areas of the country.

The objective of the project was to provide mid-day meals to school children in pre-primary and primary schools in the most affected districts and in areas where people were primarily nomadic.

The School Feeding Programme has been one of the major success stories of the partnership between Kenya and the United Nations. Enrolment in schools during the first five years of the programme went up by 300 percent. The performance of children in districts in the Kenya Certificate of Primary Examination (KCPE) also greatly improved. One of the participating districts, Baringo, was ranked among the top ten nationally, in KCPE performance in 1985.

Through WFP, the United Nations also spends millions of dollars each year feeding people where food based interventions are most useful. Apart from the School Feeding Programme in the arid and semi-arid parts of the country, WFP provides food aid to people in Nairobi's slums and to refugees and other people in emergency situations, in partnership with other United Nations agencies such as UNHCR. Over the years, the United Nations has fed hundreds of thousands of Somali and Sudanese refugees in Kakuma in northwest Kenya near the border with Sudan, and in Dadaab in eastern Kenya, near the Somali border. It has also been providing food aid to Ethiopian refugees who have been sheltering in Kenya since 1991 when civil conflict broke out in Ethiopia. In all, more than 400,000 people who have sought refuge in Kenya over the years have benefited from United Nations assistance.

Between 1999 and 2003, WFP spent US$ 32.5 million providing thousands of tons of food in support of the Government's efforts to alleviate poverty in the country and to increase primary school enrolment and prevent pupils from dropping out of school. In the arid district of Wajir, WFP and UNICEF have consistently provided vulnerable and marginalized communities with food aid to enable them to cope with natural disasters. The inhabitants of Wajir perennially suffer from drought and sometimes from flash floods. During the 1997 El Niño floods, United Nations agencies worked with NGOs to save lives and promote self-reliance in the disaster-prone district. By providing food aid, the United Nations also helps to reduce community conflicts over limited resources.

Another example comes from Marsabit district, one of the areas of Kenya most affected by drought. UNICEF continues to assist by providing supplementary foods and by training local staff. During the recent long drought that affected north-eastern Kenya, UNICEF transported emergency food supplies by air and by road. An average of 36 metric tonnes per day was moved to areas including the Mandera, Marsabit, Banissa and Rhamu regions. The drought severely strained Marsabit area's water points as nomadic tribes moved into villages already crowded with refugees from civil conflict in neighbouring Somalia and Ethiopia. UNICEF has taken over the water distribution system for refugee camps in the north-eastern and eastern provinces and continues to assist in an intensive vaccination campaign in the area.

The ultimate objective of the United Nations is to eradicate hunger and poverty and eliminate the need for food aid. To improve food security in the more arid regions of the country, the United Nations promotes research and development of drought-resistant food varieties. This has been an important aspect of the United Nations contribution to Kenya's development and has contributed to significant improvements in the agricultural sector. WFP also helps to promote the self-reliance of poor people and communities through food-for-work programmes. WFP works together with other United Nations agencies, such as FAO and UNICEF, to promote economic and social development among the country's most vulnerable communities.

Thus, international organisations have contributed towards the development of Kenyan economy in order to eradicate poverty and ensure food security.

However, there exists more to the interaction of Kenya with the outside world than just financial aid. It is among the 77 African, Caribbean and Pacific countries that negotiated with the European Union over a possible economic partnership. It is also a member of the Common Market for Eastern and Southern Africa (COMESA) and the East Africa Community (EAC) regional integration blocks.

Through these international and regional trade agreements, the country incentivises its producers to produce more and export to other countries for greater profits. It also ensures that Kenya is a viable market for the producers of other countries to provide Kenyan consumers with the best food products at competitive prices.

Conclusion

The greatest fallacy that exists in planning of both the Kenyan Government and the international agencies is their short-term focussed approach. Lack of availability of food is not a specialised area of problem which can be disassociated from the rest of the socio-economic crisis affecting the region. It is affected by the gross human rights violations that the African region is infamous for, the global climatic change, political instability, disturbances in the neighbouring countries like that of Somalia etc.

Thus, the cohesive approach to tackle the problem of food insecurity in Kenya is intricately linked with the development of the entire African continent. Internally, the government can aim to open its market to more than just member countries of the African and European Union. An economic partnership agreement or other viable trade agreements with the South Asian Association for Regional Cooperation would also benefit the country as many agricultural products of these regions are complimentary and hence benefit trade relations.

Also, pursuing a government policy to attract foreign investment would provide the agriculturalists with the required capital to push from subsistence to commercial farming. The involvement of foreign players will not only lead to commercialisation and modernisation of agriculture but also absorb the unemployed population, especially the urban unemployed.

The Kenyan government with the help of international aid devised an all round development policy network which involves the simultaneous implementation of social, economic, cultural and agricultural policies. Also, apart from its cross-sectoral plan of relief dependency and development that Kenya advocates, it will have to implement long-term self sustainable models of better agricultural output and nutritional distribution to combat food insecurity. [9]

Moreover, the U.S./India/Africa Trilateral University Partnership Program for Food Security will combine the strengths of PAU with Ohio State's expertise in agricultural capacity-building to address poverty and hunger issues in Kenya and throughout Africa. The Ohio University's College of Food, Agricultural, and Environmental Sciences (CFAES) has formed a three-way partnership designed to bring together University expertise at Ohio State, Punjab Agricultural University (PAU) in India and Egerton University in Kenya. The program is a joint effort of the U.S. government and the Government of India. It is run under the auspices of the U.S.-India Strategic Dialogue by the U.S. Agency for International Development and the U.S. Department of Agriculture's Foreign Agricultural Service.

Just like India, Kenya has a diverse agricultural potential which is unevenly concentrated in the topography and is heavily dependent on the monsoons. [10] Such unilateral dependence on climate often proves unstable as a result of human interference in the ecology. Such is the case with Kenya as well. Climate is among the most frequently cited drivers of food insecurity in African nations because it acts both as an underlying, ongoing issue and as a short-lived shock.

The low ability to cope with shocks and to mitigate long-term stresses means that coping strategies that might be available in other regions are unavailable or inappropriate. In other regions, though, such as parts of the Indo-Gangetic Plain of India, other drivers, such as labour issues and the availability and quality of ground water for irrigation, rank higher than the direct effects of climate change as factors influencing food security. [11]

However, along with climatic turbulences and aggressive policies on negotiating the most beneficial of trade agreements with countries from across the globe, the Kenyan government has to also ensure a standard of human dignity to protect its citizens from the gross human rights violations that the African Region is infamous for.

Another economic and humanitarian step that needs to be checked on is the liberalization strategy; under the aegis of either structural adjustment plans or dismantled protectionist regulations which exposed farmers to international competitors and markets, deregulated investment, and replaced state funding and planning bodies with private institutions. Although food production has been on the rise during the last two decades, the level of under-nourishment in the investigated countries stagnates or even increases.

A strong, logical and realistic strategic and implementation framework is required, with associated programmes and action plans. Actions must be purposefully linked and coordinated with one another and with sectoral initiatives of the Government and partners at national and county levels. This, however, will not be sufficient to meaningfully address food insecurity and malnutrition in Kenya over the long-term. An essential component of the implementation strategy is to create strong and lasting advocacy mechanisms. Particularly important is the role of the media, local communities and civil society which must be clearly and consistently used as strategic partners to achieve long lasting food security and improved nutrition in Kenya. A conglomeration of economic and social development of the people is the only path towards a more food secure Kenya.

Endnotes

1. Keith, A.C., "A Mapbook of Eastern Africa, Zambia and Malawi", Nairobi, Kenya: Macmillan Books for Africa, 1974, 13.
2. "Report for Selected Countries and Subjects", International Monetary Fund.
3. "Food Security: Republic of Kenya", available at: www.kenyafoodsecurity.org/index.php?option=com_content&view=article&id=48&Itemid=55, accessed February 4, 2012.
4. "Special Programs for Food Security", Website of the Ministry of State for Special Programs, Kenya, available at: http://www.sprogrammes.go.ke/index.php?option=com_content&task=view&id=268&Itemid=164, accessed on December 17, 2012.
5. "Enterprise Development: Kilimo-Biashara Partnership, Kenya", www.iblf.org/.../03129DA397824D4BA3C49E4D135DFC82.Ashx, accessed on December 17, 2012.
6. Article 25, UDHR: "Everyone has the right to a standard of living adequate for the health and well-being of himself and of his family, including food, clothing, housing and medical care…".
7. Article 11, ICESCR: (a) "The state parties to the present Covenant recognize the right of everyone to an adequate standard of living for himself and his family, including adequate food, clothing and housing, and to the continuous improvement of living conditions. The state parties will recognize the essential role of international cooperation and fulfil their commitment to act, either jointly or alone, to achieve the full realization of the right to adequate food. The state parties will take appropriate steps to ensure the realization of this right, recognizing to this effect the essential importance of international co-operation based on free consent"; (b) The state parties to the present Covenant, recognizing the fundamental right of everyone to be free from hunger, shall take, individually and through international cooperation, the measures, including specific programs, which are needed to improve methods of production,

conservation and distribution of food by making full use of technical and scientific knowledge, by disseminating knowledge of the principles of nutrition and by developing or reforming agrarian systems in such a way as to achieve the most efficient development and utilization of natural resources".

8. http://www.unicnairobi.org/photo-gallery/UN-KenyaBook/images/UN%20AND%20KENYA%20HISTORY.pdf, accessed on April 1, 2012.
9. "Food Security Situation Improves in Kenya: FAO in Emergencies", Food and Agriculture Organization of the United Nations, available at: http://www.fao.org/emergencies/fao-in-action/stories/stories-detail/en/c/176235, accessed on August 6, 2013.
10. Lacroix, Thomas (2011), "Food Security, Migration and Rural Development", in *Migration, Rural Development, Poverty and Food Security: A Comparative Perspective,* London: University of Oxford, p. 10.
11. P.J. Gregory, J.S.I. Ingram and M. Brklacich (2005), "Climate Change and Food Security".

9

Mexico: Sustainable Food Security

Supratim Guha and Amudavalli Kannan

Challenges to Food Security in Mexico

Agricultural policy, since 1989, under President Salinas, has undergone quite a change as a part of the restructuring of the Mexican economy aimed towards integration with the world market. It resulted in reorganization of the institutions with the goal of reducing state intervention in the countryside and attracting private investment in livestock, agriculture and forestry. Thus, the framework under which peasants and farmers have operated for over two decades was completely modified. Access to resources became more difficult and expensive, resulting in uncertainty for the producers.

Some of the main policy changes that had a profound impact on agriculture were:

- Reorganization of rural credit—reducing heavily subsidized credit for small and medium-scale peasants.
- Privatisation of input industries like fertilizers and seeds.
- Abolishing of support prices.
- Liberalizing trade for all crops except maize and beans.

Small farmers were excluded from the whole banking system, and received only small loans for basic crops like maize through a poverty assistance programme Pronasol, which covered only a third of production costs per hectare. Further, due to scarcity of credit, medium sized farmers became heavily indebted. Access to crop insurance diminished and deregulation was partial. There are many obstacles prevalent in the Mexican food market itself that prevent opportunities provided to the citizens from reaching them.

For instance, the income distribution still favours a small

proportion of the population; high value product consumption is still congregated in the upper income urban strata. There are approximately 15 million households in Mexico, and two-thirds are situated in urban areas. The average size of the Mexican family is approximately 5 persons per household with only 1.5 working. Milk and meat purchases represent their major food cost items. Economic growth has thus contributed to a rise in food demand. Further, Mexican consumers prefer quality over cost, and are willing to pay for quality products, subject to the limits of their ability.

Water scarcity is another major challenge to food security. The Southwest Climate Change Network (SWCCN) has observed that the volume of water available for crop irrigation has reached an all time low in the Western parts of the United States, Arizona and Mexico. The combined effect of limited water with a high potential of climate change has resulted in the possibility of some significant challenges to food security. The citizens will feel the maximum impact in rising prices; a continued trend of rising prices is predicted, that outplaces inflation. According to the U.S. Census Bureau 2010 report, Arizona and New Mexico already rank among the worst in the nation in terms of poverty and household food insecurity. [1]

This would have adverse effects on the agriculture in the South West; one of the significant aspects of climate change is the impact on the growing season which would change how irrigation water is managed. Extreme weather like droughts, wind, fire and flood could also be expected. It would also result in a shift in the vegetation patterns, resulting in an increase in non-native species of vegetation and pests. Severe freezes, particularly among pecans and onions could also be observed. Drought was prevalent in New Mexico in November 2010, during which time there was no precipitation in Las Cruces.

Further, due to poor snowpack conditions, groundwater has to be pumped out to irrigate crops, resulting in an increase in the cost of production, and a subsequent rise in prices. The community of Navolato faced serious problems in water supply in absence of groundwater to ensure adequate supply of water for irrigation etc.

Socio-economic Profile

The United Mexican States, [2] better known as Mexico, is a federal republic in North America. Home to a number of ancient civilizations such as the Mayans and the Aztecs, Mexico has a rich socio-cultural history. The Mexico of today is heavily influenced by Spanish culture: a direct result of the Spanish colonization.

Mexico's politics were dominated for 70 years by the Institutional Revolutionary Party, which made it seem like a one-party state with a democratic facade, until 1997 when there was a resurgent opposition break. However, it returned to power in 2012 promising that it will not return to its old authoritarian ways. [3]

A careful analysis of the prevailing socio-economic conditions will help in the better understanding of the food security issues faced by the nation.

Mexico is classified as an "upper middle income" country by the World Bank having a GDP of US$ 1.26 trillion in 2013. With a population of about 122.3 million in 2013, the nation had a per capita income of around US$ 10,307 (2013). Despite the healthy macro-economic figures, the Mexican economy has been hit hard by the U.S. economic crisis with poverty figures sky-rocketing to over 51 percent. Moreover, there has been a sudden spurt in unemployment with the unemployment rate crossing 5.0 percent for the first time in over a decade.

Progressive measures by the government are reflected in the improving statistics pertaining to social overheads such as health and education. The population also has very healthy life expectancy figures, comparable to those of very advanced countries. [4] The latest life expectancy figures available with the World Bank are 76 years from the date of birth. The healthy life expectancy count is accompanied with an impressive figure of 93 percent adult literacy rate.

Traditionally close to the US, Mexico has demonstrated greater independence since the 1960s, but relations with the US persist as a result of high volume of trade and extensive Mexican migration to the US. Mexico is a major recipient of foreign transfer remittances, especially from Mexicans working in the U.S. These transfers form a major part of the country's foreign exchange and is a very peculiar feature of the socio-economic scenario of the country.

The tourism industry also contributes significantly to the national income of the country and is a major source of foreign exchange.

Agriculture in Mexico economically speaking, occupies a very small part of the GDP: around 5 percent of the GDP and employs around 13.7 percent of the total workforce of the economy. The most important revenue earning crops of Mexico are: (a) maize/corn, (b) sugarcane, (c) tomatoes, (d) dry beans and (e) avocados.

However, agriculture in Mexico is mostly subsistence in nature and is characterized by agriculture on small land holdings. In recent years, the deregulation of the Mexican agricultural sector under the NAFTA (North American Free Trade Agreement) has resulted in change in agricultural patterns under the dictates of the forces of globalization and competition.

Food Security Laws and Policies in Mexico

Mexico is a signatory to the International Covenant on Economic, Social and Cultural Rights; thus it has a legal obligation to respect, protect and fulfil the right to adequate food. Mexico has thus joined the small bandwagon of states that make the right to food explicit in their domestic constitutions. It aims to improve this legal framework by adopting more laws that incorporate the right to food; this framework is recommended by the Committee on Economic, Social and Cultural Rights, under the voluntary guidelines in the context of national food security.

Programme of Direct Support for the Countryside (PROCAMPO): It was Mexico's 1992 plan to support the crop yields and the producers, by providing direct payments per hectare conditioned only to the registration of the area sown by the landowner. The number of beneficiaries was limited to those producers who registered their plots in the directory program over the past three growing seasons before August 1993. In 2003, the program rules were modified to support the new low-income producers with an area less than or equal to five hectares with plantings in the temporal mode. PROCAMPO is a program of the Ministry of Agriculture (SAGARPA), and has received the biggest budget. In 1998, its expenditure reached US$ 919 million; since 1994, PROCAMPO made payments in an area of about 14 million hectares, covering 90 percent of arable land in Mexico. The program also transferred payments to more than 300 million farmers.

Agricultural Development Programme: It was initiated in 2005 to boost productivity and competitiveness in the sector, by encouraging investment and capitalization of technology, research, transfer and integration and consolidation of producers. Its total expenditure came up to US$ 68,977,600. This program was subsidized by the Federal Government, and resulted in more farmers getting trained in newer technology, improving rainfed crops by introducing sustainable techniques, managing the scarce water resources and protection of existing trees.

Programme to Support Agricultural Insurance Fund: It directed its funds to support the complementation of the transaction cost of insurance for agriculture, animals and livestock, and guaranteed surface growth. Supporting organizations supplemented the costs on supervision, monitoring and training operations. By the end of the fiscal year 2008, 259 insurance funds were supported with US$ 2,309,517, and the community of Navolato was benefited with IUSD 4,683.54.

In 2008, Mexico launched the Programa de Apoyo Alimentario (PAL), which was a food aid programme for fighting poverty in rural areas. It was strengthened by the provision of an additional cash tranfer to its beneficiaries. Further, the Social Milk Programme (LICONSA) provided fortified milk to the individuals belonging to poor families. Also, the Rural Food Support Programme (DICONSA) sold basic food products at affordable and reasonable prices, benefiting an estimated 29 million people.

Law on Food Security and Nutrition: It was approved by the Legislative Assembly of the Federal District on August 17, 2009. It was a milestone that acted in favour of the Right to Food which was recognised as both a fundamental human right and as the main objective of this Law. According to the statistics provided by the INEGI (National Institute of Statistics and Geography), almost half a million people in Mexico City are still food insecure. This law is one of the first laws in the world implementing the right to food at the sub-national level and thus bringing the right to food protection closer to the citizens. The law thus explicity guarantees the right to food as a universal human right and takes into consideration human rights principles as well as the level of implementation required for its full realisation.

This new law established the Food Security and Nutrition System of the Federal District, and reaffirms the role of the Social Development Council in the participation of civil society in the planning, decision-making, design, programming, execution and evaluation of policies and actions. The law also creates a wide-ranging food security programme as an instrument to define responsibilities, priorities and budget allocations. It also institutes monitoring proceedings like the commission of surveillance and assessment of social policies and programmes and other such mechanisms to promote the right to food. Further, the law makes it easy to access the policies, programs and actions that are undertaken by the Federal Government. This allows the people to be an integral part of the decision-making process and hold the competent authorities responsible for their actions.

A new organization was set up in the Rio Grande Valley along the U.S.-Mexico border in order to reshape production, distrubution and consumption of food—the La Semilla Food Center. It not only grows and sells organic food, but also exposes youth to new careers and encourages value-added industries. La Semilla's business strategy involves building up a new food shed concept, which is gaining popularity; it defines the area where food is produced and distributed. La Semilla further hopes to influence the local food system by assisting in the formation of a food policy council that brings together community organizations and government agencies. [5] Such food policy councils look into pressing issues such as the nutritional value of the food served in public schools.

Furthermore, a landmark constitutional reform which has been described by Mexico's Supreme Court of Justice as one of the most important steps in the human rights field in recent years, grants constitutional ranking to human rights enshrined in international treaties ratified by Mexico. These include the International Covenant on Economic, Social and Cultural Rights, and therefore, the right to food. The reform enhances the potential of the Mexican Human Rights Commission, and is a representative of the growing trend among Latin American countries to incorporate human rights at a constitutional level. The gesture towards the reform has shown that the Mexican Congress is taking important steps in consolidating a democratic regime that is based on respect for human beings, their liberties and their human rights.

International Treaties for Food Security

Food security laws all over the world have all been influenced by the major international treaties and conventions dealing with food security.

International Food Security Treaty: The International Food Security Treaty seeks to realize the universal right of man to live a life free from hunger. The treaty came into being in order to fill the gap between food security policies and their implementation. Moreover, the treaty will compel and help countries fulfil their obligations to maintain food security. The treaty seeks to promote food security by means of a universal agreement. The fundamental principles upon which this treaty is founded are:

1. Food is a unique human resource. Everyone has the fundamental right to be free from hunger.
2. Access to food with dignity is a basic condition for the physical, psychological and spiritual well-being and survival of the human species.
3. Free market structures are not sufficient to assure global food security; basic guarantees of individual access to food are needed. International cooperation and assistance may be necessary in order to implement such access in low income food deficit countries.
4. International initiatives which enhance global food security will significantly contribute to international peace and security and the reduction of civil unrest and strife.
5. Food may never be used as a weapon to gain political or military advantage either within a state or as an instrument of foreign policy.

The IFST commits itself to:

- Enhanced access to a minimum standard of nutrition (set by the United Nations).
- Contribute to the creation of a World Food Reserve and Resource Centre. It aims to provide assistance to any nation facing an emergency.
- Establish and enforce laws. The treaty seeks to prohibit any country from denying or intending to deny minimum nutritional standards to any person.
- Support United Nations Food Security Enforcement. It seeks to initiate action against nations which are unable to enforce food security laws, or are unwilling to do so through formal investigations.

World Food Summit on Food Security: [6] This global summit was convened in the year 2009 by the Food and Agriculture Organization of the United Nations (FAO). The World Food Summit was called in response to widespread hunger and under-nourishment and the growing concern regarding the capacity of present agricultural systems to meet the needs of the future. The summit unanimously adopted a resolution towards renewed efforts to eradicate the evil of hunger from the face of earth sustainably and as soon as possible.

The participant countries undertook to work towards greater domestic and international funding in the agricultural sector and promote new investment in the sector. The summit also considered the implementation of certain reforms to existing food security laws in order to enhance governance of food security issues. Enhancing the role of PPPs (public private partnerships) in the agricultural sector was also advocated. Finally, the food security measures to be undertaken by the countries must be in consonance with the principles of sustainable development.

Tortilla Crisis

In 2007, Mexico witnessed its worse tortilla crisis in its modern history. The alarming rise in international corn prices which was caused by the demand for grain-based fuel ethanol led to the expensive tortillas. That, in turn, led to lower sales for vendors and angry protests by consumers. It raised questions about the powerful businesses that dominate the Mexican corn market and were suspected by some lawmakers and regulators of unfair speculation and monopoly practices. On January 18, Calderón announced an agreement with business leaders capping tortilla prices at 78 cents per kilogram, or 2.2 pounds, less than half the highest reported prices. This move by the then-president was a throwback to a previous era where Mexico controlled prices—the government subsidized tortillas until 1999, at which point cheap corn imports were rising under the NAFTA trade agreement.

The tortilla crisis stands as an example of the failure of the neo-liberal agricultural and food policies, overlooked by successive governments during Mexico's recent history. NAFTA's institutions modified the state's core regulatory functions and eliminated those institutions that made regulation possible. In 1999, poor consumers received a severe blow because tortilla subsidies that were given to 1.2 million families were eliminated. The shortage of corn in the beginning of 2007 was caused by three factors: one, speculation by the large monopolies that dominate Mexico's corn and tortilla markets; two, NAFTA commitments to open up the agricultural and livestock sectors totally to imports from the United States, and three, increase in corn prices in the international market due to increased demand for corn to produce ethanol, as mentioned earlier. The tortilla crisis shows that one of the NAFTA's basic assumptions—that it benefits consumers, even if it sacrifices farmers—is a macabre fallacy.

North American Free Trade Agreement (NAFTA) [7]

Prior to the 1980s, Mexico's International trade policy was characterized by high import tariffs and quotas, with restrictions on foreign investment, trade and ownership. However, after a severe economic crisis in the early 1980s, the country liberalized its protectionist policies. Since then, Mexico has implemented 11 free trade agreements, with the European Union, countries in South and Central America, Japan, and, most importantly, United States and Canada. Well before the implementation of NAFTA, successive Mexican governments embraced free trade with remarkable zeal. Beginning with its membership of the General Agreement on Tariffs and Trade (GATT) in 1987, Mexico has signed more trade agreements than any other country in the world. In 1994, Mexico joined the Organization for Economic Cooperation and Development (OECD) and that same year NAFTA was implemented.

The North American Free Trade Agreement is an agreement entered into by Canada, The United States of America and Mexico. It created a trilateral trade bloc in North America. The agreement came into effect on January 1, 1994. NAFTA was given momentum by President Ronald Reagan when he was campaigning on a North American common market. It was launched to reduce trading costs, increase business investment, and to help North America become more competitive in the global economy and market place.

Under the NAFTA, all non-tariff barriers to agricultural trade between the United States and Mexico were eliminated. It provides protection and enforcement of intellectual property rights, allows for the resolution of trade disputes, promotes fair competition, etc. In addition, many tariffs were eliminated immediately, with others being phased out over periods of 5 to 15 years. This allowed for an orderly adjustment to free trade with Mexico, with full implementation beginning January 1, 2008. In other words, the agreement between Mexico and the U.S. provides for the liberalization of the agricultural sector. This implied free-market competition in the Mexican agricultural sector and tariff-free transactions with the U.S. markets.

Over 80 percent of Mexico's agricultural exports go to the United States, and more than two-thirds of its agricultural imports come from the United States. Specifically, U.S. imports of Mexican agricultural, fish, and forestry products in calendar 2006 were valued at a record US$ 10.2 billion, and U.S. exports of agricultural, fish, and forestry products to Mexico were valued at US$ 11.5 billion. [8] NAFTA has thus become increasingly significant with the launch of the European Union and the economic growth of China and other emerging market countries.

Despite the many benefits provided by NAFTA, the Agreement has been a highly controversial issue, such that its disadvantages are pointed out during most Presidential campaigns. Indicators of rural poverty show a larger incidence of poverty, and deeper poverty in 1998 than in 1989. The numbers provided by the Mexican Agricultural Ministry, SAGARPA, state that as of 2001, 81.5 percent of people in rural areas were living in poverty. For the economically active population in agriculture, the incidence of poverty increased from 54 percent in 1989 to 64 percent in 1998. A study by Mexico's Centre for Economic Research and Teaching found that since 1992, the proportion of workers employed in agriculture has shrunk by 10 percent and that rural wages are 30 percent lower than other sectors of the economy. However, the authors have focused only on the provisions relating to agriculture as only these provisions are relevant to the discussion here.

Advantages of NAFTA:

1. It resulted in increased foreign trade, due to elimination of trade barriers. During the period of 1993 to 2007, the gross domestic product (GCP) of the United States grew by 50 percent, and that of Mexico grew by 46 percent. As the cost of imports is decreased, it results in a reduction in inflation.
2. NAFTA creates agreements on international rights for business investors. This spurs investment and growth, especially for smaller businesses. Investment in Mexico has thus helped increase the efficiency of U.S. domestic production. By shifting assembly of their products, many companies are able to reduce their costs. The U.S. manufacturing output thus increased by almost 60 percent from 1993 to 2006.
3. Mexican employment levels have been more volatile since the implementation of NAFTA. However, as of 2005, the Mexican affiliates of U.S. companies employed nearly 850,000 people, who contributed 3.3 percent to Mexico's GDP. Mexican workers' wages have also seen a steady rise since the 1994 peso crisis, and continue to increase each year. Mexico's industries that export goods or are located in regions with a high level of foreign investment also pay higher wages.

Disadvantages of NAFTA:

1. Many Mexican farmers were put out of business by the U.S.-subsidized farm products. NAFTA provisions for environmental protection and Mexican labour were not

strong enough to help the workers and prevent their exploitation. About 1.3 million farmers lost their jobs. The 2002 Farm Bill subsidized U.S. agribusiness by 40 percent of the net farm income. Upon implementation of NAFTA, however, corn and other grains were imported to Mexico at very low costs. Rural Mexican farmers could not compete with these prices.

2. NAFTA resulted in the expansion of the maquiladora program, by which U.S.-owned companies employed Mexican labourers near the border to cheaply assemble products for export to the U.S. These workers had no labour rights or health protection. They worked for about 12 hours a day or more.
3. The Mexican environment was severely deteriorated due to the use of more fertilizers and other chemicals, as rural farmers expanded to more marginal lands. This also resulted in deforestation.

NAFTA and Agriculture in Mexico: Food security in Mexico has been severely compromised by trade liberalization. Ironically, this liberalization had been undertaken in violation of the protections negotiated by the Mexican government into the NAFTA. With the onset of NAFTA, Mexican economy and agriculture came under new pressures from the U.S. exports. NAFTA was supposed to create a level playing field, but in fact tilted the scales towards the U.S. economy; an example of this would be the highly subsidized U.S. farm products. Through the dictates of economic efficiency, Mexico was deemed unfit to produce corn as its yields were way below the average yield of its neighbours, as a result of which it sought to turn over its land to niche crops such as tropical fruits and vegetables. However, this resulted in three million corn farmers being declared as obsolete; they were to be relocated to manufacturing or assembly work. This resulted in large scale migration to the U.S.

Several agricultural goods such as corn, soybeans, wheat, rice, cotton, beef, pork and poultry, were all produced in Mexico itself before NAFTA, but were, after NAFTA, imported into Mexico from the U.S. markets. Thus, the U.S. exports of the eight supported commodities mentioned above have increased dramatically since the early 1990s, rising between 159 percent and 707 percent. From January 1995 to June 1996, consumption of basic foods (corn, beans, wheat) dropped to 29 percent, and as a result one of two Mexicans did not have access to the minimum caloric requirements established by the World Health Organization. Assuming Mexican producer prices were depressed by the same percentage as the dumping margins, below-cost exports cost Mexican producers of corn, soybeans, wheat, cotton and rice an estimated US$ 9.7 billion from 1997-2005, just over US$ 1 billion per year.

Furthermore, meats were exported at below-cost prices as U.S. producers were benefited from below-cost soybeans and corn. This subsidy that was granted to meat producers resulted in dumping margins of 5-10 percent on exported meat. This resulted in an estimated loss of US$ 3.2 billion between 1997 and 2005, with the largest loss being that of beef.

The eight products had an estimated total loss of US$ 12.8 billion from 1997 to 2005. This effectively boils down to an average annual loss of US$ 1.4 billion, which is equivalent to 10 percent of the value of all the Mexican agricultural exports to the United States, and is greater than the value of Mexican tomato exports to the United States. Producer and consumer food insecurity resulted in part from the NAFTA-induced policies that put the cost of food beyond the reach of many consumers and made it impossible for Mexican farmers to sell their harvests to importers

Conclusion

The implementation of the NAFTA in Mexico led to a significant policy change with the Mexican government deregulating the agricultural sector. Moreover, the relaxation of tariff rates led to enhanced competition from food grains imported into Mexico from the U.S. These food grains were made available to consumers in Mexico at subsidized prices. Local cultivators could not compete against such low market prices and were priced out of the market by food imported tariff-free. In fact, the exodus of Mexican farmers from the countryside has been well documented.

The farmers hold other jobs to subsidize their farming. Some farmers continue to survive, thanks to money sent by relatives working in the United States. Farmers in the region have survived NAFTA by switching to modern techniques of production in order to enhance crop yields. They also lobby for government aid and band together to fight private oligopolies that sell seed and buy corn. But their landholdings remain small, sometimes not more than 10 acres, and they are at the mercy of rising costs and fluctuating prices. Hence, it is simply not possible for these marginal producers to compete against their better equipped and technically advanced counterparts in the U.S.

Moreover, the distribution of food grains in the economy is handled by 'middle-men' transnational organizations who sell such food grains at international prices. Besides influencing prices for producers and participating in imports, they can act as monopolies, as they did during the 2007 tortilla crisis. The free market economy has resulted in a reduction in the market prices. It has been estimated that the real price of corn in Mexico has declined substantially.

The present development paradigm adopted by Mexico has clearly disrupted the socio-economic fabric of the Mexican agricultural community. The agricultural sector, which is closely related to traditional life in Mexico, has been brought under stress due to the adverse backward linkages of the liberalized market.

The NAFTA, in an increasingly globalized world, is here to stay. However, it is unfair to let the small agricultural producers bargain with giant organizations dominating the distribution networks in North America. The disruption of normal socio-economic life in rural Mexico due to the inability of farmers to cope with enhanced competition is a precursor to social unrest. Moreover, the international market being volatile, Mexico is exposing itself to fluctuating prices. This does not auger well for the agricultural sector dominated by small producers who are still dependent on farming loans and subsidized farming implements. If measures are not taken at the earliest, the Tortilla Crisis of 2007 is just the beginning.

Endnotes

1. Eakin, Britain, "Climate Change Poses Challenges to Food Security in the Southwest", University of Arizona, available at: www.climas.arizona.edu/feature-articles/april-2011, accessed on March 28, 2012.
2. "Mexico", available at: http://images.rca.org/docs/mission/country-profiles/Mexico.pdf.
3. "Mexico Profile", available at: http://www.bbc.co.uk/news/world-latin-america-18095241, accessed on 1 April, 2012.
4. The World Bank, "Data: Mexico", available at: http://data.worldbank.org/country/mexico, accessed on 1 April, 2012.
5. "Producing Food Security Along the U.S.-Mexico Border", available at: http://mexidata.info/id2904.html, accessed on March 28, 2012.
6. "World Summit on Food Security, Rome", available at: http://www.fao.org/wsfs/world-summit/en, accessed on April 1, 2012.
7. "North American Free Trade Agreement", United States Department of Agriculture, Foreign Agricultural Service, available at: http://www.fas.usda.gov/itp/policy/nafta/nafta.asp, accessed on April 1, 2012.
8. "Strengthening NAFTA Through U.S.-Mexican Cooperation in Agriculture", available at: http://www.fas.usda.gov/itp/Mexico/030607StrengtheningNAFTA.pdf, accessed on April 1, 2012.

10

New Zealand: Food Security Treaty with Australia

Ankita Shankar and Shweta Adhikari

Socio-Economic Profile

Demographic Indicators: The demographic indicators indicate a relatively small population. The population density, however, has been rising steadily from 11.35 in 1980 to 16.59 in 2011. [1] The majority of the population is concentrated in urban areas, with a rising trend towards urbanisation. The sex ratio is well-balanced.

Gender Indicators: The position of women is good; however the participation in politics, higher education, job is low. Both adolescent fertility and maternal mortality rates are low.

Health Indicators: Here, arises one of the first anomalies in the socio-economic profile of the country. While the life expectancy is high and the infant and child mortality rate is low with an overall decent health index, a very small proportion of the GDP is used in the form of public expenditure on health.

Education Indicators: The public expenditure on education seems reasonable. The high enrolment rate as well as expected and mean schooling years make it evident that the education system is functioning at a satisfactory level, at least as far as primary education is concerned.

Economic Profile

Income Indicators: According to the World Development Report, 2010, any country with a per capita GNI of US$

11,906 or more qualifies as a high income country. [2] NZ's per capita income, both GDP and GNI, are over double this level, indicating very high economic development. The income index, too, is extremely favourable, with an obvious low occurrence of poverty.

Inequality Indicators: There is no large-scale inequity as far as LE is concerned. This data remains inconclusive as to the equitable distribution of education and income.

Poverty Indicators: No conclusive data has been made available regarding poverty in NZ.

Sustainability Indicators: Adjusted net savings are marginal, indicating sufficient circulation of capital to sustain development. The devastation due to natural disasters is maintained at a bare minimum, with no fatalities, all indicating excellent disaster management abilities. Various indicators of green accounting reveal that the ecological cost of development is not disproportionate or unreasonably high.

Human Development Index

The human development index is a composite index which measures human development, based on social and economic indicators, including demography, gender, health, education, income, inequality, poverty and sustainability.

As per the first Human Development Report of 1990 "People are the real wealth of a nation". [3] According to Prof. Amartya Sen, [4] "Human development, as an approach, is concerned with what I take to be the basic development idea; namely, advancing the richness of the human life rather than the richness of the economy in which the human beings live, which is only a part of it".

Over the past few decades, there has been substantial progress in many aspects of human development. Development is ultimately best measured by its impact on individual lives. Thus, it is evident that human development is not merely quantitative, but a comprehensive measure which incorporates various factors. An analysis of the level of human development of a nation through a period of time is reflective of the overall living standards of the people living there.

In NZ, the HDI Value has gone up from 0.80 in 1980 to 0.908 in 2011, showing a substantial development. Out of 187 countries surveyed in 2011, the HDI rank of NZ was 5. This indicates that the social and economic parameters used to measure development, too, have witnessed improvement. Of these parameters, food security is an essential component without which the development of any kind is not possible. Thus, prima facie, it is evident that food supply in the state has improved over the past three decades, perhaps as a result of government planning.

The HDI is calculated on the basis of certain parameters, which contribute to the overall trend the index seeks to reflect. These parameters include aspects related to health (LE at birth), education (expected years of schooling and mean years of schooling) and income (GNI per capita).

Legislative Framework

The Domestic Food Review began in 2003. Till date the review has covered all aspects of the safety and suitability of food produced, processed, manufactured, traded, transported and imported to NZ. The need for this review was felt because the country's food regime has not been reviewed for the last 30 years. The review has identified a number of problems in the food regime as it is currently applied across the country, including:

A lack of clarity in the roles of the regulators—there are inequities with the way the food industry is regulated across the country and a lack of clarity in the roles of the regulators involved, namely the NZ Food Safety Authority (NZFSA), city and district councils (local authorities) and public health units.

A rising incidence of food borne illness—food review by the NZFSA attempted to identify the most effective means of protecting consumers and harmonising food safety legislation for NZ food business operators. [5]

In response, the NZ Government agreed to an overhaul of the Food Act, 1981 and committed to providing an effective, efficient and risk-based food regulatory regime that is capable of:

- Making it easier for businesses to manage food safety.
- Minimising compliance costs for business.
- Reducing the incidence of food borne illness.
- Providing consumers with greater assurances that their food is safe.

The Food Bill reflects the outcome of the DFR. The bill not only includes the opinion of the legislature but also of the people. The outcome of the review by people was the proposals for the Food Bill. The publications and information on the Food Bill was available throughout this process on the NZFSA website and was used to supplement the consultation process.

During the public consultation on the Food Bill by the Primary Production Committee from 22nd July to 2nd September 2010, 66 submissions were received. The large turnout of people for the deliberations proves that even the public wants the food act to be reviewed. It has been so many years even after the DFR but no food act or legislation has been passed to improve the food security condition in NZ.

Food Act, 1981: The Food Act regulates the sale of food for human consumption (both domestic and imported) and is administered by the NZFSA. [6] Part 1A of the Food Act seeks to facilitate a voluntary transition from compliance with the FHR to the adoption by the food industry of Food Safety Programmes (FSP). An FSP may relate to either a particular part of the food industry or a particular person or group of persons within the food industry. FSPs are verified by approved independent auditors and regulated by the NZFSA and public health units of district health boards.

The Food Act, 1981 allows standards to be issued in relation to the composition of food, including the:

- Maximum amounts of chemical contaminants or residues

that may be present.

- Maximum or minimum amounts of additives or other substances that must or may be present.
- Microbiological status.

There are also standards for imported food. These standards must be met by producers and processors in NZ. They do this by implementing measures and controls for food safety in their businesses. This is usually done through an FSP or by operating under the FHR, 1974. The three regulations under the Food Act, which apply to food businesses in NZ, include the following.

Food Hygiene Regulations (FHR), 1974: The Food Hygiene Regulations are enforced by local councils (territorial authorities). They set food-handling requirements and describe registration and inspection of food businesses.

Food businesses that come under the Food Act meet food standards by operating under the FHR or by implementing an FSP. Under the regulations, food sold in NZ has to be made in premises that are registered and inspected by local authority environment health officials (EHOs).

There is a large area of potential overlap between the work of Food Act officers and EHOs, usually decided by local arrangements.

Food Act officers are authorised to exercise all powers defined within the Food Act except those given to EHOs. A health protection officer at a district health board can also be a Food Act officer and can be contracted to NZFSA.

Food (Safety) Regulations, 2002: These regulations include provisions relating to food containers, infected people working with food, the manufacture of low-acid canned food and provisions relating to particular foods including mutton birds, wine labels, fluoridated water and hemp seed oil. The new Food Act proposes to repeal the FHR and have only one set of Regulations.

Food (Fees and Charges) Regulations, 1997: These regulations describe the charges which MAF and other authorities may make for services they undertake for food businesses. The act also includes the concept of FSPs to identify and control food safety risk factors in order to establish and maintain food safety.

Food safety risk factors may relate to the production, manufacture, preparation, packaging, storage, handling, transport, distribution, or sale of food. The legislature is planning to repeal this act and replace it with the new Food Act. The Food Bill will implement a risk-based food regulatory regime.

Agricultural Compounds and Veterinary Act, 1997: All agricultural compounds imported, manufactured, sold or used in NZ must be authorised under the ACVM Act, 1997 and regulations.

NZ ranked 5th in the 2011 HDI, [7] 4th in the 2011 Index of Economic Freedom published by The Heritage Foundation [8] and has trade relations with many countries. In light of all these facts it can be inferred that misuse of agricultural and veterinary products and their being low standard may not only cause havoc in the economic but also social setup of the country. Consequently, these products are subject to strict regulatory controls on their importation, manufacture, sale and use. Regulatory control of these products focuses on avoiding or minimising the possible adverse effects that may result from their use.

The basic Government policy is to impose control that is 'necessary and sufficient' to manage risks while avoiding unnecessary costs of compliance. The legal definition of an agricultural compound, as stated in the ACVM Act is, "...any substance, mixture of substances, or biological compound, used or intended for use in the direct management of plants and animals, or to be applied to the land, place, or water on or in which the plants and animals are managed, for the purposes of:

1. Managing or eradicating pests, including vertebrate pests; or
2. Maintaining, promoting, or regulating plant or animal productivity and performance or reproduction; or
3. Fulfilling special nutritional requirements; or

4. Manipulation, capture, or immobilisation of animals; or
5. Diagnosing the condition of animals; or
6. Preventing or treating conditions of animals; or
7. Enhancing the effectiveness of an agricultural compound used for the treatment of plants and animals; or
8. Marking animals; and includes:

- any veterinary medicine, substance, mixture of substances, or biological compound used for post-harvest pest control or disinfestations of raw primary produce;
- anything used or intended to be used as feed for animals; and
- any substance, mixture of substances, or biological compound declared to be an agricultural compound for the purposes of this Act by Order in Council made under sub-section (2)". [9]

According to the Act, before importation, manufacture, sale and use of agricultural products, approval of AVCM group is required in NZ. The ACVM group is responsible for implementing and confirming compliance to the NZ processes under the ACVM Act, 1997, Animal Products, 1999, Food Act 1981and Wine Act, 2003.

In regard to the ACVM Act, this means:

- Authorising ACVM products and monitoring their importation, manufacture, sale and use.
- Developing, implementing, evaluating and reviewing standards relating to agricultural chemicals, veterinary medicines and maximum residue limits.
- Maintaining public registers/lists.
- Confirming compliance and investigating non-compliance.

The three core functions of the group include standards, approvals and conformance. To meet its objectives, the group consists of three teams, namely standards team, approval team and programmes team.

If one imports, manufactures, sells or uses veterinary medicines, agricultural chemicals, vertebrate toxic agents, fertilizers, pet food, stock feed and supplements in NZ, the ACVM requirements apply to them. The rules enshrined in the

ACVM are strict one and attract heavy liability in case of breach. However, a few amendments are required in the act as it is too consumer centric and thus excessively harsh on the producers.

Animal Products Act, 1999: The Animal Product Act establishes a risk management system that requires all animal products traded and used to be 'fit for intended purpose' through meeting NZ animal product standards. The Act was passed with the following two objectives:

- Minimise and manage risks to human or animal health arising from the production and processing of animal material and products by instituting measures that ensure so far as is practicable that all traded animal products are fit for their intended purpose; and
- Facilitate the entry of animal material and products into overseas markets by providing the controls and mechanisms needed to give and to safeguard official assurances for entry into those markets.

The risk management system comprises the following main types of controls.

Risk Management Programmes (RMPs): An RMP is a written document, specific to a particular operator's business, which sets out how the operator will identify and control, manage and eliminate or minimise hazards and other risk factors in relation to their production and processing of animal material and animal products in order to ensure that the resulting animal product is fit for the intended purpose. These are programmes implemented by businesses processing animal material to identify and manage potential hazards in order to ensure that the resulting animal product meets relevant standards and is free from any prospective hazards.

Section 13 of the APA requires the following persons to operate under a RMP:

- All primary processors of animal material;
- All secondary processors of animal products intended for human or animal consumption, except to the extent that

they are subject to the Food Act regime;

- Retail butchers who are dual operator butchers, and
- Such other persons as may be specified by Order in Council under Section 15 as required to operate under an RMP. [10]

However, there are certain operators who are exempted from having RMPs, they are dairy processors of dairy products consumed on premises, processors of certain dairy products that are multi-ingredient foods, domestic dairy processors, processors of food for animal consumption, fish premise processors and egg producers.

When a business operates under an RMP, it is covered by the APA and the provisions in the Food Act regime do not apply for the operations covered by the RMP. This means the premises detailed in the RMP are not subject to the FHR or the Health (Registration of Premises) Regulations, 1966 for the operations covered by the RMP.

Regulated Control Schemes: These are schemes imposed by NZFSA to manage risks. An example is the national scheme for monitoring residues in meat. Regulated control schemes are tools intended to be used to manage hazards both at individual and company level. It also ensures that cost effective methods are employed for hazard management.

Exporter Controls: These include the issuing of official assurances and the publishing of export requirements. Most exporters of animal material and products are required to be registered with the NZFSA. The APA provides for the issue of official assurances to be given by the Government (usually in the form of certificates) when required by authorities in importing countries. The Act also provides for the government to issue statements as to NZ animal product standards in other situations.

Recognising Agencies and Persons: The NZFSA recognises persons involved with key functions to ensure competency and performance.

The APA contains NZ's requirements for game estates to

facilitate the tracing and proper treatment of animal material and product derived from such estates. Also, the Act sets out what is allowed in NZ in regard to home kill and recreational catch activity. While allowing for this activity, there are strict requirements to prevent the unlawful trading of this unregulated product. The risk management system as proposed by the Act is sound and ensures that unfit animal products are not marketed either in domestic market or abroad. It maintains food safety along with acknowledging the individual's right to rear animals and butcher them at a domestic scale. But like other legislations, this also needs review to remove its obsoleteness.

Wine Act, 2003: The new Act replaced the old Wine Makers Act, 1981 and the Wine Makers Levy Act, 1976 which had become obsolete and were no longer in use in NZ. With time, the wine industry of NZ expanded and need was felt to frame comprehensive legislation for the regulation of manufacture and export of wine. The Wine Act establishes a new integrated regime for the production and export of wine. The objectives of the Wine Act are as follows:

- To set standards for identity, truthfulness in labelling, and safety of wine.
- To minimise and manage risks to human health arising from the making of wine and ensuring compliance with wine standards.
- To facilitate the entry of wine into overseas markets by providing the controls and mechanisms needed to give and safeguard official assurances issued for the purpose of enabling entry into those markets.
- To enable the setting of export eligibility requirements to safeguard the reputation of NZ wine in overseas markets.
- To promote consultation with industry organisations on the regulation of the industry, as an aid to fostering efficiency and growth in the NZ wine industry.
- To enable levies to be imposed on winemakers for payment to entities representing their interests for the

funding of industry-good activities. [11]

According to the Act, a winemaker is "a person who, for reward (otherwise than as an employee) or for purposes of trade, makes wine". [12] This means a person who undertakes any or every process or action from the receipt of the commodity through to the dispatch of wine.

The Act requires the winemakers to act under a Wine Standards Management Programme. A WSMP is a set of documents that demonstrates how the standards and requirements of Wine Act are met. It is linked to a particular winemaking place or places—a winery. A winery may have more than one winemaker associated with it, or more than one business using it. It is not necessary for each winemaker who uses a single winemaking place to have an individual WSMP.

Plans and Programmes

Food Control and Safety Plans: An FSP sets out the process by which the safety of the food product can be assured. The business owner/operator, an employee, or an outside agent may design the FSP. A variety of factors influence food safety and each FSP must be tailored to the specific food operation or process in each business. The programme must be approved by the NZFSA and is subject to an independent audit by a suitably qualified and NZFSA approved auditor. Premises with approved FSPs are exempt from the requirement to be registered by the Council. Food businesses that are within the Food Service and Catering sectors of the food industry (restaurants, takeaways, cafes/lunch bars, and catering businesses), can be exempted from the FHR, 1974 by adopting an OP-FCP.

The Food Control and Safety plan ensures that adequate safety and control measures are taken during the manufacture and processing of food. The plans include even small businesses like cafe etc. so as to ensure safety even at the lowermost level. The provisions of the plan are excessively stringent, therefore, not favourable for owners of small-scale food processing units, thus discouraging them and effecting food production. Like all other legislations and programmes, this too needs review.

Role of International Agencies

World Trade Organization (WTO): The World Trade Organization is an international organisation of countries that deals with global rules of trade—it determines and oversees the multilateral trade rules that underpin NZ's trading relationships with the 152 other member countries. It not only provides trade rules but also acts as a judge in case of disputes. NZ being an open economy and being keen in making trade relations with other countries, it benefits from clear trade rules that are common to all. When making decisions, WTO members are guided by the fundamental principles that international trade should be:

- Without discrimination—a country should not discriminate between its trading partners and should not treat foreign goods, services or people differently from the way it treats its own. In the WTO, all parties are granted this "most-favoured nation" status.
- Freer—to remove barriers of trade through negotiations.
- Predictable—so foreign companies, investors and governments are confident that trade barriers will not be raised arbitrarily.
- More competitive—by discouraging "unfair" practices such as subsidies and dumping.
- More beneficial to developing countries. [13]

Since a major part of NZ's export includes food product, the rules of the WTO directly or indirectly influence the food security in NZ. Since the WTO provides a common platform of similar laws to be applicable to all, it is conducive to the development of international trade.

United Nations: The broad work agenda of the United Nations covers many issues of importance and interest to NZ. The United Nations, Human Rights and Commonwealth

Division of the Ministry of Foreign Affairs and Trade liaise with other divisions in the Ministry, as well as other government departments to facilitate NZ's interaction with the United Nations. [14]

The UN provides funds to NZ through its various arms namely UNDP, WHO, UNFP, FAO, etc. NZ is committed to maintaining human rights of its citizens and for this purpose it has signed seven core human rights treaties. Safe and healthy food free from all contaminants is also one of the basic human rights of the people; the United Nations helps NZ to achieve this goal through its different arms. [15]

Recently, the United Nations World Food Programme and Japanese electronic entertainment company Konami Digital have teamed up to release an online game that can support the fight against hunger.

The funds accumulated as a result of this endeavour will be donated to run a WFP school meal programs. NZ being an extremely rich country, there is not much which the United Nations can donate to NZ. Iin contrast, NZ funds various projects of UN like Libya relief project, Mindana etc.

Commonwealth Group of Nations: The Commonwealth is the outcome of an ongoing evolution. It began to emerge in the nineteenth century as countries shifted from colonial to dominion status culminating in the 1931 Statute of Westminster. Through their diversity, Commonwealth countries have a strong sense of kinship and unity. The members due to common past have similar systems of law, education, government and some common cultural traditions.

The Commonwealth is an intergovernmental organisation, with countries as its members. The people-to-people links are supported by the Commonwealth Foundation, acting as an umbrella organisation for some 30 Commonwealth associations of professionals.

NZ being a part of this group is committed to its aims and objectives—one of them being food security. Recently, a joint statement was issued by Australia, Canada, NZ and the United

Kingdom in support of the Perth Declaration on Food Security Principles. All these countries agreed to help the countries of the region of Horn of Africa to achieve food security. Not only this, NZ is also a signatory of L'Aquila Food Security Initiative and the declaration of the World Summit on Food Security in 2009 which aims at helping the under developed countries to achieve food security.

International Treaties

Australia-New Zealand Cooperation: The only food security related international treaties signed by NZ have been bilateral ones with its neighbour, Australia. For over 15 years, the Australian and NZ governments have been working in close collaboration to align food security requirements and develop its standards.

In 1983, the Australia NZ Closer Economic Relationship Free Trade Agreement (CER) was signed by the governments of these respective states. This comprehensive agreement underpins a number of auxiliary agreements, which includes the Food Standards Treaty and the Trans-Tasman Mutual Recognition Arrangement. The Food Standards Treaty, 1995, committed both countries to the development and implementation of a single system of joint food standards. It provides for an agency to undertake this task, with the underlying objective being to consider the needs of both the states in protecting public health and reducing unnecessary trade barriers.

There following were the two main outcomes of the treaty: establishment of the FSANZ and the development of the Code.

The Food Standards Australia and NZ is responsible for developing, varying and reviewing food standards for the available food products.

The Australia NZ Food Standards Code (a.k.a. 'the Code') sets requirements for the labelling and composition of food and food-related products. The Code was adopted in NZ in 2001, and took full effect from 2002. At this time, a series of regulations were also introduced in NZ to cover food safety requirements outside the joint system.

The Trans-Tasman Mutual Recognition Act, 1997, came into effect from 1998, as part of an agreement between NZ and Australia. It has implications for the sale of goods, including food predicts. Where food standards that cover both countries have not been decided on, they are mutually recognised under the TTMRA.

Apart from these agreements, other steps have been taken to promote Australia-NZ cooperation on food security matters. The Codex Alimentarius Commission is a forum which coordinates international food standards. Through FRANZ, Australia and NZ have been closely cooperating on a wide number of issues as part of this forum. Both states participate in the Quadrilateral Group alliance for promoting food security.

Leading Judgements

In the age of the obesity epidemic, it is common for food manufacturers to try to influence consumer purchasing decisions by touting a product's nutritional, natural or health qualities. But if the product's contents do not deserve the producer's claims, the consequences can be severe as we have seen in the high profile Ribena case. Ribena is a British brand of fruit-based uncarbonated soft drink, carbonated soft drink and fruit drink concentrate produced by Glaxo SmithKline.

In 2004, Anna Devathasan and Jenny Suo, two high school students from Pakuranga College in Auckland, NZ, conducted a science experiment to determine the vitamin C levels of their favourite fruit drinks. As Ribena advertising referred to "four times the vitamin C of oranges", they were surprised to discover the levels of vitamin C were much lower— 22 mg/100ml—in the syrup, compared with another product, Just Juice—72 mg/100ml. After contacting the manufacturers of Ribena, their concerns of 'intentionally misleading and quite inappropriate' claims were dismissed, and they were told the claim related only to the blackcurrant fruit, not the product.

Their case was taken up by a television consumer affairs show, Fair Go, which broadcasted the story nationwide on TV ONE in October 2004. Following further testing, in March 2007, the NZ Commerce Commission brought 15 charges in the Auckland District Court against Glaxo SmithKline under the Fair Trading Act. In addition to the misleading representations that the Ribena range "contained four times the vitamin C of oranges" in its advertising and packaging, cartooned ready to drink Ribena falsely claimed on the label to have 7 mg of vitamin C per 100ml, or 44 percent of the recommended daily intake, when it had no detectable vitamin C content.

The Commerce Commission argued that this claim, while literally true, was likely to mislead consumers about vitamin C in Ribena and orange drinks. As an example of the true comparison, Ribena syrup diluted in the recommended way had only one and a half times the vitamin C of orange juice. GlaxoSmithKline pleaded guilty to 10 charges of breaching the Fair Trading Act in relation to these 'four times' claims and a further five charges over the incorrect labelling of the ready-to-drink product which contains no detectable level of vitamin C. Glaxo SmithKline was fined NZ$ 227,500 and ordered to undertake a nationwide campaign of corrective advertising for misleading its customers about the blackcurrant drink 'Ribena'.

The case brings to light the health conscious attitude of the people of NZ. The soft drink giant had to pay a hefty amount of NZ$ 227,500 for the misrepresentation made by it. Not only this they were forced to take corrective measures so as to make the people of the land aware about the misrepresentation made by them. It can be inferred from the above mentioned facts that the food laws of NZ are strictly implemented by the judiciary.

Recommendations

From the peculiar nature of the problem, it seems unlikely that a complete de-privatization of the food sector is in order. Such a step will only burden the government exchequer more, and lead to a loss of efficiency, which is characteristic of many public ventures. The government, though adequately capable of dealing with the potential financial burden at present, may face a serious depletion of funds in the future. That the population is growing steadily has been established. With an increase in population, demand for food and other resources, too, will increase. Historically, government resources rarely manage to increase proportionately with population growth, whatever be the stage of development. Over time, if the entire burden of food production is placed on the government, it may face paucity of funds due to the increased demands of a growing population.

Additionally, the violation of private producer's basic right to occupation is unjust. The proposed de-privatisation will not only revoke the producer's right to grow food for commercial purposes, but also for sustenance. While preventing commercial food production can be seen as a violation of the right to occupational freedom, and may still be justifiable, preventing subsistence agriculture will be deprivation of the right to food, which is absolutely unwarranted.

A wiser step would, therefore, be to implement financial incentives for setting up more storage and distribution outlets, which will deal primarily with the distribution of fresh, unprocessed food. There is no shortage of food production in NZ, however, there is no proper distribution system either. Food products are therefore often required to be converted into processed forms to increase durability. This has formed the cause of the unhealthy reliance on processed food, and resulting malnutrition. Thus, policy measures which promote the establishment of cold storages and distribution systems (including transportation) would help ensure that fresh food products are distributed more efficiently. This would reduce the dependence on packaged food, and also solve the other problems of distribution of production faced in the region. Malnutrition rates would, therefore, naturally, decline.

Mass awareness via education regarding nutritious diet

plans must also be taken up as a government initiative. The importance of a balanced diet must be inculcated in the minds of people, ideally during childhood.

Conclusion

It was hypothesised that the high level of malnutrition in New Zealand is due to inequitable distribution and excessive reliance on processed food products and that the de-privatization of the food sector will not improve the peculiar food security problem faced here.

At present, the socio-economic indicators point towards a positive trend. The HDI has been improving steadily and substantially. Given the flourishing state of the economy and the food security-oriented aid provided to other regions, food scarcity seems to be an improbable risk. Even as far as international agencies go, New Zealand has not required any support for food security, having, instead, extended support to these organisations. However, as the analysis has revealed, malnutrition and obesity are still a problem in the region, thereby hindering food security. The major reason for this is too much reliance by the people on canned food. This in turn is due to the poor distribution system. This problem can be effectively coped by opening outlets offering distribution of fresh food at a reasonable rate.

An analysis of the food legislations offers the proof that one of the main causes behind this can be attributed to faulty legislative policies on the part of the government. There is a pressing need for renewal of some of the obsolete policies still in existence. There are some laws which have been in force since the last thirty years without any significant amendment; however a majority of the legislations are otherwise theoretically sound but difficult to implement. A lot of hopes are being attached to the upcoming food review.

The proposal of the government to take over food production can be seen as a setback for those who practice agriculture as their main occupation. If this is done, a lot of people will be rendered jobless and the food prices will rise sharply in future.

From the peculiar nature of the problem, it seems that financial incentives for setting up more storage and distribution outlets, which will deal primarily in the distribution of fresh, unprocessed food, would be a wise move. Mass awareness via education regarding nutritious diet plans must also be taken up as a government initiative. Another suggestion for NZ could be to increase its horizon of relations with other countries in this regard. These simple and easy steps will go a long way in ensuring food security and better health in New Zealand.

Endnotes

1. "Population Density in New Zealand", *Trading Economics*, 2011, available at: http://www.tradingeconomics.com/new-zealand/population-density-people-per-sq-km-wb-data.html.
2. "World Development Report, 2010" available at: http://siteresources.worldbank.org/INTWDR2010/Resources/5287678-1226014527953/Statistical-Annex.pdf.
3. "About Human Development", Human Development Reports, available at: http://hdr.undp.org/en/humandev.
4. Professor Amartya Sen, Professor of Economics, Harvard University; Nobel Laureate in Economics, 1998.
5. Moyles Michael, "Domestic Food Review", p. 3.
6. "A Guide to Food Act", *New Zealand Food Safety Authority*, available at: http://foodsafety.govt.nz/elibrary/industry/Guide_Animal-Clarifies_Requirements.pdf.
7. United Nations, "Human Development Index", available at: http://hdr.undp.org/en/media/HDR_2011_EN_Table1.pdf.
8. "2012 Index of Economic Freedom", *Heritage,* available at: http://www.heritage.org/index.
9. Agricultural Compounds and Veterinary Medicines Act, 1977, Section 4.
10. Animal Products Act, 1999, Section 13.
11. The Wine Act, 2003, Section 2.
12. The Wine Act, 2003, Section 11.

13. "New Zealand and WTO", New Zealand's Ministry of Foreign Affairs and Trade, available at: http://www.mfat.govt.nz/Trade-and-Economic-Relations/NZ-and-the-WTO/Doha/0-about.php#whatisthewto.
14. "The United Nations", New Zealand's Ministry of Foreign Affairs and Trade, available at: http://www.mfat.govt.nz/Foreign-Relations/2-International-Organisations/United-Nations/NZ-engagement-with-the-UN.php.
15. "UN Food Aid Agency Helps Create Online Game to Fight Hunger", *Scoop World*, available at: http://www.scoop.co.nz/stories/WO1112/S00020/un-food-aid-agency-helps-create-online-game-to-fight-hunger.htm.

11

North Korea: Climate Change, Famines and Food Security

Rajat Arora and Prithviraj Chauhan

1. Introduction

Current Food Security Scenario: The UN Food and Agriculture Organization and World Food Programme released a new report on food security in North Korea based on a crop assessment undertaken in September and October of 2012. The report estimated a total 2012-13 crop of 5.8 million tons from collective farms, individual plots, and household gardens, with staple food production up by about ten percent from the previous year. [1] Acute malnutrition rates seem to have decreased, the report said, although chronic hunger continues to be a major problem and the population remains susceptible to production shocks.

The report stated that food production improved despite a dry spell and several instances of flooding over the agricultural season, with the impact of the dry spell partly staved off by increased irrigation efforts. However, the report noted that the dry spell impacted the harvest of soy beans and other early crops, leading to possible protein deficiencies in the country's diet.

The FAO and WFP recommended that the international community continue to address the preclusion of malnutrition in North Korea by providing nutritional support to helpless groups and promoting the production of protein sources. The report also recommended that North Korea improve its incentives for agricultural production and provide support for household food production.

However, there were bright spots on the prospect as annual staple food production has been rising over the past few years, effectively extenuating the amount of acute malnutrition in the population. Overall, the FAO was satisfied with the improvements their targeted aid has made in specific areas, yet considerable progress still remains in combating children's vulnerability to shock and pregnant and nursing mothers' levels of under-nourishment.

Challenges to Food Security in North Korea: There are four major factors that have contributed as challenges to the DPRK food security.

The first factor is economics. North Korea has seen its agriculture and industrial base worsen noticeably during the past five years, primarily because of high investment in the military, centrally controlled economic management, environmental mismanagement, economic isolation, and the end of the Cold War (and subsequent loss of a client relationship with the former Soviet Union which conventionally provided Pyongyang with substantial economic and military aid). [2] Moreover, the Asian economic crisis has also had an impact by hindering progress on the creation of joint ventures and free trade zones. [3]

The second major factor relates to North Korea's domestic political choices. The authoritarian nature of North Korea's political system has perhaps exacerbated the food crisis. Democratic (or semi-democratic) governments tend to be more responsive to famines or food shortages. [4] In many ways, the food insecurity in North Korea reflects the failure of a political system to be accountable to the people that it governs. North Korea's pattern of persistent food shortages reflects the experiences of other non-democratic countries such as China during the Great Leap Forward.

The third factor influencing North Korea's food security situation is the environment. A series of back-to-back natural disasters (floods, droughts, tidal waves, and a typhoon) have overwhelmed North Korea's agricultural infrastructure. North Korea now blames its massive crop failures on abnormal weather—and not on environmental mismanagement or other economic policy failures. This has also given the North Koreans an excuse to continue to request foreign assistance.

The fifth factor relates to the tension that exists within the international community on how to respond to North Korea. On the one hand, there is a humanitarian imperative or moral duty to save lives. On the other hand, some foreign governments appear to be pursuing a policy of seeking to starve North Korea into submission. [5] In other words, some political decisions to withhold food assistance to North Korea may be rooted in a perception that famine may offer a regime an occasion to consolidate its power.

Socio-economic Profile

Government Overview: North Korea has a centralized government under the rigid control of the communist Korean Workers' Party (KWP), to which all government officials belong. A few minor political parties are allowed to exist in name only. Kim Il-sung ruled North Korea from 1948 until his death in July 1994 as Secretary General of the KWP and President of North Korea. The latter post was abolished following Kim Il-Sung's death and the title of the Eternal President of the Republic was established and given to Kim Il-Sung. Little is known about the real lines of power and authority in the North Korean Government despite the formal structure set forth in its constitution.

Following the death of Kim Jong-Il in December 2011, his son Kim Jong-un became the supreme leader of North Korea. In December 2011, the Politburo of the KWP officially appointed Kim Jong-un as the Supreme Commander of the Korean People's Army.

Three key entities control the government of the D.P.R.K. The cabinet, formerly known as the State Administration Council (SAC), administers the ministries and has a significant role in implementing policy. The cabinet is headed by the premier and is the dominant administrative and executive agency. [6] The NDC is responsible for external and internal security, and under the leadership of Kim Jong-Il, the NDC assumed a significant role in influencing policy. The Politburo of the Central People's Committee is the top policymaking body of the KWP, which also plays a role as the foremost social institution in North Korea.

Economy Overview: North Korea has long had a socialized, centrally planned, and mainly industrialized command economy isolated from the rest of the world. The means of production, which are largely outdated, are owned by the state through state-run enterprises or collectivized farms. Prices, wages, trade, budget, and banking are under strict government control. Traditionally, poor domestic economic performance was offset with infusions of Soviet aid. But after the collapse of the Soviet Union in 1991, the aid stopped and the economy was adversely affected. This situation was then further complicated by severe food shortages that began in 1995-96 and continued in 2007. [7] Massive international food aid deliveries have allowed North Korea to escape mass starvation since the mid-1990s, but the population remains the victim of long-lasting malnutrition and dwindling living conditions. [8] This situation was brought about by a shortage of arable land, collective farming, weather-related problems, and unceasing shortages of fertilizer and fuel. In addition, large-scale military expenditures consume resources needed for investment and civilian consumption. [9]

Agriculture: Agriculture has long been the traditional source of employment and income but, under state control, secondary to industry in emphasis. The agricultural sector was collectivized by 1958. An estimated 30 percent of the land was in agricultural use in 2002, and agriculture produces approximately 30 percent of the gross domestic product. [10] Most agricultural land is on plains in the south and west and was subject to flooding in 1995 and 1996 and to drought in 1997 and 2000. The principal crops, according to the size of the yield in 2002, are rice, potatoes, corn, cabbages, apples, soybeans, pulses, and sweet potatoes.

In the early 1990s, agricultural production in North Korea began a precipitous decline that finally resulted in a famine from which perhaps 5 percent of the population died. Since the worst years of 1996 and 1997, food production has recovered somewhat, and international aid has helped ward off the worst consequences. Yet farm production in the DPRK still remains far below its potential, despite substantial and continuing efforts by farmers, the government, and international aid organizations.

North Korea is planning to allow farmers to keep more of their produce in an attempt to advance agricultural output. The plan hopes to boost supplies, help cap rising food prices and ease malnutrition. The move to liberalise agriculture under new leader Kim Jong-un, who took office in December 2011 after the death of his father, would reverse a crackdown on private production that started in 2005. The country needs about five million tonnes of grain and potatoes to feed its people and since the early 1990s its annual harvest has been 3.5-4.7 million tonnes. [11]

Legislative Policies

The cropping season started favourably in 2012. The winter was less severe and less drawn out than in the previous two years, and rainfall in April was promising. However, this was followed by a prolonged dry spell during May and June, which had a chiefly serious effect on winter and spring cereals and on early vegetables, the yields of which were significantly depressed. July saw some serious flooding, mainly in the agriculturally important provinces of North and South Pyongyang, and at the end of August the country was hit by Cyclone number 15 (Bolavan) which caused some crop damage, especially in North and South Hwanghae and South Hamgyong. [12]

On the other hand, there was much more sun shine the following year and temperatures were favourable to good crop growth. The amounts of most inputs received by cooperative farms this year—seed, fertilizer, diesel, pesticides—were similar to those of last year but the timeliness of delivery was much improved. These factors and the huge effort put into minimizing the adverse effects of the dry spell at the beginning of the season have been the chief contributors to this year's better harvest. [13] The expectations for the winter and early crops which will be harvested in the first half of 2013 were lowered somewhat from the usual target due to the shortage of winter and spring cereal seed resulting from the poor harvest this year.

For 2012-13, an overall production of 5.8 million tonnes (in cereal equivalent) was estimated, an increase of about 10 percent over the last year. This figure included main-season crops and winter and early crops produced on cooperative farms, and production from sloping land, home gardens and kitchen gardens; it excluded production from state farms. Considering the planned Government imports of 300,000 tonnes, it was forecasted to cover a food deficit of 207,000 tonnes. This was much lower than the usual food gap and was mainly explained by better harvest.

Policy Framework in the Light of Various Famines: The PDS has been a key political-cum-economic institution in North Korea. Prior to the great famine of the mid-1990s, the government set production quotas of the cooperatives, distributed farmers' rations at the time of the harvest, and distributed food to urban residents through the PDS at nominal prices; markets played virtually no role in the allocation of food. During the famine, households relied on distribution through work units, the market, barter, private farming activities, and even foraging. The army and some unknown share of the upper civil service and workers at advantaged state-owned enterprises supposedly enjoyed the benefits of distribution through separate channels, although these channels did not deliver full rations during the famine either.

The incursion of foreign aid in the late 1990s incompletely

revived the PDS as donors had no autonomous channels for distributing food. But marketization also continued apace, driven by partial reforms such as allowing some private plots and farmers markets, as well as de facto marketization through diversion of food aid and cooperative output and commercial trade across the Chinese border. The calculations suggest that roughly 50 percent of total consumption in North Korea was sourced through the market in the early 2000s, and WFP reports have suggested that poor households were spending up to 80 percent of total income on food.

Historically, the North Korean government's supply-side response to urban food shortages has been to seize food in rural areas. In late 2005, reports emerged of the government extracting food by force in contravention of the rules determining the disposition of cooperative farm output, though it is unclear just how widely this occurred. In the wake of the 2007 floods, it appears that such moves were intensified in improved efforts to impose direct levies for additional supplies. First, the government increased production quotas for the next crop cycle. Second, the government began to crack down on misappropriation and fraudulence on the part of cooperative managers and the growth of trade and barter of rice among the administrators charged with managing food distribution. Although spiralling prices no doubt created incentives for corruption, some of these activities may simply have reflected an effort on the part of cooperative managers to protect their members. Third, the government began to express concern that cooperative farmers would divert effort from the current cooperative planting into the tending of private plots; as a result, new precincts were placed on some of these activities as well.

In a noteworthy development in April 2008, the central government dispatched a team of 200 investigators to Sinuiju in the name of an Anti-Socialist Conscience Investigation to inspect the books of foreign trade organizations, necessarily disturbing market activity as a result. [14]

In July 2013, WFP started a new operation—Nutrition Support to Children and Women in the Democratic People's Republic of Korea (DPRK). As regarding the previous operation, it did not seek to reduce the food gap in the country, but rather to address the nutrition gap that existed among young children and pregnant and breastfeeding women.

The new operation had a particular focus on the prevention and cure of moderate acute malnutrition among children (6 months-4 years old) and their mothers.

Collective Farms' Distribution System: At the onset, the government purchases the state's quota at a very low price from the collective farms at the harvest. The total cash income for the collective farm comes from this government purchase. The remaining production after government purchase is the farmers' share. Production costs and other management costs are deducted from the total cash income because all the inputs except labour are supplied by either government or the collective farm. These inputs include electricity, oil, chemical fertilizer, insecticides, etc. Several collective funds are also deducted from total cash income. What remains, after deducting production costs, management costs, and collective funds, is distributed among the farmers.

A farmer can get his or her income through basic distribution and collective incentive distribution. Basic distribution, which is mainly in grains, is intended to reimburse the workers for their labour, and is distributed according to an individual's accrual of working-points. For example, when a farmer transplants rice seedlings on 0.17 acre, he gets 1.5 working-points and when a farmer carries 500 rice sheaves, he gets 1.25 working-points. Farmers' working-points are revaluated according to the production team output. Since under the basic distribution system, farmers are interested in increasing their own working-points, the North Korean government adopted the collective inducement system, which is designed to increase labour productivity and to endorse collaboration. If the output of a working brigade exceeds the planned production output, the surplus would be distributed to the brigade members as cash, drawn from the final total cash income of the farm. This incentive distribution had little effect on productivity, however, because, to get the collective incentive distribution, farmers had to meet several other conditions and the government purchasing price is very low.

Climate Change, Famines and Food Security: There have been a number of different reasons proffered as the cause of the famine and the current food shortage in North Korea. [15] By the early 1980s, however, the economy began suffering from the lack of market incentives (as did other socialist economies) and the Soviet Union's collapse in 1991 exacerbated what became North Korea's "severe economic decline". Soviet exports drastically fell from US$ 1.97 billion to US$ 0.58 billion in just one year from 1990 to 1991; and by 1993, export levels had declined to a mere 10 percent of its previous contributions. [16] The shock was obvious: North Korea suffered severe supply shortages for their agricultural needs, including its petroleum supply, which in turn failed to satisfy North Korean demand for fuel and feedstock for petrochemical plants.

In the early 1990s, a cold front hit the Korean peninsula, damaging crops and creating pest problems. In 1995, this situation was further exacerbated by a series of floods that shattered over 400,000 hectares of arable land. Grain production as a result was reduced by 1.9 million tons, or about 30 percent of the total amount of grain necessary to feed the people. Then in 1996, another set of floods hit the "breadbasket" section of North Korea, that is, the area responsible for producing 60 percent of the country's food grain; loss of grain production was estimated at about 300,000 tons. By 1996, the agronomic problems obstructing production efforts were deemed chronic.

A recent study by the U.S. Committee for Human Rights in North Korea reiterated that the famine crisis of the 1990s was avoidable, if only North Korea had made more humanitarian policy choices. For instance, rather than using foreign aid to supplement its domestic production and importation of food supplies, the government chose to substitute such aid. This study extrapolated North Korea's food supplies using the country's 1993 commercial food import levels and concluded that, at both the high-end and low-end estimations, North Korea would have exceeded the average human consumption need if it had continued its usual rates of production and received imports. Yet when North Korea began receiving aid, the saved expenses were allocated elsewhere, namely to the North Korean military. This contributes to one among the several reasons why the government is the primary culprit.

Land Reforms and Development: To the foreign eye, North Korea's persistence on food self-sufficiency at all costs seems difficult to understand (and, perhaps, doomed to fail given that 80 percent of North Korea's 12 million hectares of land is mountainous, with only 14 percent arable land). In order to understand why food self-sufficiency is such a central objective, it helps to know something of both the history of North Korea's agricultural development and the concepts of Juche and Chajusong, which drove socialist development in North Korea.

Juche entails a blend of self-reliance, self-sufficiency, and self-confidence, while Chajusong stresses the responsibility of the individual over his or her life. Together, they are also understood as national or ethnic independence, including an independent economy—the opposite of serving and relying upon foreign powers.

In the spring of 1946, North Korea carried out "the most rapid and thoroughgoing land redistribution efforts in Korean history". According to historian Charles Armstrong, land reform in North Korea was swift and relatively non-violent because of its restrained policy of redistributing land to the farmer versus an immediate state collectivization, and because South Korea gave former landlords and other dissidents refuge. Between March and June 1946, land reform redistributed nearly 50 percent of total farmland in the north.

[17] From 1945 to 1953, North Korean agriculture comprised mainly of farm households that owned on average 1.6 chongbo of land and farmed for private consumption or for market.

During this period, the government institutions overseeing food and agriculture, the Ministry of Food Administration (MFA) and the Ministry of Agriculture (MOA), were established. The MFA was charged with ensuring that adequate food was grown to supply enough food to feed all North Koreans and support the country's rapid industrial development. Its means included an agricultural tax of 25 percent of the harvest, a system whereby industrial goods were traded for agricultural products, and a state food rationing system to feed industrial workers. The remaining harvest after taxes was traded in farmer's markets. The MOA was charged with rising agricultural resources and productivity, and it achieved this by monopolizing agricultural resources such as fertilizer, water, farm equipment, and so on. It imposed production quotas on villages and farm households and encouraged the formation of production teams and labour pools, and the sharing of animals and farm tools. These policies helped lay the foundation for North Korea's evolving socialist system.

In 1949, the North Korean government announced the nation would move towards collectivized farming, but the policy was not implemented until after the war. From 1953 to 1958, North Korean agriculture was collectivized. In 1953, private farms produced 92 percent of agricultural goods. By 1959, all farms had been collectivized into cooperatives and state farms. Collectives helped North Koreans organize and maximize the use of their limited resources after the massively destructive U.S. war, and they later became a pillar of North Korea's ideological commitment to socialism.

North Korea's post-war agricultural policy, known as chongsanri, was established in response to the rural food crisis in 1954 and 1955. Chongsanri promoted communal cooperation and political conditioning of the masses. Specifically, state grain marketing institutions were created, and private grain production and trade were forbidden. Farmer's markets still existed, but they were officially discouraged and only non-grain items were sold in them. State food rationing was expanded to the entire population and a new agricultural management system was established which decentralized responsibility to provincial administrators.

Despite the country's disadvantages in food production—mountainous land, high elevation, and a cool climate—North Korea doubled its agricultural output between 1961 and 1988. This was a massive effort that required tremendous coordination.

Future of Food Security: The famine that struck North Korea in 1994 has had and will continue to have terrific consequences—many of them beyond our knowledge. We know for certain that hundreds of thousands died and fled and that persistent food shortages will have lasting impacts on the development of North Korea's children and the health of its entire people. We also know that the famine brought foreign aid agencies and non-governmental organizations to North Korea, affecting its food and economic systems in innumerable ways. What we do not know is the direction North Korea will take next in its agricultural and economic development.

North Korean food production is today a stressed system undergoing rapid change. The 2002 economic reforms that raised food prices, legalized farmer's markets, and gave greater autonomy to farms to grow crops of their choice are a big part of this change. According to Randall Ireson, devolving decision-making to where the "palm meets the dirt" and increasing opportunities for farms to obtain inputs will help North Korea achieve greater food security. For now, the urban working poor are less food secure than before.

The overwhelming message governments and aid agencies are directing at North Korea is to open their markets and play monopoly if they want peace and prosperity. Unless North Korea develops its agricultural infrastructure and can trade with other nations, its food security will be subject to the vagaries of politics-driven food aid and the vicissitudes of weather.

The high value North Korea places on feeding its people has shaped the nature of its food crisis. North Korea's crisis differs from those of other countries that suffer from persistent food shortages, such as India, which has food reserves and exports food to other countries while its own people are starving. According to Meredith Woo-Cumings, although North Korean malnutrition rates were high at the height of famine, they weren't any higher than they are in India and Bangladesh in "ordinary" times.

As it emerges from the famine years with an agricultural system that has broken down, North Korea is at a crucial juncture. It has the opportunity to be an example to the world, as one of the few nations with an agricultural policy aimed at ensuring food for everyone, not just maximizing profit. As they map the way forward for their agricultural and trade policy, North Korean leaders should heed the wisdom of farmers' movements around the world: food sovereignty is an option to corporate-driven economic globalization and runaway free trade policies that demolish rural communities around the world".

The leading model that encourages export-focused agriculture, free trade, and importing cheap food also supports a chemical-intensive, large-scale monoculture, with genetically modified (GM) crops. The industrial agriculture model worked for years to feed all of North Korea's people, but it has ended in diminished yields and ravaged soils. It does not make sense for North Korea to relapse to this failed model.

Adherents of the food sovereignty model believe these industrial farming practices that destroy the land for future generations should be replaced with genuine agrarian reform and a mixture of traditional knowledge and sustainable, agro ecologically based farming practices. North Korea, like the rest of the world, needs sustainable agriculture, not just open markets, which run counter to their juche ideals. The international community should help North Koreans achieve food sovereignty, not isolate, vilify, or strong-arm them.

International Agencies

The United Nations Office for the Coordination of Humanitarian Affairs (UNOCHA) coordinates the response of the United Nations system to major humanitarian emergencies, both natural and man-made, and promotes action to improve disaster prevention and attentiveness. UNOCHA coordinates field missions sent by United Nations operational agencies to assess needs in crises areas and UNOCHA also issues consolidated inter-agency appeals for funding humanitarian assistance. After launching appeals, it organizes donor meetings and follow-up arrangements and monitors the status of contributions in response to the appeals. It also issues situation reports to keep donors and others apprised of developments. Since September 12, 1995, UNOCHA (formerly UNDHA) has issued a UN Consolidated Inter-Agency Appeal for North Korea seven times at the request of the government of North Korea. The appeal has been formulated on the basis of need assessments, data, and substantive contributions of various UN agencies in the provision of emergency and development relief to North Korea.

Among UN agencies, World Food Program (WFP) has played the most important role in emergency relief to North Korea. WFP began operations in North Korea in 1995 in response to the demand for emergency assistance. Instead of simply channelling international food aid through the Flood Damage Rehabilitation Committee (FDRC), WFP has tried to move in more rehabilitative directions by expanding Food for Work (FFW) in key agricultural and rehabilitation activities.

The Food and Agriculture Organization (FAO) is a UN agency that aims to get better living conditions of farmers and agricultural productivity. It works to help farmers re-establish production following floods, outbreaks of livestock diseases, and similar emergencies. With WFP, FAO has done crop and food supply assessment missions twice a year.

The United Nations Development Programme (UNDP) acts to help the UN become a powerful force for sustainable human development. In order to achieve sustainable human development, it carries out improvement programs in poverty eradication, the creation of employment and sustainable livelihoods, the empowerment of women, and the protection and rejuvenation of the environment. To meet the food security challenges, UNDP developed the Agricultural Recovery and Environmental Protection Program (AREP) to phase out the cost of international food aid programs through the restoration of sustainable food production. In 1998, round table meetings on AREP approved the overall objectives and strategic options over 1998-2002 period. Despite the growing international concern for long-term recovery and development in North Korea, UNDP has not attracted proper donors' support for AREP.

The World Health Organization (WHO) division of emergency and humanitarian action (EHA) manage the international response to emergencies in the area of health. WHO provides expert advice to member states on epidemiological surveillance, control of communicable diseases, public health information, and health emergency training. EHA is responsible for emergency relief that includes the stipulation of emergency drugs and supplies, the fielding of technical emergency assessment missions, and for technical support. In emergency preparedness, it also aims to fortify the national capacity of member states to reduce the adverse health consequences of disasters. [18] With the Ministry of Public Health, UNICEF, IFRC and NGOs, WHO has carried out important health programs such as immunizations to control epidemics and TB, and for improving community-based health services.

The European Commission Humanitarian Office (ECHO) was set up in 1992 to oversee and coordinate the European Union's humanitarian operations in non-member countries. It responds to all types of crisis through emergency aid, food aid, and aid to refugees and displaced persons. Instead of carrying out its own projects, ECHO operates through partners, NGOs, and the specialized agencies of the United Nations by supporting operation funds. The EC's directorate general for development has focused its activities on support to agricultural rehabilitation through a number of projects for soil conservation, rehabilitation of irrigation systems and sustainable upland hillside conservation and reforestation.

The Swiss Agency for Development and Cooperation (SDC) has distributed relief goods such as rice, frozen meat and baby foods, both bilaterally and through NGOs.

Conclusion

Although the North Korean government will and should make its own decisions about how to achieve food self-sufficiency, it appears that North Korea can choose among the probable paths: moving to a more sustainable model of agriculture and expanding trade via removal of U.S. sanctions.

Most agricultural experts agree that a move to sustainable agriculture is the surest road to greater food security in North Korea. Theodor Friedrich, senior agriculturalist at the FAO, opined, "considering the land area, food self-sufficiency will be a challenge and only possible using preservation of agriculture techniques, otherwise North Korea will lose too much land by erosion and soil deprivation". [19]

By building an agricultural system that produces more with fewer inputs, North Koreans will get much closer to achieving sustainable agriculture and the food self-sufficiency they so crave for.

Endnotes

1. "New Report on Food Security in North Korea", last modified July 15, 2013, available at: http://www.ncnk.org/resources/dprk-news/2012/new-report-on-food-security-north-korea.
2. Bruce Cumings, "North Korea: Another Country", New York, *The New Press*, 2004, p. 178.
3. United Nations World Food Program (WFP), "Rapid Food

Security Assessment: Democratic People's Republic of Korea", WFP Rome, June-July 2008.

4. "Hunger Politics", available at: http://www.northkoreanow.org/hunger-politics/#3, accessed on July 15, 2013.
5. "Humanitarian Aid in North Korea", Friends Committee on National Legislation, available at: http://www.kpolicy.org/documents/policy/050531christineahnnk foodsecurity.pdf, accessed on August 12, 2003.
6. "Countries and their Cultures", available at: http://www.everyculture.com/Ja-Ma/NorthKorea.html#b, accessed on July 15, 2013.
7. "North Korea: Economy", available at: http://globaledge.msu.edu/Countries/NorthKorea/economy, accessed on July 15, 2013.
8. Lee Suk, "Food Shortages and Economic Institutions in the Democratic People's Republic of Korea", University of Warwick, Department of Economics, accessed in January 2003, p. 211.
9. Dick K. Nanto and Emma Chanlett-Avery, "North Korea Politics: Nuclear Threat", Economist Intelligence Unit Views Wire, available at: http://fpc.state.gov/documents/organization/125938.pdf, accessed on May 27, 2009.
10. Amnesty International, North Korea: Amnesty International submission to the United Nations Universal Periodic Review, Human Rights Council, United Nations, December 2009.
11. Kim, Woon-Keun. "Food Situation and Agricultural Reform in North Korea", *Journal of Rural Development*, Korea Rural Economic Institute, 1998, p. 10.
12. FAO/WFP Crop and Food Security Assessment Mission to the Democratic People's Republic of Korea, available at: http://www.ncnk.org/resources/publications/FAO_WFP_CFSAM_2012.pdf, accessed on July 14, 2013.
13. Lee Sang Yong, "Rodong Moves to Shift Food Security Blame", *DailyNK,* available at: http://www.dailynk.com/english/read.php?cataId=nk01700&num=10547, accessed on July 15, 2013.
14. A. Lankov, "North Korea Reaps a Rich Harvest", *Asia Times Online*, January 16, 2009, accessed on April 29, 2009.

15. Daniel Goodkind and Loraine West, "The North Korean Famine and Its Demographic Impact", *Population and Development Review*, 2001, pp. 219-221.
16. Sue Lautze, "The Famine in North Korea: Humanitarian Responses in Communist Nations", Feinstein Int'l Famine Ctr., Feinstein Int'l Famine Ctr., Working Paper, June 1997.
17. Charles Armstrong, "The North Korean Revolution", 1945-1950, Cornell University Press, 2003, p. 77.
18. "International Organizations' Assistance to North Korea and Inter-Korean Cooperation", Paper submitted for International Seminar Organized by the KINU and the Korean National Commission for UNESCO, 2001, available at: http://www.kinu.or.kr/upload/neoboard/DATA02/2001-061.pdf, accessed on July 15, 2013.
19. "Funding Shortfalls of Hunger Crises in 2004", accessed July 15, 2013, available at: http://www.globalpolicy.org/socecon/hunger/tables/2004/largest crises.

12

Norway: Nutrition and Food Supply Policy

Advait Narayan and Shivangi Singh

Socio-economic Profile

Living Standard of the People: Norway has been ranked the best country to live in by the United Nations Development Program (UNDP) [1] several times during the past decade. In addition, Global Gender Gap Report of the World Economic Forum has ranked Norway as one of the world's leading countries in closing the gender gap between men and women. The general health of the population is very good, and the infant mortality rate is low. [2]

Literacy is virtually 100 percent and most of the adult population has completed upper-secondary schooling. In Norway, there is no extreme poverty and the relative poverty level is low compared to other OECD [3] countries.

The GDP per capita is high, and wealth is relatively equally distributed among the population. Gender equality prevails at all levels of society. In keeping with its welfare policies, Norway has implemented a public health service financed by tax revenues which is universal in nature and a national insurance scheme, which is applicable to all citizens and resident and provides a host of social benefits. As a result of modernization and urbanization, traditional settlement patterns have been replaced by trending greater mobility, with people moving and changing jobs more frequently.

Employment in Agricultural Sector: Norway is one of the most sparsely populated countries in Europe, with a large area covered by mountains and high terrains. Only 3 percent of the land area is arable. Agriculture employs approximately 53,000 full-time equivalents, 2.1 percent of the country's total employment, and 0.3 percent of gross domestic product (GDP). Over the past decades, the agricultural sector has witnessed significant structural changes towards fewer, but larger and more efficient holdings. The arable area has however, remained fairly stable during this consolidation process.

The Ministry of Agriculture altered its name in 2004 and became the Ministry of Agriculture and Food. This change signalled a wider scope of the agricultural policy, increasing attention to the complete value chain, from biological production to food and other products that are based on agricultural resources, including knowledge production. The past decade has also witnessed mergers between different agricultural research institutes.

The main objectives of the agricultural policy include: national food security; development shall be sustainable; socio-politically by maintaining farming throughout the whole Norway and a basis of living; economically by providing a basis for increased value creation; and environmentally friendly by managing resources, taking climate change into account. During the past years, food security, climate change and relations to adjacent industries have been given greater emphasis in policy development.

The labour market for workers in the Norwegian agricultural sector varies according to the time of the year. Agricultural jobs include general farm work in milk and animal production (sheep, cattle and swine) and plant crops like wheat, barley and hay. During summers, agricultural work mainly includes planting, weeding, trimming and harvesting of fruits and berries, vegetables, flowers and plants, trees and plants. As compared to other countries, Norway has a relatively short growing season. Even though farmland covers just three percent of the Norwegian land area, there are farms in virtually every part of this rugged country. Due to great geographical and climatic variations in Norway, choice of crops and how they are grown can vary a great deal.

Farmer's Market was launched as a pilot project for nine different locations in the autumn of 2003. Currently, there are 18 markets all over Norway. Farmer's Markets have proven to give very positive results for the producers involved and provide an opportunity for Norwegian consumers to obtain food products which are not found in grocery stores. Sales at Farmer's Market have increased from 5.5 million in 2006 to 22.3 million norwegian kroners (NOK) in 2009. For many manufacturers, organic farmers markets have turned into an important sales channel.

Export and Import Policy: Norway is a highly developed, industrial country with an open, export-oriented economy. Known to be one of the richest countries in the world, it also has a very high standard of living, life expectancy and overall health and housing standards. Abundance of natural resources and Norway's inclusion in the industrialization of Western Europe because of its close proximity to the major markets are the reasons why the level of material wealth is high in Norway. [4]

Norway has successfully applied the restructuring measures required to achieve economic growth. Because of extensive trade and contacts with other countries, Norway has been able to establish a foundation on which they can develop an advanced economy. Major investments in production equipment, improved and extended education as well as technical and organizational expertise in industry and public administration have also helped to promote growth. The 20th century represented a period of continuous vigorous economic growth in Norway. Since the 1970s, the offshore oil industry has played a dominant role in the Norwegian economy. Only 21 percent of Norway is productive land (3 percent cultivated land and 18 percent productive forest). Norway is not a member of the European Union (EU), but participates in the EU common market as a signatory to the European Economic Area (EEA) Agreement between the countries of the EU and the European Free Trade Association (EFTA).

Norway accounts for less than 0.1 percent of the world's population, and is thus a small country. Norway's economic importance, however, is greater than its population would otherwise indicate. According to WTO statistics, Norway was the world's 28th largest merchandise exporter, and the 37th largest importer, in 2004. [5] Foreign trade amounts to approximately 37 per cent of Norway's GDP. [6] Norway enjoys substantial market shares in certain sectors. It is currently among the world's top five exporters in the seafood, crude oil and shipping services sectors, and has significant market shares in the light metals and ship equipment sectors, as well as in a number of maritime services such as classification, consulting and marine insurance.

The makeup of Norway's foreign trade sets it apart from other industrialized nations. According to OECD statistics, industrial products make up 85 percent of the OECD countries' total goods exports, whereas the figure for Norway is around 28 percent. Norway's reputation as raw materials supplier must, however, be understood in light of the fact that major segments of its raw materials industry are highly knowledge- and technology-intensive, even though the end products are not considered to be processed industrial goods.

A good example is the petroleum industry, in which technology and know-how have in them become an increasingly important business with a share of goods and services exports that has reached a significant level. Although exports of traditional goods rose throughout the 1990s in absolute terms, their share of overall export income fell from 36 per cent in 1991 to 31 percent in 2001. This share was, of course, significantly affected by fluctuations in the price of oil. Norwegian service exports have increased substantially in recent years, to around NOK 176 billion in 2004. [7] The shipping sector accounted for around half of the service export revenues.

Of other types of services, commercial and financial services have shown the greatest increase in the past decade, although petroleum-related services have also grown strongly. The increase in oil and gas revenues resulted in a reduction in the share of export revenues attributable to services, from around 28 percent in 1991 to around 24 percent in 2004. Services account for a growing share of world trade. The opposite trend in Norway is due to the fact that its petroleum exports are growing even more strongly than its services exports. Geographically, Norwegian exports focus on the developed markets of Europe, North America and Asia.

Percentage Expenditure on Food: While the household consumption has tripled since 1958, Norwegian households are spending increasingly less of their budget on food. According to Statistics Norway, an average household spent a modest 11 percent of their budget on food in 2009 as compared to 40 percent in 1958. Not only Norwegians have started eating out more often, they also have started buying other types of food. For instance, the consumption of fish and potatoes has fallen considerably since 1958 and consumption of meat has increased. Also, there has been a ten-fold increase in the consumption of mineral water and soft drinks and sale of wine.

Legislative Framework

Nutrition and Food Supply Policy: In 1975, the Norwegian Parliament created a comprehensive food supply and nutrition policy [8] intended to bring agricultural production in tandem with national goals for healthy lifestyles and world food needs. Specifically, it sought to:

1. Bring about a change in diet by encouraging consumption of healthy foods and reducing that of fats (especially saturated fats) by replacing them with polyunsaturated fats, whole grains and vegetables;
2. Promote domestic food production and reduce food imports to increase national self-sufficiency from 39 percent to 52 percent by 1990;
3. Promote agricultural development in the poorer outlying regions while conserving the environment; and

4. Contribute to world food security by promoting food production and consumption in poor countries.

Since the commencement of Norway's food security programs, its efforts have attracted the attention of various international food security organisations. [9] Many detailed reports have been made of the food situation in Norway, and one of these concluded that economic conditions, including the uncertainty of imports of essential components of a balanced diet in the mid-1970s, gave motive for drafting policies to ensure a greater degree of food security. But in actual fact, the political action was only taken at the time when the perceived threat of difficulty faced by the economy was removed by external factors such as the new found wealth of oil in the North Sea; and it was found that the public had once again to be made aware of the food problems and policies of the country, which had previously had little impact on them. Interest groups and policy-makers tried to bring to the forefront the economic and political realities of the nation. It was a successful plan as all the organisations worked in tandem and with the aid of well-established and fruitful organizational links between mutually dependent government and interest groups. [10]

Therefore, even though Norwegian food security and nutrition policies such as maintaining a balanced diet (also an integral part of food security), were not originally considered significant, they became so at a later stage, and this appeared to gain momentum in the early 1980s as a revival of nutrition and health priorities was attempted.

White Paper Policies

First White Paper: After World War II, an outbreak of various cardio-vascular diseases broke out in the Scandinavian region, and in the 1960s, the link between cardiovascular diseases and consumption of fats was recognised. The extensive subsidies given to producers of milk products were challenged, and from a status as essential foods, full-fat milk and butter became nutritional problems. In an attempt to strike a balance between nutrition recommendations and agricultural interests, the revised nutrition recommendations were presented in the first white paper of 1976, from the Ministry of Agriculture, 'Report on Norwegian Nutrition and Food Policy', with one of its objectives being to reduce consumption of fat but only to a moderate extent. It was considered a political success but the policy was quite ambivalent and too generalised as it tried to match the needs of improved health through food behaviour changes with those of the agricultural sector dominated by dairy industries. This first white paper was "closely linked with policies of agricultural self-sufficiency and regional development". The goals of the policy were divided into 4 broad sections as follows: [11]

- Health: Encourage healthy dietary habits, with the specific objective of decreasing fat consumption from 42 percent to 35 percent of total calorie intake, and a decrease in the ratio of saturated to polyunsaturated fats in the diet from 3.5:1 to 2:1 by reducing consumption of whole milk and margarine. The aim was an increase the consumption of complex carbohydrates, fish and skimmed milk.
- Global Aid: To help stabilise world food supply in accordance with the recommendations of the World Food Conference (Rome, 1974) and decrease reliance on imported food which could be diverted to developing countries.
- Food Production: Promote consumption of domestically produced food and strengthen national food self-sufficiency.
- Rural Economy: Strengthen the rural economy and halt decline in the number of small farms by making farming more profitable.

Second White Paper: In the early 1980s, a new white paper was presented by the Norwegian Ministry of Health and Social Affairs, in which the link between nutrition and health was emphasised and placed nutritional problems on the political agenda. The policy stressed "that the alteration in diet should take place by voluntary changes in food habits" and that it was "a public and community responsibility to ensure that circumstances are optimized to enable people to choose a nutritionally favourable diet". [12] A wide range of measures were used to improve the diet including legal, economic, organisational and educational. There was a definite shift "towards implementation strategies emphasizing health education and individual responsibility for change". [13] Nutrition, at this time, was regarded as an issue of knowledge and behaviour rather than a problem of food supply. This second white paper, acting in tandem with the nationalised Everyday Food nutrition (and food security) campaign started in 1982 was seen to be very successful in its own right, but did not have quite as far of an outreach and impact as envisioned.

Third White Paper: In the early 1990s, the Norwegian Ministry of Health and Social Affairs, in order to emphasise the link between nutrition and health, published the third white paper, 'Challenges in Health Promotion and Prevention Strategies'. The policy became much more concerned with the prevention of diseases other than cardiovascular disease (such as cancer), which was the only one for which provisions had been enacted so far, and promoted the consumption of fruits and vegetables. However, with regard to the white paper policy it was expressed that "far from being incorporated into a general health promotion agenda, nutrition policy seems to have retained a considerable part of its characteristic approach. Even now, indirect influence on the food market by negotiating with and influencing other sectors and actors is exercised with explicit ambitions, expressed by the statement—Healthy food should be easy to procure and consume".

Everyday Food Nutrition Campaign: In 1982, the 'Everyday Food' Nutrition Campaign was launched. [14] Its main objective was to encourage people to have a balanced diet—an integral aspect of food security. The dietary goals of the campaign were presented as a series of small changes in the daily meal routine, for example, spreading butter thinly and using low fat varieties of traditional dairy products. Prohibitions were avoided and it was encouraged that a balanced diet be had during weekdays so that individuals would be free to eat anything they wished on weekends. Educational material for young children developed this idea of 'everyday food' and food to enjoy at weekends in books entitled "Best Friends and Saturday Friends".

The campaign was launched with a press conference, television and radio items and articles in the press. Posters were displayed in streets and on public transport. Fact sheets, school books, wall charts and games were produced. The centre piece was the widely advertised book 'Everyday Food'. The campaign placed a strong emphasis on involving people at local levels including worker's organisations, works canteens, institutional caterers, women's organisations, libraries and small food shops—all were encouraged to hold discussion groups, redesign menus, display posters and stock brochures. [15]

Spis Med Glede (Enjoy Eating Campaign): In 1990-94, the Norwegian National Association for Public Health together with the National Nutrition Council and other voluntary and professional organisations, implemented a nation-wide campaign called 'Spis med glede' (Enjoy Eating). The campaign specifically targeted the retail sector and people from both the young and old age groups, with emphasis on school going children. It focused on the enjoyment of food and highlighted positive messages focusing on the foods people should consume more of. Activities included 'action weeks' for the promotion of consumption of bread, cereal, fish, fruit and vegetables, meat, milk and poultry, including television advertisements, brochures, in-shop demonstrations and exhibitions. The goals of the campaign were to: [16]

- Stimulate local activities which could change diet and exercise habits;
- Find key groups to disseminate information on diet and health;

- Stimulate collaboration between authorities, voluntary organisations, industry and the media in activities related to improving food habits;
- Increase understanding of the cultural and social meanings of food; and
- Target the retail sector to establish collaboration among food suppliers, wholesalers, retail chains and organisations.

Other Important Measures: Other significant and more recent measures to ensure food security in Norway included the Nordic Plan of Action for Better Health and Quality of Life through Diet and Physical Activity, adopted in July 2006, and the Action Plan on Physical Activity (2005-2009), working together for physical activity. Norway has in recent years seen a new food-related problem in the increase of sugar consumption, especially among young people. Also now on the Norwegian agenda is school catering.

There are no public school meals in Norway and children bring lunch from home. They can subscribe to milk and in some schools to the delivery of fruit. Through the Action Plan on Physical Activity (2005-2009) schools are considered a key setting for health-promoting interventions and models for school meals and daily physical activity at school are being tested. There are ongoing discussions around including one hour of daily physical activity as a national requirement and providing free school meals.,[17]

Agencies Working for Food Security

Inter-Ministerial Council and the National Nutrition Council: The statutory bodies responsible for implementing the nutrition policy were the Inter Ministerial Council (IMC) and the National Nutrition Council (NNC). [18] The IMC's function was to prepare plans for implementation of nutrition policies, define time periods for completion of the plans, define specific tasks and oversee the activities of the government ministries for those plans. It was therefore meant to be a body for implementation of policies that was politically accountable. The NNC, meanwhile, was meant to be an advisory body of four to six people that would discuss nutrition and food security policies, with educational, monitoring, analysing and information collection functions, and powers to take initiatives within its remit and resources.

The NNC was situated in the Health Directorate's Food Control and Nutrition Section of the Government. The IMC also had an office in this section. In the absence of any powers besides the strategic use of information, and dependent on a larger system of government for limited resources, the IMC and NNC realised that their policy-keeping task of ensuring the implementation of the food supply and nutrition policy was quite challenging.

Thus, at the beginning of the 1980s the policy, as represented by the IMC and NNC, was in a weak strategic position compared with 1975 when it had been adopted. They were facing the challenges of an aging, better educated population exposed to wider viewpoints and expressing a potentially more critical opinion; and powerful organizations whose interests were more likely to collide than coincide with the objectives and guidelines of the nutrition policy. Proponents of the policy argued that the reasonable way to gain effective control of its implementation was to develop a second white paper for the Parliament that would assess progress and propose further steps. This was tabled in Parliament in July 1981.

Food and Agricultural Organization (FAO): In Norway's view, FAO should be a cornerstone of the global architecture for food security and agriculture. Thus, it is of great importance that the FAO's reformed Committee on World Food Security is strengthened and given a prominent role. Norway also considers it important that FAO strengthen its activities relating to climate change and climate adaptation and their impact on world food security. Norway plays a proactive role in this work. In Norway's view, more attention must be focused on fisheries and aquaculture in FAO's efforts to achieve world food security.

FAO is the main institution for forestry issues in the UN system. FAO has for years worked to build specialised competence, develop knowledge of global forest resources and promote the sustainable management of the world's forests. Norway wants these efforts to be further developed. FAO's expertise in the field of forest monitoring will provide an essential foundation for efforts to combat deforestation. Norway attaches importance to the key role played by FAO in creating a coherent understanding of sustainable management of land and forest resources, which is also essential to addressing climate-related challenges.

FAO, the UN Development Programme and the UN Environment Programme have jointly established a UN collaborative programme to combat deforestation, which is a key channel for Norwegian funding under Norway's Climate and Forest Initiative. FAO heads global efforts to safeguard genetic diversity in agriculture and food production. Norway is strongly committed to this work and participates actively in forums under the International Treaty on Plant Genetic Resources for Food and Agriculture.

Norway is also an active participant in the FAO Commission on Genetic Resources for Food and Agriculture, including its implementation of the multi-year work plan which covers forest and fish genetic resources as well as plant and livestock genetic resources. In Norway's view, FAO should emphasise the necessity of adequate nutrition as part of its food security work and in connection with activities relating to food production. FAO also has important functions in terms of promoting food security, among other things through the Codex Alimentarius Commission which develops global food standards. In the past three years, through its seat in the Council, Norway has advocated that FAO must be rationalised and modernised in line with the recommendations in the evaluation of FAO carried out in 2007. Norway has called for quicker follow-up and better management with greater focus on performance.

As a result, Norway decided in 2009 to reduce its voluntary contributions to FAO and not to enter into a new partnership agreement for 2010-2011. In 2010, Norway chose to earmark voluntary support for a small number of selected programme areas where, FAO can demonstrate results and where it has special qualifications and capabilities for contributing in accordance with the priorities of Norway. This applies particularly to FAO's projects on the impacts of climate change on agriculture, forestry and fisheries, and its efforts to ensure the right to food. In Norway's view, FAO must give priority to completing the reform and strengthening cooperation with the two other Rome-based agencies, the International Fund for Agricultural Development (IFAD) and the World Food Programme (WFP). As part of the UN reform process, Norway considers it very important that FAO participates in efforts to achieve a more coherent UN at the country level.

United Nations: Owing to the strong position of Norway in terms of food security, it has provided a lot of help to various organizations of the UN rather than actually receiving help. The World Food Programme (WPF), an organization whose mandate is to fight hunger and ensure hunger is supported by Norway in the form of flexible and short-term relief and food aid during and after crises and disasters. Norway provided a total contribution of USD 41.6 million to WPF in the year 2010. [19] The Food and Agriculture Organization also got an assistance of US$ 21.1 million by Norway.

International Treaties

Food Aid Convention: Norway, being a relatively prosperous and agriculturally self-sufficient nation, is in a position to provide food aid to third world countries rather than to receive it. Norway is, therefore, one of the donor countries under the Food Aid Convention of 1999. The Food Aid Convention is an instrument for the promotion of multilateral cooperation. It has been in operation since 1967 and is a separate legal instrument under the current International Grains Agreement, 1995, which also comprises the Grains Trade Convention. It is administered by the Food Aid Committee, using the services of the Secretariat of the International Grains Council.

Under the FAC, donors pledge to provide annually specified minimum amounts or values of food aid to developing countries in the form of grains and other eligible products. The objective of the Convention is to contribute to world food security and to improve the ability of the international community to respond to emergency food situations and other food needs of developing countries. [20] The donors of the Convention make sure that quality food aid is made available to the neediest of nations irrespective of fluctuating world economic conditions such as food prices and import or export tariffs.

As a framework of cooperation between food aid donors, the FAC aims to achieve greater efficiency with respect to food aid operations. It also emphasizes on monitoring and evaluating the impact and effectiveness of food aid operations, in support of food security in developing countries.

Food Aid Committee: The Food Aid Committee consists of all parties to the Food Aid Convention. Donor members oversee that the Convention is implemented and information on food aid needs and operations is exchanged. The Committee holds two regular meetings annually.

The Food Aid Committee's sessions may also be attended by observers from international organisations concerned with food aid including the UN Food and Agriculture Organisation (FAO), the World Food Programme (WFP), the World Trade Organisation (WTO), the Organisation for Economic Cooperation and Development (OECD) and the UN Conference on Trade and Development (UNCTAD).

The Committee monitors the performance of members' undertakings under the Convention, based on the records maintained by the IGC Secretariat. Information on policy developments affecting food aid is shared and the world food situation and prospects in developing countries are discussed.

Ways in which donors' aid efforts may best achieve their objectives are also considered, emphasizing on evaluating needs and the effectiveness and impact of food aid operations. As of December 2009, the signatories of the Convention included Argentina, Australia, Canada, the European Union, Japan, Norway, Switzerland, and the United States. According to a statistical fact sheet published by the Food Aid Committee in 2009, Norway supplied approximately 145,586 metric tons of food aid in 2004-05 and in 2009-10 it supplied approximately 62,774 metric tonnes.

In conclusion, it can be said that the hypothesis behind the project to show that Norway has successfully worked toward a sustainable food security policy that is being effectively implemented by statutory bodies of Norway and international agencies is proved to be true. From the statistics provided in the previous pages it can be clearly seen that Norway is among the most prosperous nations in the world, with high human development, economy and food security indicators, and therefore serves as a contributor and supplier of provisions for world food security under multiple treaties including the Food Aid Convention of 1999. Subsequent information on the analysis of legislative framework in the country, including the various food security policies and the Parliament's 'White Paper regulations' to guide and give direction to food policies, shows that Norway as a country has made an honest effort to ensure food security.

Endnotes

1. "United Nations", Global Development Network, available at: http://cloud1.gdnet.org/cms.php?id=gdn_development_research, accessed on June 12, 2013.
2. "Norwegian Krone", FX Rate, available at: http://fx-rate.net/NOK, accessed on June 12, 2013.
3. Organization of Economic Co-operation and Development is an international economic organization of 34 countries founded in 1961 to stimulate economic growth and international trade.
4. "Food Support for NOK 1 Billion", Norway, available at:

http://www.norway.org/News_and_events/Press-releases/Food-Support-for-NOK-1-Billion-Approx-US-173-M, accessed on June 12, 2013.

5. "Norway in International Trade", Norway, available at: http://www.norway.org.vn/aboutnorway/economy/trade, accessed on June 16, 2013.
6. "Norway Stories" Norway, available at: http://www.norway.ae/?querystring=&navigators=locations percent2CS percent2C^Norway percent24 percent2CS percent2CLocations percent2CS percent2CNorway&offset=230, accessed on June 4, 2013.
7. "Norway", World Trade Organization, available at: http://stat.wto.org/CountryProfile/WSDBCountryPFView.aspx?Language=E&Country=NO, accessed on June 14, 2013,
8. "European Food and Nutrition Policies in Action", World Health Organization Regional Publications, available at: http://www.euro.who.int/__data/assets/pdf_file/0005/96458/QU14598EU.pdf, accessed June 04, 2013.
9. "Factsheet for Norway", European Topic Centre on Sustainable Consumption and Production, available at: http://scp.eionet.europa.eu/facts/factsheets_waste/2009_edition/factsheet?country=NO, accessed on June 13, 2013.
10. The IMC and NNC.
11. K.I. Klepp, and J.L. Forster, "The Norwegian Nutrition and Food Policy", *Journal of Public Health Policy*, 1985, p. 449.
12. G. Roos et al., "Dietary Interventions in Finland, Norway and Sweden: Nutrition Policies and Strategies", *Journal of Human Nutrition Dietet,* 2004, p. 102.
13. K.I. Klepp, and J.L. Forster, "The Norwegian Nutrition and Food Policy", *Journal of Public Health Policy,* 1985, p. 449.
14. "Proceedings of the Nutrition Society", Cambridge Journals, available at: http://journals.cambridge.org/action/displayAbstract?fromPage=online&aid=673240, accessed on June 12, 2013.
15. C.R. Blythe, "The Norwegian Nutrition Campaign: Setting Goals and Assessing Results", London: Cambridge University Press, 1984, p. 239.
16. G. Roos et al., "Dietary Interventions in Finland, Norway and Sweden: Nutrition Policies and Strategies", *Journal of Human Nutrition Dietet,* 2004, p. 104.

17. "New Guidance on Promoting Physical Activity" World Health Organization, available at: http://www.euro.who.int/eehc/implementation/20071218_28, accessed on June 14, 2013.
18. "European Food and Nutrition Policies in Action", World Health Organization Regional Publications, available at: http://www.euro.who.int/__data/assets/pdf_file/0005/96458/QU14598EU.pdf, accessed on June 4, 2013.
19. "Norway", World Food Programme, available at: http://www.regjeringen.no/upload/UD/Vedlegg/FN/faktaark_wfp.pdf, accessed on June 23, 2013.
20. "Contributing to World Food Security", Food Aid Convention, available at: http://www.foodaidconvention.org/en/index/aboutthefac.aspx, accessed on July 12, 2013.

13

Thailand: Paddy Pledging Programme

Catherine Ayallore and Garima Jain

Introduction

Despite remarkable success in economic growth and poverty decline in Asia, a large proportion of the Asia-Pacific region experiences food-related problems. Most countries manage policies for ensuring that basic foodstuffs, in particular staple food grains, are available at the national level. Agricultural development is a key element in maintaining food security. This is done by increases in productivity and incomes.

Thailand, in the past has not just been concerned with its own food security. Global food security has played its part in its agricultural developmental policy. As a result we see that the availability of food supply in Thailand, especially of rice has increased tremendously more than the domestic demand and the surplus has been exported. However, the problem that we have identified is that despite being a food surplus country at the macro level, food accessibility at the household level is problematic. This is manifested above all, in rural remote areas. The food availability and accessibility have been challenged:

- by the global economic crisis;
- by climate change;
- by food-fuel crops; and
- rise in global food prices in recent years which has inevitably induced a sharp increase in the domestic food price, causing a high inflation rate.

For the poor, food constitutes a considerable portion of the expenditure. There is a direct reflection of high food price and inflation rate in their living standard.

Food security is considered differently depending on whether the focus is at the macro or the micro level. Food security, at the macro level means that enough food has to be available to cover the whole population's nutritional necessities. At the micro level, for households and individuals, three conditions need to be considered: sufficient food at the macro level, stability in supply, and a regular access to food for all households and their members.

Various studies emphasize food availability at the macro level by focusing on the market elements such as production inputs, labour, consumer goods and credit, quantities supplied and demanded, and prices. On these terms, food security is achieved if subsistence production and market supplies are sufficient to meet total household food requirements. However, in order to successfully provide food security to all citizens, two additional elements of the domestic food system have to be considered. First is that the individual households are able to have the funds for the food that is produced. Factors that play an important role here are employment opportunities and the distribution of income by the household. The second element is food prices. Short-run food price fluctuations and shocks make low income households especially vulnerable to food insecurity.

Even when sufficient food for the entire population is available, food insecurity may persist. Poverty is often the culprit. The poor do not have adequate means to secure their access to food even when food is available in local or regional markets.

Socio-economic Profile

Demographics: The population of Thailand was 67,091,089 as per estimation of July 2012 with the population growth rate of around 0.543 percent. Birth rate was 12.81/1,000 while the death rate was estimated to be 7.38/1,000 population. 34 percent of the total population was urban. The sex ratio of the total population was fairly favourable with 0.98 males/females. The infant mortality rate is 15.9 deaths/1,000 live births. The life expectancy rate is

73.83 years, wherein females have more expectancy as compared to males. The rate for males is 71.45 years while it is 76.33 for females. Literacy in Thailand is the ability of a fifteen year old person being able to read and write. The literacy rate is as high as 92.6 percent and is 94.9 percent in males and 90.5 percent in females.

The government spends approximately 4.1 percent of its GDP on the education sector while 4.3 percent is spent on health sector. [1] As per data derived from the 1995 National Nutrition Survey by the Division of Nutrition, Ministry of Public Health revealed that the average calorie intake of the Thai population was 1,751 kcal per person. Prevalence of under nutrition has reduced from 10 percent in 2007-09 to 7 percent in 2010-12.

Thai climate is tropical and is characterized by monsoons. There is a rainy, warm and cloudy southwest monsoon from mid-May to September, as well as a dry, cool northeast monsoon from November to mid-March. Southern part of the country is usually hotter and humid.

Thailand is an agricultural economy, able to produce food that is sufficient not only to meet the domestic demand but also to export to other countries. Public and private investment in agricultural research and development has led to significant increases in yields and land productivity providing Thai agricultural products with a competitive edge in global markets. In addition, the quality of agricultural products has been enhanced in term of its cleanliness and hygienic standards. The Food and Agriculture Organization (FAO) has ranked Thailand the 15th largest world food exporter. But the fact remains that despite this entire food surplus and a sound economic development record, Thailand still has considerable malnutrition.

FAO estimates that 17 percent of Thailand's total population is undernourished. Sufficient production of food in itself is visibly not enough to cope with the rising challenge of feeding the people. Indeed, due to uneven prosperity in Thai society, Thailand is now enduring a new chapter of nutrition-related health threats. While food availability is not the main issue for Thailand, food accessibility remains a big challenge. This problem has yet to be fully examined and understood. However, other studies from both developed and developing countries have shown that the ability of households to access food is not limited to these factors but varies in accordance with numerous demographic and socio-economic characteristics.

In this report, the authors use Thailand's Household Socio-economic Survey 2007 [2] from the National Statistical Office, Ministry of Information and Communication Technology to examine the relationship between a household's ability to access food and a variety of social, economic and demographic characteristics. Instead of focusing on the availability of food as most studies do, we have attempted in this study to provide an in-depth perspective on the household's ability to access food by using the data set to investigate the effect that different household socio-economic characteristics have on the probability of a household living under the food poverty line.

Current Food Security Status: Thailand has made steady progress in economic development and in food production since their first National Economic and Social Development Plan (1961-66). The agricultural share in the country's gross domestic product has continuously declined from one-fifth in 1980 to around one-tenth in 2007. [3] Nonetheless, like in India, the country's resources, predominantly land and labour, are still being used up for agriculture and food production. Agriculture is a source of the country's export earnings. Hence, it is not just only an income source of farm households. In 2007, Thailand exported agricultural and food products to international market at a value of 612.87 trillion baht (17.76 trillion US$) and imported those from the international market to the domestic market at the value of 181.41 trillion baht (5.26 trillion US$). As a result, Thailand is not only a net exporter of agricultural and food products, but also one of the tenth major suppliers in the world food trade. [4]

Food Access: Even with such high availability at macro

level, food insecurity is evidently seen in the household levels. In Thailand, as in other Southeast Asian countries, rice is the major staple food and is grown throughout the country. The central plain and lower north of Thailand are considered the country's commercial rice bowl. [5] The rice for export mostly comes from this region. Rice production steadily increased at an average annual rate of 3 percent. This growth of production is due to Thailand's rice cropping intensity and adoption of modern rice varieties. For quite some time, the production of food in Thailand, particularly rice production, has been increasing at a rate far greater than that of domestic demand, with the surplus being exported. In 2006-2007, about 42 percent of the country's rice output was exported. Rice exports increased from 1.3 million tons in 1971-1975 to 8.14 million tons in 2006-2007.

However, with the global economic crisis, climate change and the expansion of food-fuel crops, the availability of food as well as the identified problem of food accessibility has been significantly impacted worldwide. While Thailand is able to produce more than enough rice to support its population, some vulnerable households do not have enough food to meet their energy and nutritional needs, particularly in the rural areas. Based on the household national food poverty line of 779 baht (US$22.58)/person/month, [6] some 416,410 households were below the food poverty line in 2007. This represents about 2.62 percent of all households in Thailand.

The number of people affected by food poverty increased during 1998-2000 in the wake of the 1997 financial crisis, and during 2004-2006 with food price inflation. The UN World Food Programme (WFP) has expressed concern over the rising price of food in Thailand. [7] As prices go up, more people have difficulty accessing sufficient food and face the possibility of food starvation.

Agriculture can play a significant role in enhancing food security. About 87 percent of those who were affected by food poverty in 2007 were agricultural households. Among agricultural households, the farm operator, who mainly rents land less than 1.6 hectares and engaged in fishing/agricultural services/forestry in rural areas turned out to be the most vulnerable group affected by food poverty. This is the inherently blatant fallacy seen in the food security scenario of Thailand. This problem of food accessibility has been analyzed below and policy recommendations need to be in place as suggested.

Current Import/Export Status: Thailand today, is classified as a middle-income country in Southeast Asia with its economy being heavily export-oriented. Exports account for more than 2/3rd of the gross domestic product. Thailand has made the transition from a low-income to a middle-income country with per capita income of approximately US$ 3,000 within a span of few decades.

Thai economy is agriculture based with rice as the leading crop. Thailand in fact is the world's largest exporter of rice, earning it the name of 'Kitchen of the World'. In the year 2010 alone, 8,939,625 tonnes of rice was exported by Thailand. [8] Agriculture contributes to around 11 percent of the GDP with other major crops being rubber, corn, cotton, sugarcane and jute.

Legislative Framework

The major change in government agricultural policy occurred in 1986 when the pro-consumer policy was replaced by the now prevalent pro-producer policy. The export taxes and export restriction [9] which penalized the farmers were removed, which resulted in an almost neutral nominal rate of protection for most exportable crops, except a few imported competing crops such as palm oil and soybean. Since then, the governments have increased the agricultural subsidy through the agricultural price support program with the aim of improving farmers' income.

Paddy Pledging Programme: The paddy pledging programme had an initial objective to provide a soft loan at low interest rate for farmers who needed cash at the early harvesting season so that the farmers can keep their products from the market at harvest and delay sales until prices rise later in the season. The farmers choose to pledge their paddy with the BAAC [10] at the price of 80 percent of the target price. It was later adjusted to be 90 percent of the market price in 1990-91 and to 95 percent in 1998-99. The farmers receive the loan for their pledged paddy at the net interest cost of 3 percent per annum but applied only pledging period normally not beyond 7 months.

The major change in the schemed occurred in 2001 when the government by that time drastically raised the pledge price to 120 to 130 percent of the market price, thus changing the program to the price support one. Nipon Poapongsakorn, distinguished fellow/director for Sectoral Economic Program on Industrial and Rural Development Policy indicated that the program only increases the farm price in the harvesting period but depresses the market price later in the season when the government releases the rice in the market. Furthermore, the increase in the share of pledged paddy has reduced the supply of paddy to be handled by the market, thus, reducing the number of local rice traders and central paddy markets which are operated by the private sector. It would certainly create the instability of food supply and food price in the long-run as a result of market inefficiency. [11]

Export Promotion Policies: In the year 2010, the Export Promotion Department, in discussion with related state agencies and private sectors, agreed to issue the export promotion measures of the year 2010 in preparation with the economic recovery and the promotion of sustainable export value by focusing on strong export promotion for agricultural products and foods, promoting the reduction of capital cost in the trade logistics system to lift up the export competitive competencies for entrepreneurs, promoting the export of goods and services under the 'Creative Economy and the Kitchen of the World 2012 Project', Thailand.

All these policies were mainly regulatory in nature; Thailand has few restrictions on exports except when dealing with national security, environmental protection, cultural issues or concerning trade agreements. Laws to ensure that domestic needs are met before exports can be permitted, reserves certain items, principally food staples. But as we can see the problem is of food accessibility.

Export Financing: Thailand has several programs that benefit manufactured and processed agricultural producers. These usually take the form of preferential financing, tax certificates and rebate of taxes and import duties. The Thailand Export-Import Bank has taken over many of these programs and has recently offered an expanded credit program to stimulate export activity during the economic downturn in Thailand.

Major Determinants of Food Security

As noted earlier, food security at the household level is a function of many factors that empower individuals to access nutritionally adequate and safe food in appropriate ways. These include a host of socio-economic, demographic and community-related variables. It is important to recognize that economic security is an essential precursor to permanent food security.

Furthermore, economic security is itself a complex outcome related to steady, adequate income, family stability, affordable expenditures and access to a social safety net in times of need. In formulating policy directed at maintaining and enhancing domestic food security, it is therefore critical to consider economic security as a prerequisite of this condition. [12]

In any given year, national food availability is determined by a country's own food production, its stocks of food, and its net imports of food, including food aid. [13] Studies show that ownership of land is crucial to the food security of rural households, and that the landless tend to be the poorest in rural society. The percentage of the population below the poverty line in rural areas is typically around twice that found in urban centres. Despite the fact that most food is produced in the countryside, those in towns and cities have the greatest access to it. This may seem counter-intuitive, but it graphically illustrates the difference between food availability and food access. [14]

The important factors are as follows.

Income: The decline in the percent of income spent on food as incomes rise is rooted in the fact that even though food is a necessity, its consumption is limited by the size of the human stomach. Human beings simply cannot continue to increase their food consumption in proportion to the increase in their income.

Household Size: There is considerable evidence of a strong negative correlation between household size and income per person in developing countries. It is often found that people living in larger and generally younger households are typically poorer.

Gender: According to FAO (1996) Report, women account for approximately 50 percent of overall regional food production. Over 60 percent of the agricultural labour force in Thailand is female. The report also depicts that the direct responsibility for household food production falls, for the most part, on women. The improvement of household food security and nutritional levels are therefore closely related to women's ability to earn income and their roles in household expenditure decisions.

Education: The general education level of the homemaker has been found to have a substantial impact on food expenditure. It is essential that awareness about how to avoid and face illnesses is generated and acquired since people with diseases require more calories to be food secure. Education also helps develop an understanding pertaining to intake of an adequate and diversified diet in order to build a stronger immune system. Thus, people with only a minimum level of education can properly access and understand food related information.

Self-sufficiency and Change in Land Use Pattern: Substantial part of economic growth recorded by Thailand in the 1970s and the early 1980s was owed to the steady extension of the agricultural sector. This sector provided adequate food for the rapidly growing population and also produced substantial surpluses of some commodities for export purpose. Agriculture has been instrumental in Thailand's economic development and to some degree continues to shape Thai identity and support Thai lifestyles. It is a strong element of the image the country presents to the world. About 1/3rd of Thailand's total land area (about 51 million hectares) is dedicated to agricultural production. [15] Rice is the country's largest crop, but the main cash crops are sugarcane and cassava. There are several annual crops including maize and also perennial crops such as oil palm, rubber, coconut and various fruits.

Roughly 2/5th of Thailand is covered by mountains and hills, the steepness of which generally precludes cultivation. Nevertheless, perhaps as much as a 10th of this area might also be converted to agricultural purposes once detailed information is obtained through surveys. Estimates in the 1970s of overall land-use suitability classified roughly 58 percent of mountainous and hilly regions as cultivable soils throughout most of the country which are of low fertility, largely as a result of leaching by heavy rainfall. Differences between various soil types is the result of differences in parent rock material, variations in the amount of rainfall, length of wet and dry seasons, type of vegetable cover, and other natural factors. In general, stony and shallow soils characterize the hill and mountain terrain of the North. Large portion of this mountainous area is traditionally used by hill people for shifting cultivation.

The Northern Region comprises 3 physiographic zones:

- The lowlands (15 percent of the area), which are relatively flat with fertile alluvial basins, and which produce paddy rice.
- The uplands (45 percent of the area) which are undulating to hilly in terrain to 500 ma.s.l. Principal land use is upland rice, maize, grain legumes and other field crops.
- The highlands (40 percent of the area) which range in

altitude from 500-2500m, comprise rugged steep sided mountains which are dissected by high valleys. Crops include upland rice, maize and opium which are cultivated in swiddens.

Soils of the uplands and highlands are mostly derived from granites, gneiss, shales, limestones and sandstones.

In the Northern Region, rainfall varies from 900 to 2,000 mm. At Chiang Mai (300m altitude), temperatures vary from 29°C/13°C in January to 36°C/21°C in April. Temperatures decrease at approximately 0.5°C per 100m altitude and frosts occur in sheltered highland locations.

The central plain rice growing area and the delta of the Mae Nam (river) Chao Phraya has clayey soils of high to moderate fertility. Low-lying and flat, much of the area is flooded during the rainy season.

Higher areas on the edges of the plain are generally well-drained soils of high to moderate fertility that are suitable for intensive cultivation. These lands are used extensively for maize and sugarcane. Among other highly useful soils are the well-drained clayey and loamy soils in parts of the peninsula where rubber is grown. [16]

Southern Region: The Southern soils are derived from a variety of parent materials such as limestone, bedded sediments and granites, and vary from clay loam to sandy loam. There are also large areas of alluvial soils, beach sands and acid peats. The region is dominated by plantation agriculture, principally rubber, oil palm, fruit trees and coconuts, although rice and horticultural crops are also grown.

Shifting cultivation was the principal mode of production for many people in Northern Thailand for a long time. It for the most part, only means of growing food for most of the people who lived in the mountains. It also provided for an essential supplement to wetland rice cultivation. The numerous forms of shifting cultivation that were described and characterised in the 1960s, however, are hardly recognisable in the 1990s. As a crop production practice involving the slashing and burning of natural vegetation, shifting cultivation can still be found in northern Thailand, but is no longer the most important mode of production. Almost no one now is solely dependent on shifting cultivation.

In the 1960s, when the population of Thailand was not quite 30 million, it was estimated that more than one million people were engaged in some form of shifting cultivation. In just over 30 years, shifting cultivators who were lowland Thais, have completely disappeared. Farming by hill tribe "shifting cultivators" is now totally different from that described in the 1960s. The last frontier of shifting cultivation in Thailand was the northern mountains. The people who live in the mountains largely belong to groups who are ethnically distinct from the majority Thai population of the lowlands. Two basic types of shifting agriculture were practised before 1970: pioneer and rotational types.

However, during the past 30 year, the Thai economy as a whole has seen many changes and, for all practical purposes, the short fallow-short cultivation system of lowland by Thais has completely disappeared. There have also been major changes in land-use patterns in the mountains. By 1990, voluntary village relocation and the setting up of new villages had become very rare. Shifting cultivation has now largely disappeared, but rotational shifting agriculture can still be found. [17] The extensive area where the majority of villagers are still largely dependent on rotation shifting agriculture covers only a few provinces. The fallow period is often shortened by increased population pressure and restriction on the use of forest land by the Royal Forestry Department.

Many fields remain perennially cropped, some even growing two, sometimes three, crops a year. Along with land-use intensification, technology adopted for increasing productivity included irrigation, and the use of fertilizer and pesticides. Irrigation for wetland rice paddies, which has expanded to cover dry season soybean which follows the rice, has come from the Karen and lowland Thais. Sprinkler irrigation for fruit trees and vegetables has become widespread in the past 10 years or so. Chemical fertilisers, especially nitrogen and phosphorus, and pesticides, for controlling weeds as well as insects, are routinely applied to cash crops.

While Thai agriculture evolved from wet rice systems, modern irrigation systems were generally imported. Large dam projects were implemented with the aim of increasing rice area and production. Additional dams have become a common policy response to perceived need for additional water resources both in agriculture and hydro-power sectors. In addition, the increased availability of credit for farmers and the creation of the BAAC facilitated the types of investment necessary to realize the benefits of technological progress within the sector. Thailand is now one of the world's foremost suppliers of sugar, rice and cassava. Modern mechanization, chemical pesticides and fertilizers in association with large scale irrigation facilities have been crucial in facilitating the regular cycle of agricultural output required to meet the needs of export markets. At present, 77 percent of the value-added in crop agriculture arises from the production of traded goods. Exports of agricultural products amounted to almost 10.5 percent of the total Thai exports in 2004. [18]

Price Rise Crisis of 2008: "In Thailand, food vendors say inflation is biting into their daily profit. One man says he raised the price of noodles by 16 cents or 5 baht because fuel, cooking oil, chicken and pork prices have all gone up. A banana fritter vendor says he reduced the number of bananas he sells for 32 cents from 20 pieces to 15 pieces. "What we see is because the economy is doing well, people feel like they should be able to pass along some of those increases but you'll never be able to pass a 100 percent", noted Frederico Gil Sander, an economist at the World Bank in Thailand. Bad harvests, political tensions and higher demand have wreaked havoc on many families' budgets. Many are getting less for their money".

The rise in food prices are mainly a sign of input costs

going up rather than the domestic economy heating up. It cannot be understood to be the case of too much demand for too few goods, which happens when wages amplify and producers find it difficult to keep up with consumer demand. Instead, prices have been increasing principally because of factors outside of Thailand—the increase in global prices for energy (fuel) and agricultural commodities (including food). Adding to it, there was uncertainty as to if this rise was a temporary spike in prices, or whether increases was part of a long-term trend.

The price rise was not due to crop failure or a particularly tight global rice supply condition. Instead, various reasons culminated to result in inflation situation. These included trade restrictions by major suppliers, "panic buying" by numerous large importers, a weak dollar, and record oil prices, which were the immediate cause of the rise in rice prices. The 2007-08 rice price increase was followed by price hikes for other major agricultural produce such as wheat, corn, and soybeans. The primary cause of the rise in prices for these commodities during 2006-08 was rising global incomes, dietary changes, increased use of bio-fuels, tight grain supplies, and increased participation in futures markets by non-traditional investors. [19]

The fluctuation in fuel price in 2008 was even greater. An analysis of inflation in 2008 revealed some interesting findings. [20] It is found that food price rise contributed more to the overall inflation than the rise in energy price. Rural areas tended to have higher inflation than the urban counterparts, in both general inflation and food inflation. Since almost 90 percent of poor people lived in countryside areas, rising food price therefore posed a threat to the overall situation of poverty and vulnerability in Thailand. Whether or not it is a real threat and, if it is, how it affects different groups of people is an important issue to address. To this end, we found that the impact could be both positive and negative, depending on whether the rural dwellers are net buyers or net sellers of food whose price hikes. For rice, there were both rice-surplus farmers (3 millions) and rice-deficit farmers (2.5 millions) among the poor households in 2007.

When rice price increase, there were thus gainers and losers among the poor, making the impact on poverty to some extent unclear and ambiguous. Interestingly, the distribution of rice surplus was biased in favour of richer farmers, making the benefit from price rise, or price support policy, more than proportionately. There is also evidence that price increase in other food products since 2007 provided net benefit to the producers even after higher cost of energy and fertilizers were already taken into account.

People adjust when prices rise. Available data from household surveys since 2007 to the first half of 2008 reveals that poor households lowered their food consumption with price elasticity close to unity, meaning that spending on food in money term remained unchanged. Since poverty lines are derived with minimum food intake just sufficient for normal daily functions, cutting food consumption by the poor (who were defined poor by poverty lines) means their nutrition intake might be insufficient, which could cause both short-term and long-term negative impacts. There are other coping mechanisms apart from adjusting consumption model. A recent survey by the National Statistical Office shows that reducing debt was the most sought of measure next to reducing overall spending. This is somewhat surprising as one might expect households to create more debts to meet the higher cost of food and energy. Perhaps most households expected prices to rise further and were more cautious of their future repayment ability.

Higher agricultural prices are generally positive for the Thai economy, but the benefits are not evenly circulated among various sections of the population. Many vulnerable urban and rural households may be pressed into poverty when food prices go up. In 2008, poverty spiked up for the first time in Thailand since the Asian financial crisis. Although a majority of the poor were helped by higher agricultural incomes, they also spent most of their earnings on food. So, on an average, the effect of price increase completely eroded what was a healthy income gain for the bottom 20 percent of the population.

The year 2008 was of great political and economic upheaval for Thailand. With the global economic meltdown pushing up the prices of food grains, it was a difficult task to ensure food availability for the Thai population, especially the rural Thai population. Adding to the obstacle, there was instability at the central level. There had been three governments already in power and with the fall of the third one, fourth government was established. Since the source of higher prices is, for the most part, external to Thailand, the standard medicine for inflation (higher interest rates) may not be that effective in slowing down price increases. In fact, higher interest rates may attract foreign capital and slow the recovery, which depends heavily on the strength of the domestic market.

In order to tackle the food price rise, first, a proposal of issuing food coupons to the poor was introduced. From the initial stage, the details of the proposal were not clear and since the discussion of the same was short-lived, the plan never did materialize. From the reports it appeared that under the proposal, the urban poor were to get food coupons that they could use to exchange for food at certain specified stores. Rural poor were to get cash instead of coupon as administering food coupon program in rural areas would be too costly an affair. The main reason this proposal was finally turned down, according to the then Finance Minister, was because the government did not have accurate information to identify poor households. The program would therefore have been subject to serious targeting problem.

The government later introduced a 'Six Measures for Six Months' policy package. [21] Under this package, total subsidy of around 50 billion baht was divided among six measures, namely subsidy for transportation, fuel, water, electricity, bus and train services. The biggest chunk of subsidy, around 30 billion baht, went to the subsidy of fuel sales. This posed a serious problem of targeting, as it tended to prove more advantageous for well-to-do population than the poor and the vulnerable ones.

The policies announced targeting rice was utterly chaotic. This is because, as pointed out earlier, here is some ambiguity regarding the impact of rice price changes on the poor. The long-standing conventional wisdom dating back many decades is that Thai rice farmers are poor. And that has been the motivation that drives the government towards supporting the price of rice for the last two decades when the price of rice was low. But, over the years, while it remains true that most of the poor people are rice farmers, but many of these farmers are now in deficit in rice. Further, it is not true that all rice farmers are poor. In particular, if they contribute more than their share (41 percent) of the rice surplus produced, much of the benefits of the previous rice price support policies would accrue to them.

In any case, as a result of these previous price support policies, Thailand entered 2008 with a stock of rice amounting to 2.1 million tons of rice. When the price surge took place in the early part of 2008, the government that just came to power (the second of the four governments) decided in April to release that rice stocks and sell it in limited quantities at well below market prices (about 40 percent below) "to help the poor consumers".

Unfortunately, Thailand never had the infrastructure (say, ration shops) to target its policies towards the poor in a systematic fashion. This limited the government's ability to implement the policy of releasing rice stocks without lowering market prices, which it decidedly did not want to do. In the event, only 1,500 tons of the 2.1 million tons were released to supermarkets where long lines quickly formed. Those long lines were there despite the fact that the rice sold was of lower quality than the rice mostly consumed in urban areas.

In the event, it was people's tolerance for the low quality and for the long waiting time that rationed the small amount made available. Soon after the price began to ease, but when it was still well above the previous levels, farmers began to pressurise the government to prevent it from falling further. Uncharacteristically, the government moved with alacrity on this front, and set a price support, well above the market price. The price then set is still in place now, even though the prices elsewhere in the world have sunk below the Thai government's set price, naturally affecting Thailand's ability to export its rice.

Self-sufficiency: The New Theory

The agriculture sector is also an important source of crisis resilience, self-sufficiency and rural social support for poorer rural communities. Continued development within the sector is necessary to preserve rural livelihoods. The rapid expansion of agriculture was generally made possible by the conversion of forest land to agriculture.

The philosophy of sufficiency economy in Thailand, which is called the new theory in agriculture sector, is a practical way of living and engaging in agriculture that His Majesty the King has initiated to help the farmers to improve their quality of life and well-being. It is divided into 3 stages: first stage is widely known in the name of "The New Theory in Agriculture" which includes production for self-sufficiency; second stage is to cooperate or to form a group to support production, marketing, society and social welfare; and third stage is to launch their production activities into business. The advantages of the sufficiency economy include: (i) use of land with high efficiency, (ii) different production, (iii) reducing risks, (iv) reducing cost of production, (v) increase in income, (vi) balancing of natural environment, (vii) greater activities, (viii) reduction in migration, and (ix) better life quality. [22]

In short, the self-sufficiency economy and its expected outcomes are best summarized, by His Majesty himself; "Sufficiency economy is a philosophy that guides the livelihood and behaviour of people at all levels, from the family to the community to the country, on matters concerning national development and administration. It calls for a 'middle way' to be observed, especially in pursuing economic development, in keeping with the world of globalization. At the same time, we must build up the spiritual foundation of all people in the nation, especially state officials, scholars, and business people at all levels, so that they are conscious of moral integrity and honesty and they strive for the appropriate wisdom to live life with forbearance, diligence, self-awareness, intelligence, and attentiveness. In this way we can hope to maintain balance and be ready to cope with rapid physical, social, environmental, and cultural changes from the outside world". [23]

Policy Recommendations

With limited resources for policy implementation, and given the urgency of the issue due to external factors such as rising food prices, the government has to act in quick response to the needs of households that are most vulnerable to food poverty. This study provides policy makers with information that they should find useful in targeting households most at risk of being food insecure. In addition, the study demonstrates the importance of a more comprehensive approach to sustainable food security in Thailand. The evidence noticeably suggests that a household's ability to access food can be strengthened through social policies, such as family planning and improved education.

Household size and income significantly affect a household's ability to access food. While rising household income decreases the probability of food poverty, a larger household size raises that probability. These findings support the theory that as household size increases, the proportion of income spent on food also rises. Members of the larger family have more dependents to take care of. This negative effect, however, can be reduced if the proportions of income earning members in the household increases as more members are added.

- Improve family planning programmes to cover not only birth control but also day-care services.
- Grandparents or women of the house are responsible for taking care of the children at home. Day-care services are rare and not commonly used. However, the cost is high since at least one family member has to stay home to take care of the children instead of entering the job market. As mentioned earlier, an additional member in the family suggests that more income is needed.
- Although female heads of household tend to spend more on food, they usually have limited access to income and therefore often need to rely on male members of the family for this purpose. Empowering women by increasing their access to other assets is, therefore, a more effective means by which to reduce food insecurity in Thailand.
- The inclusion of nutrition instruction in school curricula would mean that people are able to access nutrition and health-related information. With this information, they can learn how to take care of themselves and also their family members, thus, reducing the risk of household food insecurity.
- The Household Socioeconomic Survey is not sufficient to examine details of nutrition and food intake, thus it should be merged with Thailand's Health Survey since Household Economic Survey looks only at socio-economic data. An amalgamation of the two would be necessary for getting a more comprehensive picture.

For overcoming future impacts of high food price and rising production cost on rural poor, the government policy must target small farmers and the rural poor.

Endnotes

1. "Thailand Demographics Profile", available at: http://www.indexmundi.com/thailand/demographics_profile.htm accessed on November 12, 2012.
2. "Household Economic and Social Survey", available at: http://web.nso.go.th/survey/house_seco/socio.htm, accessed on

November 12, 2012.

3. The value of gross domestic product at 1988 prices was 4,259.63 trillion baht or approximately 123.47 trillion US$.
4. Poapongsakorn, N., "The Political Economy of the Thai Rice Price and Export Policies in 2007-08", a paper presented at a Workshop on Rice Policies in Asia, Organized by FAO, February 10-12, 2009, Chiang Mai.
5. Graeme MacRae, "Thailand's Rice Bowl: Perspectives on Agricultural and Social Change in the Chao Phraya Delta", available at: http://www.iias.nl/nl/36/IIAS_NL36_25.pdf.
6. The food poverty line is approximately 54 percent of the total poverty line.
7. "Thailand: Rising Rice Prices Fuel Fears of Food Shortages and Starvation", available at: http://www.irinnews.org/report/77608/thailand-rising-rice-prices-fuel-fears-of-food-shortages-and-starvation.
8. http://faostat.fao.org/site/342/default.aspx.
9. Export taxation was implemented before 1986. The purpose was for controlling the export flow. It was abolished in 1986.
10. Bank of Agricultural and Agricultural Cooperatives.
11. Poapongsakorn, N., "The Political Economy of the Thai Rice Price and Export Policies in 2007-08", paper presented at a Workshop on Rice Policies in Asia, Organized by FAO, February 10-12, 2009, Chiang Mai.
12. Iram, Uzma and Muhammad Butt, "Determinants of Household Food Security: An Empirical Analysis for Pakistan", *International Journal of Social Economics,* 2004, 31:753-766.
13. Smith, Lisa, Amani El Obeid, and Helen Jensen, "The Geography and Causes of Food Insecurity in Developing Countries", *Agricultural Economics,* 2000, 22:199-215.
14. Gill, Gerard, John Farrington, Edward Anderson, Cecilia Luttrell, Tim Conway, N.C. Saxena and Rachel Slater, "Food Security and the Millennium Development Goal on Hunger in Asia", working paper 231, 2003, Overseas Development Institute.
15. "Worldstat Info, Thailand", available at: http://en.worldstat.info/Asia/Thailand/Land, accessed on November 12, 2012.
16. "Thailand Land Use and Soil Last", available at:

http://www.photius.com/countries/thailand/economy/thailand_economy_land_use_and_soils.html, accessed on November 12, 2012.

17. Rerkasern, K. and Rerkasem, B., "Shifting Cultivation in Thailand: Its Current Situation and Dynamics in the Context of Highland Development", IIED Forestry and Land Use Series, 1994, No. 4. 140.
18. "BEPS Analytical Framework in Thailand", available at: http://www.fao.org/docrep/013/i1739e/i1739e01.pdf, accessed on November 12, 2012.
19. Siamwalla, A. and J. Somchai, "Protecting the Poorest: Rising Food Prices and the Vulnerable Groups in Thailand", 2009.
20. "Bank of Thailand, Inflation Report, 2008", available at: http://www.bot.or.th/English/MonetaryPolicy/Inflation/Download/Pages/2008.aspx, accessed on November 12, 2012.
21. Poapongsakorn, N., "The Political Economy of Thai Rice Price and Export Policies in 2007-2008", in Rice Crisis: Markets, Policies and Food Security, (ed.) D. Dawe, 2010 191-217, Earthscan, London/Washington D.C.
22. His Majesty the King initiated the establishment of the Chaipattana Foundation, aiming to help his people through development activities in various forms, www.chaipat.or.th, accessed on November 12, 2012.
23. "King Bhumibol and His Enlightened Approach to Teaching", available at: http://thailand.prd.go.th/ebook/king/intro.html, accessed on November 12, 2012.

14

United Kingdom: Food Security Policies

Rahul Dave and Sankeerth Vittal

Socio-economic Profile

Food security is one of the major concerns of any world economy. Every government has to think of how it can feed its population and how it can protect the domestic agricultural sector from external threats. The United Kingdom is one of the major economies of the world and is a global player in every major issue. Food security in the UK dates back to the 17th century when industrial revolution was at its formative stage. Throughout this period, UK would export food grains across the world. However, the lack of foresight proved a bane as increased industrialisation led to rapid urbanisation and hence less focus on the agricultural sector. It was during 1947 that UK passed a major legislation on agriculture in the form of the Agriculture Act which provided new grants and also the introduction of machines and other modern food production techniques. However, for all the fool proofing, UK still faced the impact of the global food price rise in 2008. This paper attempts to analyse the food security measure of the UK through ages and also looks at the opposition of the UK to the CAP regime.

Demography: Every nation, province, city and for that matter, every society is different and as distinct from the other, hence, before setting forth on a voyage of discovery of a profile of a country on any topic, let alone it be that on its food security, it is most important to first put forth the demographics and give an opportunity to the reader to understand the unique problems and the varied solutions that are offered to it and the advantages that a nation possess over others. Thus, given below are the bare facts of the demographics of the United Kingdom to help the reader in drawing inferences based on the factors that affect the country.

History of Food Security in the UK: The period from 1600 to 1750 saw a dramatic change in the nature of agriculture in the UK. Subsistence farming which had dominated for much of the preceding 6,000 years gave way to an industry in which innovation and technology became the drivers of output.

The agricultural industry was changing with many innovations and new crops, that found their way into practice. Specialization was the name of the game with each farmer taking advantage of the soil and topography of his own area. This led to regional specializations which to this day have remained largely unchanged. Soon agricultural societies sprang up and began to communicate the innovations and technological advances to a wider farming community.

Despite this progress, conservatism was still prevalent among the farmers in adopting these ideas. They generally followed some of these ideas once they were established in the low countries. The practice of enclosure reached a new level of activity and small farmers often found themselves landless and dispossessed having been forced to sell out to much larger and rich farmers who were now coming to dominate agriculture.

The 1750s saw the advent of industrialisation and the growth of towns saw a radical change in the social structure of Britain. These towns were no longer market places for local goods; instead they provided goods of both national and international origin in addition to professional, cultural and recreational services. International trade and financial services were well advanced. It was upon the back of this trade and the supply of services, that the professional middle classes emerged and where the primacy of land declined within an increasingly commercialised economy.

Between the 18th and the 19th centuries, the industrial revolution transformed the landscape and led to Britain becoming the world's first urban nation. Railways, new roads and an improved transport infrastructure provided fresh impetus for fast growing towns while imported produce from around the world provided a greatly more diverse diet. Increasingly however, the countryside became a remote and distant environment to an industrialised society.

The Corn Laws were among the first legislations in the world that hoped to help the local farmers by protecting them against increasing international trade. These laws however ended up pushing the prices of wheat and made bread expensive. These laws were unpopular amongst the manufacturers as costly goods saw a consequent increase in wages. In 1846, the Corn Laws were repealed amidst the potato famine and widespread pressure from the manufacturers. Imports resumed as a consequence of this repeal. Even though agricultural interest had been checked but in a period of advances in technology, the industry was able to ride out the competition with increasing yields and lower production costs. Capital spending on drainage, buildings, machinery and roads linking to the railways all fuelled the agricultural revolution with British farmers at least twice as efficient as their European contemporaries.

History has shown that periods of progress are often punctuated with crisis. The Potato Famine of 1846 is an illustration of that. During 1845, 1846 and 1848 blight decimated the potato crop in Ireland and up to a million died from malnutrition and in the decade that followed a further 2 million emigrated. [1] In 1860, 80 percent of food consumed was still produced in the UK but by the 1870s, after a series of bad harvests and the arrival of imports from the prairies, farm gate prices fell dramatically and the great agricultural depression followed. Lasting for nearly thirty years, significant rural depopulation resulted and where previously the workforce had known, understood and been involved in country ways, the new workforce were migrants with only a transient interest. There were few to speak for agriculture and as rural Britain became depopulated so the countryside became a plaything for the rich. By 1900, the majority of food and raw materials were imported.

The 20th century technological revolution which was underway led to an increased output and greater security of supply. With rationing still fresh in the public's mind, the industry responded to government initiatives derived from the 1947 Agriculture Act. Improved stock and plant breeding, the greater use of fertiliser and pesticides and a move away from more extensive forms of production saw yields rise.

Agriculture was supported by various Acts, initially the 1947 Agriculture Act and grant funding and price support greatly empowered the modern era of agriculture with new technology, specialisation, improved breeding and management, all pushing output in the new revolution. [2] Not all was well however, and Rachel Carson's book "Silent Spring" [3] paved the way for a wider concern about farming and the environment. In 1972, Britain joined the EEC and after a transitional period, agricultural policy fell within the remit of the CAP which encouraged wasteful surpluses and amidst only slow reforms, widened the gulf between agriculture and the consumer.

Agriculture was still an important industry in the economy and represented some 3 percent of GDP, but where output was rapidly rising on the back of new technology and mechanisation, the agricultural workforce declined and rural depopulation resulted. The era of globalisation saw a gradual disconnect between the urban and rural population. The urban class were unconvinced by the need for support of an industry that provided less than 1 percent of GDP and employed only 2 percent of the workforce. Despite this, agriculture still accounted for 70 percent of UK land and provided an overall sufficiency in food products of 65 percent.

New techniques like integrated farming and organic farming were increasingly adopted amidst calls for a new direction that was sought by policy makers and farmers alike. Severe financial pressure still existed with nominal prices for products often the same as those three decades earlier despite the inflation costs rising by 5 times in the period. Agriculture was continuing to decline as a land use (down 5 percent in 40 years) and was giving way to leisure and urban development. Patterns of ownership and management were changing too with a small number of highly mechanised contract farmers beginning to dominate production.

Employment in Agriculture

UK farming employed over half a million people, and in 2007 it contributed £ 5.3 billion to the economy. [4] A flexible, skilled and market-orientated domestic agriculture sector has showed it can thrive and compete in an international market.

Consumers in the UK and all around the world were motivated to buy 'local' produce for a range of reasons, including a desire to support local producers and the local economy, and its association with higher quality, and in some instances, perceptions of lower environmental impact. This resulted in the setting up of what is known as "Farmers' Market", following the policy of field to fridge, where the consumer can directly buy from the farmer.

There are now estimated 550 Farmers' Markets in the UK, compared to just one in 1997, and an estimated 4,000 farm shops. Turnover from direct selling by farmers, along with pick-your-own and box schemes is estimated to be around £ 2 billion a year. The United Kingdom is a net importer in the agriculture sector, with most of the imports from the European and mainly the Scandinavian countries.

As of now, no single country accounts for more than 13 percent of the UK food and drink food imports. In 2006, 68 percent of food imports into the UK were from other Member States of the EU. Maintaining a range of supply sources means that any risk to the total food supply is spread, lowering the impacts of any unforeseen disruptions involving any particular trading partner or from within the country's domestic agriculture sector. This culture of importing food from foreign countries also helps in breeding a healthy trade and production culture within the UK itself.

Currently, the UK is 60 percent self-sufficient in all foods and over 74 percent self-sufficient in foods that can be produced in this country. This is relatively high by historical standards. UK self-sufficiency peaked in the 1980s and has since declined, but is higher now than during the inter-War period. The very high self-sufficiency of the 1980s and 1990s was brought about by the CAP and its emphasis on boosting food production through direct subsidies to producers irrespective of demand from the market and was artificially maintained by trade barriers.

In the UK, self-sufficiency ranges from around 10 percent for fresh fruit to around 100 percent for cereals. As a measure of domestic food security, self-sufficiency does not cover the processing and distribution of food, it does not allow for the imported energy on which domestic agriculture is directly and indirectly reliant, and it does not take account the resilience of the supply chain.

Impact of Rising Global Food Prices: The impacts of price rise in global food commodities have been felt in the UK as well. Overall inflation in June 2008 was 3.8 percent but food price inflation stood at 9.7 percent. Yet over the past 40 years or so, and until the recent price rises, UK has witnessed a long-term decline in real food prices, reflected in the decline in the proportion of household expenditure spent on food. In 2007, an average household spent 9.2 percent of its weekly expenditure on food. In the 1960s, this figure was around 20 percent. If food prices stay on the current upward trend, expected proportion of expenditure spent on food for 2008 overall would be around 10 percent; the level seen at the end of the 1990s.

Recent price rises have hit family budgets and low income households spend a greater percentage of their household income on food. In the UK, the poorest 10 percent of the population spends 15 percent of their household income on food compared to 7 percent spent by the richest 10 percent.

People on low incomes have been affected more significantly than others by recent food price rises. The same people have also been affected the most by recent rises in energy, fuel and housing costs. The Government has introduced a number of measures to support low income groups. For example, approximately £ 100m is spent on Healthy Start [5] which provides support to around half a million pregnant women, and children under four in low income and disadvantaged families across the UK.

The overall food supply chain in the United Kingdom can also be considered robust because of the number of different supply chains and manufacturing and retail businesses. Having domestic and international food supply chains increases the options available to the retailers when a particular link in the chain is disrupted. Lean, low-inventory, just-in-time logistics systems adopted by the UK retail sector bring benefits in terms of efficiency, but are potentially vulnerable to direct or indirect disruption through, for instance:

- Extreme weather.
- IT systems failures.
- Interruptions to fuel and other energy supplies.
- Failures in transport infrastructure.

The government's food resilience policy focuses on ensuring that critical elements of food supply chain work. This includes maintaining communication, transport and energy networks.

Legislative Framework

Corn Laws: Corn Laws were the regulations governing the import and export of grain. Records mention the imposition of Corn Laws as early as the 12th century. [6] The laws became politically important in the late 18th century and the first half of the 19th century, during the grain shortage caused by Britain's growing population and by the blockades imposed in the Napoleonic Wars.

The first English Corn Laws, dating from the time of the Norman Conquest in the 11th century, were intended to prevent shortages of grain in England by prohibiting or controlling exports. Beginning in the 17th century, with the House of Commons dominated by landowners, this policy was changed. Imports, not exports, were tightly controlled, and the object was to keep the prices high in England, thereby protecting the farmers. The most famous of these laws were passed in 1815 at a time when Great Britain's landholding class was threatened by falling prices and by the danger of a flood of cheap foreign grains.

The 1815 Corn Laws brought hardship to the labouring class, which had to pay a high price for bread. The laws were opposed by manufacturers who believed they forced higher wages. Opposition took the form of an Anti-Corn Law League, headed by such men as Richard Cobden and John Bright. The Corn Laws were finally repealed in 1846, a triumph for the manufacturers, whose expansion had been hampered by protection of grain, against the landed interests. Popular uprisings and a potato crop failure also led to the reluctant repeal of the Corn Laws in 1846 by Prime Minister Robert Peel's Tory party. A new law (1849) permitted the buying and selling of food grain without restriction. This was an important step toward Britain's free-trade policy of the later 19th century.

Although proficient farmers on good lands did well, farmers with mediocre skills or marginal lands were at a disadvantage. This gradual yet alarming rise of agricultural exports saw a consequent decline in the employment rates in the agricultural sector. The lacunae of the repeal of the 1815 Corn Laws was that Britain entered into an era of cheap exports from foreign lands which led to a decline in the production of locally grown produce. Many farmers relocated to the cities, and unprecedented numbers emigrated. Many emigrants were small, undercapitalized grain farmers who were squeezed out by low prices and inability to increase production or adapt to the more complex challenge of raising livestock. Similar patterns developed in Ireland, where cereal production was labour intensive. The reduction of grain prices reduced the demand for agricultural labour in Ireland, and reduced the output of barley, oats, and wheat. These changes occurred at the same time that emigration was reducing the labour supply and increasing wage rates to levels too great for arable farmers to sustain.

Agriculture Act, 1947: At the end of the WWII, the 1947 Agriculture Act laid the foundation for post-War farm policy in the UK, establishing guaranteed prices for most farm products and deficiency payments which made up the difference between the guaranteed price and the market price, paid by the exchequer, thus preserving the access to domestic markets for foreign supplies at world prices and maintaining food prices to consumers at world levels. The guaranteed prices were set annually by close negotiation between the government and the National Farmers Union. [7] In the words of Agriculture Minister, Tom Williams, "to promote a healthy and efficient agriculture capable of producing that part of the nation's food which is required from home sources at the lowest price consistent with the provision of adequate remuneration and decent living conditions for farmers and workers, with a reasonable return on capital invested". [8]

During the 1950s and 1960s, the primary concern was with food security and improved self-sufficiency, and latterly with balance of payments arguments. This Act strongly protected the interests of the domestic sector. By 1957, the budgetary cost of the policy forced some limits on guaranteed price increases, and by 1964, minimum import prices had been introduced to further limit the extent to taxpayer cost. This period also saw major technical revolutions in agriculture, [9] doubtlessly fostered by the relative security of agriculture under a favourable policy regime. The mechanical revolution was already under way before and during WWII, rapidly replacing labour and horses (as the major motive power source) with machines, leading to substantial economies of scale in the farm business and associated growth in farm sizes.

The chemical revolution, including the dramatic improvement in plant and seed varieties and animal breeds and strains able to respond to an increasingly controlled environment, gathered pace after the War and progressed throughout the 1960s and 1970s, further reducing labour and machinery requirements and associated with increasing specialisation of farming systems. Much of this revolution was fostered by direct government support of research institutes, while the private sector was quick to respond to a securely supported industry's demands for new and more commercially efficient techniques, supplies and equipment. The shift of the burden of support was completed in 1973 through the UK's entry to EC and CAP.

In effect, accession to the Common Agricultural Policy and its primary system of farm support through the imposition of import levies (and export refunds or subsidies) to defend internal prices well above world prices, signalled the return of the Corn Laws to the UK, and the end of agricultural free trade and 'cheap food'. By 1986, an amendment [10] to the Agriculture Act allowed for the implementation of the EC structures regulation on environmentally sensitive areas (ESAs) and the funding of management agreements associated with these areas. The amendment also included explicit reference to the MAFF's responsibility for the 'conservation and enhancement of the natural beauty and amenity of the countryside'.

Common Agricultural Policy: The Common Agricultural Policy (CAP) is a policy proposed by the European Commission. It came into existence following the Treaty of Rome in 1957. Article 39 [11] of the CAP stated that the objectives of CAP are:

1. To increase productivity, by promoting technical progress and ensuring the optimum use of the factors of production, in particular labour;
2. To ensure a fair standard of living for the agricultural community;
3. To stabilise markets;
4. To secure availability of supplies; and
5. To provide consumers with food at reasonable prices.

The CAP recognised the need to take account of the social structure of agriculture and of the structural and natural disparities between the various agricultural regions and to effect the appropriate adjustments by degrees. The aim of the Common Agricultural Policy (CAP) is to provide farmers with a reasonable standard of living, consumers with quality food at fair prices and to preserve rural heritage. By 1962, three major principles had been established to guide the CAP: market unity, community preference and financial solidarity. Since then, the CAP has been a central element in the European institutional system. It represents 48 percent of the EU's budget. This policy covers cereals, rice, potatoes, oil, fodder, milk, milk products, honey, etc. as part of the common agricultural policy price intervention.

The CAP offered subsidies and systems guaranteeing high prices to farmers, providing incentives for them to produce more. Financial assistance was provided for the restructuring of farming, for example by subsidising farm investment in favour of farm growth and management of technology skills so that they were adapted to the economic and social conditions at the time. Certain measures were introduced in the form of help for early retirement, for professional training and in favour of less favoured regions.

Many important changes to the CAP were already made in the 1980s but, above all at the beginning of the 1990s. Production limits helped reduce surpluses (milk quotas in 1983). A new emphasis was then placed on environmentally sound farming. Farmers had to look more to the market place, while receiving direct income aid, and to respond to the public's changing priorities (MacSharry Reform of 1992). This shift of emphasis, which was effected in 1999 (the "Agenda 2000" reform) and which promotes the competitiveness of European agriculture, also included a major new element—a rural development policy encouraging many rural initiatives while also helping farmers to restructure their farms, to diversify and to improve their product marketing. A ceiling was put on the budget to reassure taxpayers that CAP costs would not run out of control.

Finally, in 2003, a further fundamental reform was agreed. The 1999 Berlin Council reformed the CAP further, under Agenda 2000. These reforms, which came into effect in March 2003, replaced production subsidies with a scheme of direct payments linked directly to compliance with a set of standards on food safety, animal rights and environmental concerns. The most fundamental new element is the new 'Single Farm Payment' that replaces the vast array of existing direct payment schemes. The key thrust of the reforms has therefore been to break the link between subsidies and production, so that farmers produce for the market and not to gain financial support.

CAP has also focussed on the development of rural communities in the member states. Agro-environment schemes have been supported by the EU since they were introduced in by the CAP reforms of 1992. They encourage farmers to provide environmental services that go beyond following good agricultural practice and basic legal standards have been consolidated in one specific axis of rural development policy for the period 2007-2013. [12] Aids may be paid to farmers who sign up voluntarily to agro-environment commitments for a minimum period of 5 years. Offering financial assistance to farmers who agree to adapt their agricultural practices, in particular by reducing the number of inputs they use or the number of animals per hectare of land, leaving field boundaries uncultivated, creating ponds or other features, or by planting trees and hedges and so going beyond conventional good farming methods.

The current areas that are issues of reform in EU agriculture are: lowering prices, ensuring food safety and quality, and guaranteeing stability of farmers' incomes. Other issues are environmental pollution, animal welfare, and finding alternative income opportunities for farmers.

UK and the CAP: The United Kingdom is one of the signatories to the CAP. In 1984, the British Government led by

Margaret Thatcher got the annual UK rebates, whereby, the UK would contribute less to the CAP than expected. Under this, UK is also to receive fewer funds as the distribution of money is based on the land area of the country. The perception in UK is that whilst UK would have to pay a substantial amount of money to the CAP as part of its obligation; on the other hand, France and Germany would benefit from the subsidies as they get a high sum of money due to their greater land area. CAP costs UK taxpayers about £ 107 each a year and totals £ 47.6 bn, almost half the EU annual budget. [13] Successive Labour and Conservative governments have argued that it is inefficient, bloated and anti-competitive. However, their stance is diluted by other countries which are against any reduction of the price cap. UK has argued that the benefits of the CAP regime have always gone to the rich farmers.

Hence, the UK has been vocal against their support to the CAP. Their main contention lies on the fact that they have to pay a substantial amount of money as contribution to the CAP and in return they will get a very paltry amount due to having less area in agriculture.

Agencies Working for Food Security

DEFRA: The Department of Environment, Food and Rural Affairs, commonly known as DEFRA is the government department responsible for environmental protection, food production and standards, agriculture, fisheries and rural communities in the United Kingdom. DEFRA was formed in June 2001 when the Ministry of Agriculture, Fisheries and Food (MAFF) was merged with part of the Department of Environment, Transport and the Regions (DETR) and with a small part of the Home office. The department was created after the perceived failure of MAFF to deal adequately with an outbreak of foot and mouth disease.

The primary objective and work of DEFRA is given out as thus, "The Government believes that we need to protect the environment for future generations, make our economy more environmentally sustainable, and improve our quality of life and well-being. We also believe that much more needs to be done to support the farming industry, protect biodiversity and encourage sustainable food production". [14]

DEFRA has a budget of just less than 3 billion pounds and is primarily focussed with the work in England. They also associate themselves with the administrations of Wales, Scotland and Northern Ireland. The department is also a leading light in negotiations with the European Union and other international players.

DEFRA has a wide agenda, covering policy and legislation making, and the department also works with other agencies to deliver policies in areas such as:

- Natural environment, biodiversity, plants and animals.
- Sustainable development and the green economy.
- Food, farming and fisheries.
- Animal health and welfare.
- Environmental protection and pollution control.
- Rural communities and issues.

DEFRA also strives to support and develop farming in Britain and also promote and encourage sustainable food production. The DEFRA business plan includes helping to enhance the competitiveness and resilience of the whole food chain, including farms and the fish industry, to ensure a secure, environmentally sustainable and healthy supply of food with improved standards of animal welfare.

Sustainable Farming and Food Implementation Group: The Sustainable Farming and Food Implementation Group was set up on the recommendation of the Sustainable Farming and Food Strategy (SFFS) paper, which was published by DEFRA in December 2002

The role of the Implementation Group is to: [15]

- Agree and prioritise the issues identified by the industry group, other stakeholders and public sector to determine those most critical to the future success of the food and farming industry.

- Agree the actions to be taken, either by individual delivery partners or collectively to address the priority issues identified, incorporating partner and stakeholder priorities and resources into the assessment.
- Develop proposals for specific projects, where mainstream delivery will not address the priority issues, identifying the most appropriate delivery partners and funding streams.
- Ensure partners and stakeholders are fully briefed on each other's current and future work programmes in the region.
- Influence policy development both in the region and nationally to ensure the needs of sustainable food and farming businesses are met.
- Advise the industry group on both the availability, appropriateness and availability of resources to support interventions by the public sector.
- Provide the link to the national sustainable food and farming group.
- Provide a link with other public sector groups and organisations in the region.

Foresight Land Use Futures Project: The Foresight Project commenced a project in 2008 to explore how UK land use could change over the next 50 years and what society's future needs and values for land might be. Sponsored jointly by the departments responsible for cities, planning, housing, environment and rural affairs (DCLG and DEFRA), it aims to support the development of forward-looking, integrated land use strategies.

The main agenda of this project is to explore how governance arrangements for the land use might be improved to deliver a long-term inter-generational sustainability. The chief interest lies in who makes the decisions regarding land use and management; who influences them or who has an opportunity to do so, how decisions are made; and at what scale they are made (e.g. farm, catchment, landscape, local authority, region or nation). They also seek evidence on decisions taken at inappropriate scales and which might have a disproportionate impact on land use outcomes, on alternative approaches, and on barriers to the reshaping of governance. [16]

Food Chain Emergency Liaison Group: The Food Chain Emergency Liaison Group was established to bring together a broad constituency of key representatives from the food and grocery industry, government, trade bodies and relevant agencies to discuss and act upon crisis management issues. The group is a communications hub for the food and grocery industry on crisis matters and has provided information to government and the security services.

Farming for the Future Programme: On July 9, 2009, Hilary Benn launched a leaflet titled, "The Future of Our Farming", a leaflet for the farming community outlining the shared aims for and actions towards achieving a thriving and environmentally sustainable farming industry". This leaflet served as the predecessor to the Farming for the Future Programme.

This programme is designed to contribute to delivering the vision for English farming in 2020. It is envisaged that the farming sector will be:

- Profitable in the marketplace, continuing to produce the majority of the food we consume.
- Making a positive net environmental contribution, notably in respect of climate change and also more widely.
- Managing the landscape and the natural assets that underlie it.

The programme is aimed at delivering the behaviour change necessary to realise that vision, at the same time setting a new direction for the relationship between Government and the industry. The programme is made up of the following work streams: [17]

- Strategy and stakeholder engagement.
- The skills for farming project.
- Agricultural industry resilience.
- Climate change mitigation.
- Anaerobic digestion.

- UK/China collaboration on sustainable agriculture.
- Climate change adaptation.
- Nutrient management.
- The environmental management systems project.
- Cross compliance (including set-aside).
- Campaign for the farmed environment.

International Relations

Grants to Developing Nations: The increase in food prices is having a substantial effect on food security in developing countries, in particular in countries that are net importers of food, where food accounts for a significant proportion of people's expenditure. The urban poor in developing countries spend a higher share (up to 60 percent) of their income on food (compared to 15 percent spent by the poorest 10 percent of the population in the UK). Food shortages and high food prices have resulted in rioting and civil unrest in a number of countries (e.g. Cameroon, Niger, Mozambique, Cote d'Ivoire, Burkina Faso, Senegal, Haiti and Egypt).

To help developing countries, the UK Government announced a £ 585 million assistance package. [18] This included, amongst other things, a further £ 30 million in response to the appeal from the World Food Programme and £ 54 million for social protection in Ethiopia, Mozambique and Bangladesh and £ 6.5 million for food aid and agricultural inputs for Afghanistan. The Government has also committed £ 400 million for agricultural research over the next five years.

Agriculture and Climate Change: In the present, uncertain times, agriculture will need to adapt to changes in climate. It will need to be ready to changes in temperature and rainfall, resulting changes to water availability, flood risk, incidence of storms, and increased likelihood of pests, locusts and diseases. [19]

UK is showing leadership within the EU and beyond by promoting the role of agriculture in both climate change mitigation and adaptation. The UK is working with key EU Members States to build consensus on the priorities for action, and is working bilaterally with countries such as China to help them reduce greenhouse gas emissions from agriculture. The UK is also working with China to help them understand the impacts of climate change on agriculture and develop appropriate responses. One UK-China bilateral project has recently developed the first adaptation policy framework for agriculture in any of the Chinese regions. In addition, the UK co-chairs an agriculture subcommittee of the Methane to Markets Partnership which aims to increase the production of renewable energy from anaerobic digestion in the farming sector internationally.

The EU has committed to a 20 percent reduction in greenhouse gas emissions by 2020, rising to 30 percent if there is an international agreement. In the UK, the Climate Change Bill is currently going through Parliament. It is the first of its kind in the world, setting long-term targets to reduce the UK's emissions. [20]

Impact of Sub-prime and Euro Zone Crises: The world and especially the UK economy underwent difficult times, with the recession, thanks to the sub-prime crisis. The United Kingdom was also affected by the recession with a huge increase in unemployment figures and inflation. The Euro zone crisis has also affected the imports and export of commodities, thanks to the perceived instability of the euro and the proximity and heavy economic, cultural and geographical ties of the United Kingdom with the main centres of the Euro zone crisis. Early 2008 saw the culmination of astonishing food price rise. The price spike brought an end to the long-term decline in relative price of food in the UK, and few expect it to return to past lows.

In conclusion, Britain being one of the most developed countries of the world has focussed on the problems of food security substantially through the ages. Even though UK is a signatory to the CAP, yet it faced the brunt of the global economic recession as it spiralled into a full blown agricultural crisis with prices increasing by the day. The Common Agricultural Policy, which is one of the most important treaties of the European Union, has been a bone of contention for the UK government. For the UK, the very fact that land area is the key criterion in allocation of funds through the CAP is a major bane. Being one of the largest economies of the EU, UK is expected to contribute heavily to the CAP. But, in return, UK does not get a good amount as part of subsidies. The UK now has DEFRA which takes care of looking at the needs of the agriculture sector in the territory. The government invests heavily on ensuring that the agricultural industry of UK is safeguarded from external threats.

Endnotes

1. P.M.A. Bourke, "Irish Agricultural Production: Its Volume and Structure", *Journal of the Statistical and Social Inquiry Society of Ireland,* XX, 1959: 1-19.
2. David W. Miller, "Ireland's Great Famine: Interdisciplinary Perspectives", *Journal of Interdisciplinary History,* 39, 1, 2008: 114-115.
3. Milne. L. and M. Milne, "There's Poison All Around Us Now: The Dangers in the Use of Pesticides Are Vividly Pictured by Rachel Carson", *New York Times Book Review*, September 23, 1962, 26.
4. P.D. Smith et al., "Agriculture in Climate Change Mitigation" Contribution of Working Group III to the Fourth Assessment Report of the Intergovernmental Panel on Climate Change, New York: Cambridge University Press, 2007, 22.
5. "Reducing Obesity and Improving Diet," Department of Health, UK, available at: http://www.dh.gov.uk/health/category/policy-areas/public-health/maternity-public-health/healthystart, accessed on June 12, 2013.
6. J. Dennis, "Influence of Corn Laws on Manufacturers and Commerce: A Letter", London: Rivington Longman and Co., 1841.
7. "An Abbreviated UK-EU Agricultural Policy History", Newcastle University, available at: http://www.staff.ncl.ac.uk/david.harvey/AEF372/History.html, accessed on November 6, 2012.

8. "Memorandum by the Minister of Agriculture and Fisheries", Britannic Majesty's Government, available at: http://filestore.nationalarchives.gov.uk/pdfs/small/cab-129-4-cp-273.pdf, accessed on November 6, 2012.
9. H. Frankel, "Economic Changes in British Agriculture: 1959-1964" London: Oxford University Press, 1964, 210-212.
10. "Legislation", Natural England, available at: http://www.naturalengland.org.uk/ourwork/regulation/wildlife/policyandlegislation/legislation.aspx, accessed on June 13, 2013.
11. Treaty establishing the European Economic Community, 1957.
12. Terry Marsden and Roberta Sonnino, "Rural Development and the Regional State: Denying Multifunctional Agriculture in the UK", *Journal of Rural Studies,* 24, 2008: 422-431.
13. W. Moyer, "Agricultural Policy Reform: Politics and Process in the EU and the US in 1990's", *Journal of Rural Studies,* 2002: 42.
14. Home Department of Environment, Food and Rural Affairs, available at: http://www.defra.gov.uk, accessed on June 2, 2013.
15. "Sustainable and Food Strategy Sub-Group Terms of Reference", East of England Rural Forum, available at: http://www.eerf.org.uk/sffs-termsofref.shtml, accessed on June 12, 2013.
16. "Land Use Futures", Department for Business Innovation and Skills, available at: http://www.bis.gov.uk/foresight/our-work/projects/published-projects/land-use-futures/reports-and-publications, accessed on June 12, 2013.
17. "Sustainable Agriculture: Future of Farming in the UK", UK Agriculture, available at: http://www.ukagriculture.com/farming_today/sustainable_agricultu, accessed on June 12, 2013.
18. "A Preliminary Analysis of European Assistance to Agriculture in Sub-Saharan Africa", Imperial College London.
19. "Severe Weather and UK Food Chain Resilience", Global Food Security, available at: http://www.foodsecurity.ac.uk/assets/pdfs/frp-severe-weather-uk-food-chain-resilience.pdf, accessed on June 3, 2013.
20. D. John Shaw, "Global Food and Agricultural Instructions", London: Routledge, 2008, 128.

15

Vietnam: Reunification of Vietnam and Collective Agriculture

Suktika Banerjee and Maulika Hegde

Economy of Vietnam

Vietnam economy is one of the developing countries with the World Bank calling it a development success story. Vietnam has transformed with a per capita income below US$ 100, to a lower middle income country with per capita income of US$ 1,130 by the end of 2010. The poverty rate has fallen from 58 percent in 1993 to 14.5 percent in 2008, with improvement in most indicators of welfare. Vietnam has attained five of its ten original Millennium Development Goal targets and is well on the way to attaining two more by 2015. The Socio-Economic Development Strategy (SEDS) 2011-2020 emphasises on "structural reforms, environmental sustainability, social equity, and emerging issues of macroeconomic stability. The overall goal for Vietnam is to lay the foundations for a modern, industrialized society by 2020. [1] Vietnam's economy expects to promote liberalization while also preserving the socialist one party status", [2]

Challenges

Economic: Vietnam appointed its sovereign credit ratings adviser Standard Chartered after it was downgraded by the three main credit rating agencies several notches below the investment grade—Fitch Ratings, Moody's Investors Service and Standard & Poor's—because of soaring inflation, pressure on the balance of payments and the collapse of Vinashin, a heavily indebted state-owned shipbuilder in 2010. Economists say Vietnam's central bank and finance ministry are far less transparent than their regional peers and that shortage of data and communication, dissuades potential investors". [3]

Inflation: Domestic prices for rice, the main staple food in the country, have been rising since July 2010 and reached record levels in November 2011. Export prices of Vietnam rice (Ho Chi Minh 25 percent broken), also rose from the beginning of July 2011 following the general trend in the international market but the increase is less marked than for domestic prices. The general inflation eased slightly but Vietnam still struggles with the fast rising prices; the consumer price inflation in August 2011, a year-on-year increase, was estimated at 20 percent. The declining purchasing power of the poor is expected to affect food security of the most vulnerable people.

Agriculture: Heavy rains since July 2011 and downpours in October caused severe flooding in the central region of the country. In spite of this localized flood damage to the summer/autumn paddy crop, the annual aggregate production in 2011 was estimated by the Ministry of Agriculture at a record level at 42 million tonnes (equivalent to 28 million tonnes of milled rice), or 5 percent higher than the previous year's bumper harvest. There has been a steady increase in rice production in Vietnam over the past several years. Vietnam is the world's second-largest rice exporter following Thailand. With the expectation of a good production in 2011, the 2012 rice exports at 7.3 million tonnes were forecast to rise.

In urbanised areas, farmers gave up farming because of narrowing land, low income, hardship and labour scarcity. Farming service providers were also affected—they chose new non-agriculture jobs.

Vietnam aims to reduce the percentage of people working in the agricultural sector from the current 70 percent to 30 percent of the total workforce by 2020, aggregating to 19 million people. The Programme on Vocational Training for Rural Workers through 2020, which was approved in 2009 and was the largest project ever to target rural workers, was expected to make a difference as it mobilised efforts by the government, enterprises, scientists and the community to ensure sustainable development. Land management and re-training for people in suburban areas to adapt to urbanisation were crucial to ensuring urban sustainability.

Role of International Organisations

There are a large number of UN Organisations currently working in Vietnam. The new One Plan [4] is the framework for cooperation programmes of UN agencies and IOM in Vietnam over the next five years. The One Plan outlines three broad focus areas where the UN and the Government of Vietnam will jointly implement work in the period from 2012 to 2016.

This includes supporting the Government to achieve inclusive, equitable and sustainable growth; access to quality essential services and social protection; and enhanced governance and participation. Work in these areas responds to Vietnam's priorities, as outlined in the 2011-2020 Socio-Economic Development Strategy [5] and the 2011-2015 Socio-Economic Development Plan. [6] The United Nations Country Team (UNCT) in Vietnam consists of all planning framework for all the UN organizations in Vietnam participating in the One Plan UN Initiative. The UN agencies funds programmes in Vietnam. The UNCT works "as one" to support Vietnam in achieving the Millennium Development Goals (MDGs) and Vietnam's own National Development Goals through a people-centred, rights-based approach to development as outlined in the One Plan.

World Food Programme: The World Food Programme (WFP) of the United Nations is mandated to combat global hunger, which afflicts one out of every seven people on earth. "Vietnam has now reached a level of national food security where we at WFP are confident we can close our programme here and devote our food aid to people who are in greater need, said Vietnam country director Julian Lefevre [7]...Vietnam can feed its people...but there are far too many other nations that cannot, and it is those that we need to help". The agency has been Vietnam's largest grant donor of the entire UN system, investing approximately US$ 500 million of food and non-food aid in the country between 1974 and 2000. Vietnam is one of the 23 countries to 'graduate' from WFP over the past five years to achieve food security and economic progress that enables WFP to close its office there. In the case of Vietnam, the return to food self-sufficiency and productivity results from a fundamental change of policy direction in the late 1980s. The achievements are reflected in a string of remarkable statistics.

Vietnam has progressed from being a significant importer of rice in the early 1980s to the world's second-largest rice exporter.

Poverty has been reduced from more than 70 percent in the mid-1980s to about 37 percent in 2000. Average per capita income has more than doubled over the same period. Per capita food availability has increased from 190 kilograms/annum in 1988 to over 400 kilograms/annum in 1999. Furthermore, Vietnam is the second largest exporter of rice in the world and the second biggest producer of robusta coffee in the world as of 2011. WFP has stated that they would continue to maintain contact with Vietnam and offer them help as and when required.

International Fund for Agricultural Development: The International Fund for Agricultural Development (IFAD), a specialized agency of the United Nations, was established as an international financial institution in 1977 as one of the major outcomes of the 1974 World Food Conference. IFAD is dedicated to eradicating rural poverty in developing countries. IFAD's goal is to empower poor rural women and men in developing countries to achieve higher incomes and improved food security. There are five ongoing IFAD funded projects in Vietnam. [8]

- Project for the Economic Empowerment of Ethnic Minorities in Poor Communes of DakNong Province.
- Agriculture, Farmers and Rural Areas Support Project in Gia

Lai, Ninh Thuan and Tuyen Quang Provinces.

- Pro-Poor Partnerships for Agro forestry Development Project.
- Developing Business with the Rural Poor Programme.
- Programme for Improving Market Participation of the Poor in Ha Tinh and TraVinh Provinces.

In 2007, IFAD and the Government of Vietnam developed a country strategic opportunities programme (COSOP). The COSOP targets the uplanned areas and focuses on creating links between remote production areas and markets and ensuring the participation of poor rural people. Interventions are tailored to reach ethnic minority groups and women.

Food and Agricultural Organisation (FAO): The Food and Agricultural organization is a specialized UN agency that leads international efforts to fight worldwide hunger. Serving both developed and developing countries, it is also a member of the Group.

The overall objective is to enhance the capacity of the agricultural sector to respond to the challenges and opportunities posed by the new market environment. Within this mandate, it seeks to promote new livelihood options via diversified commercial agriculture, income-generating strategies, introduction to modern technologies and household food security for the rural communities whose main economic activity is agriculture.

To date, FAO has been involved in the implementation of more than 400 projects in the areas of sustainable agricultural development, food security and nutrition, forestry and fisheries.

As a result, the scope of the current work is extensive, ranging from highly pathogenic avian influenza (HPAI) control and prevention, integrated pest management (IPM) and farmer field school, the control of other animal diseases, national capacity building in food quality and safety, sustainable forest management, aquaculture management and conservation, emergency relief to the support for agriculture-related studies and policy-oriented research. The year 2008 marked the 30th anniversary of FAO's presence in Vietnam. Despite the contribution to Vietnam's development in the past three decades, FAO acknowledges that there is still considerable work to be done, given the emerging challenges and increasing demands in this period of transition. Certainly, Vietnam's economic success accompanied by rapid urbanisation should not overshadow the importance of the rural sector in which 70 percent of the population reside and their livelihoods are dependent on agriculture.

Some of the projects that are and have been carried out by the FAO in Vietnam related to food security are as follows: [9]

- Food safety information, education and communication.
- Capacity building for the food inspection system in Vietnam.
- Integrated nutrition and food security strategies for children and vulnerable groups in Vietnam.

World Health Organisation: The World Health Organization (WHO) is a specialized agency of the United Nations (UN) that is concerned with international public health and is the leading international authority on health matters. Eliminating hunger and malnutrition is technically feasible. The means are there.

The challenge lies in generating the requisite political will, developing realistic policies and taking concerted actions nationally and internationally. The nutritional status of Vietnam's population has improved significantly during the past two decades. The food security situation in the country is better than ever and severe child malnutrition has been reduced substantially.

The programmes for controlling micronutrient deficiencies (iron, vitamin A, iodine) have been making progress. WHO advocates that nutrition and food safety should be placed higher on the development agenda. WHO supports the Ministry of Health and the National Institute for Nutrition and other key stakeholders in their work to develop policy to improve the nutritional situation in Vietnam.

WHO also provides technical support to nutrition

activities, particularly those targeting women of reproductive age and young children.

Millennium Development Goals (MDGs): Vietnam has made very impressive progress towards achieving the MDGs and has been successful in meeting some of them—such as MDG 1 on eradication of extreme hunger and poverty—way ahead of the 2015 deadline.

"From a poverty rate of 58.1 percent in 1990, the country has successfully reduced poverty to an estimated rate of 14.5 percent in 2008—a reduction of 75 percent. The food poverty rate has been reduced by more than two-thirds, from 24.9 percent in 1993 to 6.9 percent in 2008". [10]

World Bank: The World Bank is a vital source of financial and technical assistance to developing countries around the world. Vietnam currently receives over US$ 5 billion a year from more than 30 bilateral and multilateral donor institutions.

The World Bank has been able to mobilize additional resources for Vietnam through co-financing or parallel financing arrangements for various investment and development policy operations.

On the December 30, 2009, The State Bank of Vietnam and the World Bank signed the credit agreement for the WB's biggest ever loan to Vietnam. The approved loan was a US$ 500 million development policy loan that supported a program of public investment reforms in Vietnam. [11]

It was also the first loan given to Vietnam by IBRD (International Bank for Reconstruction and Development) showing that Vietnam was a step closer to its goal of reaching middle-income status by 2010—however, Vietnam will continue to take help from the IDA for an indefinite period of time.

International Rice Research Institute: IRRI, or the International Rice Research Institute, is a non-profit independent research and training organization. Since 1963, Vietnam and IRRI have enjoyed a long, fruitful history of collaboration, starting with the release of IR8 in both the northern and southern delta rice-growing areas. Through IRRI and Vietnam partnerships, Vietnamese farmers are now able to maximize the full potential of the high-yielding rice varieties being grown in the Mekong and Red River Deltas. Vietnam placed high value on their collaboration with IRRI. From their initial areas of collaboration, Vietnam and IRRI are expanding their partnership to include rice production in the upland ecosystem, environmental issues, and grain quality.

IRRI and Vietnam have been working together since 1963. About 70 percent of rice planted in Vietnam traces its roots to this partnership. The first IRRI variety, IR8, is known as "Honda Rice" in Vietnam because many Vietnamese farmers could buy a Honda motorcycle with the extra income they made from growing it. 2,979 types of rice from Vietnam are conserved at IRRI's International Rice Gene bank. [12]

Colombo Plan for Cooperative Economic and Social Development in Asia and the Pacific: The Colombo Plan is a regional organisation, consisting of member countries in the Asia-Pacific Region, and promotes collective inter-governmental effort to strengthen economic and social development in the region. The Colombo Plans activities .primarily focus on human resources development. [13] South Vietnam joined in 1951 and on July 2, 1976 was succeeded by Socialist Republic of Vietnam which withdrew in 1978. Vietnam was a provisional member from November 5, 2001 to November 18, 2003 until it was accepted in 2004.

International Treaties

Goods and services exports now constitute around 70 percent of Vietnam's GDP, up from a 30 percent share recorded in the mid-1990s. Vietnam's major exports include crude oil, textiles, footwear, sea food, timber products, rice, rubber, coffee, cashews, pepper and coal. Its major merchandise export destinations in 2009 were the United States, Japan, China and Switzerland. Vietnam's major imports are machinery and spare parts, refined petroleum products, urea, steel ingots, pharmaceuticals, textile and garment inputs, plastics and chemicals. The top three sources of imports in 2009 were China, Japan and the Republic of Korea.

US-Vietnam Bilateral Treaty: The US-Vietnam Trade Council has worked to promote economic and political normalization between the two counties since its founding in 1989. On December 10, 2001 after the U.S. Congress and the Vietnamese National Assembly voted for its approval, the U.S.-Vietnam Trade Agreement went into force. [14]

Vietnam has agreed to open up the right to import and export for the first time. It will allow: (i) all Vietnamese companies the right to trade immediately; (ii) all U.S. invested companies the right to trade, in connection with their operations, immediately; (iii) U.S. invested companies the right to trade any products (subject to some exceptions) in 3 years; and (iv) U.S. persons to form joint ventures for the purpose of trading, in three years, with a maximum 49 percent share; in six years, the maximum U.S. share is 51 percent. There are limited product exceptions to these rights, where the phase-in period for trading rights is longer.

MFN Treatment: Vietnam commits to Most Favoured Nation tariff treatment on all U.S. imports (it imposes a 50 percent tariff surcharge on countries with whom it does not have MFN relations).

Tariff Cuts: Vietnam has agreed to cut tariffs (typical cut is by one-third to one-half) on a broad range of products of interest to U.S. exporters, including toiletries, film, air conditioners and refrigerators, electrical motors, valves, mobile phones, pagers, video games, lamb, cheese, potatoes, tomatoes, onions, garlic, other vegetables, grapes, apples and pears, other fresh fruits, certain flours, soybeans, vegetable oils, prepared meats and fish, pasta, fruit juices.

Non-tariff Measures: Vietnam has agreed to eliminate all quantitative restrictions on a range of industrial and agricultural products (e.g., auto parts, citrus, beef), over a period of 3-7 years, depending on the product.

International Food Security Treaty (IFST): The International Food Security Treaty is a proposed international law initiative which would place the human right of freedom from hunger under the security of enforceable international law. Based on existing international covenants, the IFST aims to establish enforceable international law, guaranteeing the right to be free from hunger, and to oblige countries to establish their own related national laws. The IFST has been recognized as a crucial missing link in the world's efforts to eliminate hunger by leading figures in the United Nations, anti-hunger organizations, the U.S. Congress and court system, and national religious groups. The four essential principles of this treaty are as under:

- Provide access to a minimum standard of nutrition.
- Contribute to a world food reserve and resource centre.
- Establish and enforce law.
- Support United Nations food security enforcement.

This treaty has not been ratified and is still in the formulation stage, however the ratification of this treaty will deal with establishing an enforceable international legal guarantee of the right to be free from hunger, and oblige governments to establish and implement their own related national laws. The treaty specifies legal responsibilities nations share to prevent starvation and malnutrition, and associated monitoring and enforcement mechanisms. This will help the nations to develop better and faster.

WTO Agreement on Agriculture and Food Security: The Agreement on Agriculture is an international treaty of the World Trade Organization. Four main portions of the Agreement include: the agreement on agriculture itself; the concessions and commitments members are to undertake on market access, domestic support and export subsidies; the agreement on sanitary and phytosanitary measures; and the Ministerial Decision concerning least developed and net food importing developing countries.

Overall, the results of the negotiations provide a framework for the long-term reform of agricultural trade and domestic policies over the years to come. It makes a decisive move towards the objective of increased market orientation in agricultural trade.

The rules governing agricultural trade are strengthened which will lead to improved predictability and stability for importing and exporting countries alike. [15]

Vietnam being a member of the WTO is a party to this Agreement. The following has been done by Vietnam in respect to this agreement.

In the area of market access, Vietnam would apply border protection for agricultural products in a manner consistent with WTO Agreements (in particular with Article 4 of the AoA).

In the area of export subsidies, Vietnam has changed its outlooks, as before 1998, the Vietnamese government did not award any export subsidies to agricultural products.

Largest component of export subsidies are provided to rice export enterprises at the rate of VND 180 per US$ 1 of export value (equivalent to 1.2 percent of the exported value). The second largest export subsidy component was interest rate support to assist export enterprises to purchase coffee at the rate of VND 220 per US$ 1 of export value (equivalent to 1.46 percent). [16]

Other than these, three very important treaties are related to food security. Vietnam is party to the International Covenant on Economic, Social and Cultural Rights. Article 11 recognises the right of everyone to an adequate standard of living. This includes, but is not limited to, the right to adequate food, clothing, housing, and the continuous improvement of living conditions. It also creates an obligation on parties to work together to eliminate world hunger.

The right to adequate food, also referred to as the right to food, is interpreted as requiring 'the availability of food in a quantity and quality sufficient to satisfy the dietary needs of individuals, free from adverse substances, and acceptable within a given culture". [17] This must be accessible to all, implying an obligation to provide special programmes for the vulnerable. The right to adequate food also implies a right to water.

Legislative Framework for Agriculture

Despite many challenges of natural calamities such as droughts, storms and flooding, widespread disease and unfavourable market changes, especially in the international market, Vietnam tried to maintain their focus on agriculture and rural development by issuing policies to create enhanced motivation for mobilizing internal resources, expanding international cooperation relations, etc. so that the agricultural and rural development sector could manage its remarkable development i.e. a more mechanized agriculture sector.

Reunification of Vietnam and Collective Agriculture: When Vietnam achieved independence from France in 1954, the Geneva Accords divided it into two countries with opposing ideologies—the Democratic Republic of Vietnam in the north adopted a socialist ideology influenced by China and the Soviet Union, and the Republic of Vietnam in the south pursued a capitalist ideology influenced by the United States. After the unification of the North and the South in 1975, the Vietnamese economic policies focused on the nationalization and centralization of the national economy, and prioritized heavy industry. However, the wars waged against Kampuchea (1978) and China (1979) led to the shortage of foreign exchange, falling production, and rising inflation. Rice production in Vietnam was stagnant in the 1960s and 1970s.

During these periods, the socialist regime in the North reinforced the collective production system through enlarged agricultural cooperatives under the state control. Post-reunification of Vietnam in 1975, rural collectivism was extended to the south part of Vietnam as well with little success; only 25 percent of farm households belonged to a co-operative in 1980, much lower than the figure of almost 97 percent in north Vietnam. To correct this, renovation and rehabilitation of large scale irrigation systems has taken place in both the Red River and Mekong River Deltas.

Agricultural Policy Reforms of 1980s: Following reunification in 1975, Vietnam entered a period of central planning. Collectivization of farms and state owned enterprises were well established by 1980. Agriculture in the period up to 1981 was exclusively based on the collectivised system wherein village level cooperatives organized the labour allocation and distribution of external inputs and outputs.

Falling agricultural output in the late 1970s led to the introduction of a system of household contracts in 1981, relinquishing control of at least part of the factors of production to the household level. Up to 1981, the cooperative allocated all land, labour and essentially acted as the representatives of the central government; organized into production brigades, consisting of a neighbourhood of twenty to forty households, setting production quotas and planning future targets.

Doi Moi Reforms: In 1986, Vietnam adopted a policy of renovation (doimoi) in an effort to make it a market economy. Legal reforms had been a key component of this policy. It aimed at last transforming Vietnam's overall economy from a centrally planned to a decentralised market economy. It was characterised by a system based on market competition, private individual farms, improvement in foreign relations and the promotion of agricultural exports. The price controls over rice were abolished in line with the market liberalization and, at the same time, restrictions on internal rice trade began to be lifted.

These measures included cutting government subsidies for social services and basic consumer goods as well as other measures to reduce the already high unemployment rate. The problem facing the country at that time was as to how to finance an economically viable system of health care in a country of few resources, while at the same time remaining true to the principle of equity. There were ideological doubts about moving towards a market-based economy as well as concern about the social impact of the transformation. Decollectivization in the early phase of doimoi had an important positive impact on broad-based growth and equity. The advent of the doimoi reforms and the relative equality of the distribution of land holdings enabled so many rural households to broadly participate in the process of economic growth. Households made immediate productive use of the assets that were devolved to them in the process of decollectivization.

Endnotes

1. "Vietnam: An Overview", available at: http://www.worldbank.org/en/country/vietnam/overview, accessed on March 31, 2012.
2. Carol V. Rose, "The 'New' Law and Development Movement in the Post-Cold War Era: A Vietnam Case Study", Blackwell Publishing on behalf of the *Law and Society Association Law and Society Review* , Vol. 32, No. 1, 1998, pp. 93-140.
3. Ben Bland, "A Job for StanChart: Upgrade Vietnam", *Economic Times,* March 22, 2012.
4. "UN Initiative in Vietnam", available at: http://www.un.org.vn/en/the-one-un-initiative-in-viet-nam-mainmenu-265/one-plan/2110-one-plan-2012-2016.htnl.
5. "Vietnam's Socio-economic Development Strategy for the Year 2011-12", available at: http://www.economica.vn/Portals/0/MauBieu/1d3f7ee0400e421 52bdcaa439bf62686.pdf.
6. "UN Vietnam Annual Report 2011", available at: http://mdtf.undp.org/document/download/9016.
7. "Economic Success in Vietnam Allows WEP to Close Up", available at: http://reliefweb.int/report/viet-nam/economic-success-vietnam-allows-wfp-close-doors.
8. "IFAD Rural Survey in Vietnam", available at: www.ifad.org/governance/replenishment/briefs/vietnam.pdf.
9. "FAO Projects in Vietnam", available at: http://www.fao.org.vn.

10. "MDG-1 Factsheet for Vietnam", available at: http://www.undp.org.vn/digitalAssets/24/24197_MDG1_Eng.pdf.
11. "World Bank, Vietnam Sign $ 500 Million Loan to Reform Public Investments", available at: http://go.worldbank.org/FWKMUEBAW0.
12. "Vietnamese President visits IRRI", available at: http://irri.org/news-events/media-releases/vietnamese-president-visits-irri.
13. The Colombo Plan Report.
14. "US-Vietnam Bilateral Investment Treaty", available at: http://www.usvtc.org/trade/bta.
15. "Agreement on Agriculture", available at: http://www.wto.org/english/docs_e/legal_e/ursum_e.htm#aAgreement, accessed on March 28, 2012.
16. "Agricultural Trade Policies and the Commitments of Vietnam to WTO in Agricultural Sector" Dao The Anh and Hoang Thanh Tung.
17. UN Economic and Social Council, available at: http://www.unhchr.ch/tbs/doc.nsf/(Symbol)/3d02758c707031d58025677f003b73b9?Opendocument.

Appendix

Appendix

Aanganwadi (Kindergarten) Schemes in Gujarat

Ranita Nagar

Aanganwadi schemes are a part of the ICDS schemes of the Central Government of India. It is a scheme that provides 'package services', that is, both pre-school facilities and food facilities to children between the ages 3-6 years. Also, as part of the scheme, health benefits are provided for pregnant and lactating mothers and nutrient supplements to newborn infants and children up to the age of 6 months. Kishori Shakti Yojana is for girls below 18 years of age.

This report is a review on the functioning of 40 aanganwadi schemes in urban Gandhinagar, rural Gandhinagar and urban/slum areas in Gandhinagar. As part of the research, responses were sought from three different groups of people that are involved with the aanganwadi scheme. The first set comprises of responses of the aanganwadi workers and staff, the second set is by parents sending their children to anganwadi schools and the third is from the village panchayat.

The questions raised range from the rate of attendance in the aanganwadi schools, the food provided, the responsibilities of the aanganwadi Worker, the most encouraging reason for parents to send their children and so on.

The hypothesis of this research is to understand how a state with a high GDP encompasses within itself high levels of malnutrition. During the period 2005-10, the real GDP growth in Gujarat was 11.3 percent as against 11 percent in Haryana, 9.6 percent in Bihar, 8.5 percent in Karnataka, 8.1 percent in Kerala and 7.4 percent each in Andhra Pradesh and Tamil Nadu. Gujarat has witnessed growth at the rate of 11 percent as compared to the all-India growth average of nine percent as stated by the report of Mckinsey & Co. The Human Development Report 2011, released by the Centre, finds Gujarat performing poorly on two key social indicators. 44.6 percent of children below the age of five suffer from malnutrition whereas nearly 70 percent of the children in the state suffer from anaemia. The results look graver when compared to states like Uttar Pradesh and Bihar which have fared better than Gujarat on malnutrition levels as reported by NDTV Correspondent in October 2011.

One of the parameters to unravel this dichotomy is to look into how well the aanganwadis in Gujarat are aligned to Supreme Court guidelines. These parameters go on to indicate the efficacy of aanganwadis in Gujarat. The findings are an overview of the report. The details of the report are beyond the scope of this paper.

The first part of the paper deals in brief with the aanganwadi's within the ambit of the ICDS and the various Supreme Court judgments on the working of the aanganwadis. In the subsequent part, an overview of the findings has been presented.

The survey opens up further areas of research. The findings of the survey do not support the findings of the Human Development Report (44.6 percent of children below the age of five suffer from malnutrition) which appear to be on the higher side. Further research will need to be taken up to substantiate the overview findings of this survey.

Funding

ICDS is a Centrally-sponsored scheme implemented through the State Governments/UT Administrations. Prior to 2005-06, 100 percent financial assistance for inputs (other than supplementary nutrition), was being provided by the Government of India. Since many States were not providing adequately for supplementary nutrition in view of resource constraints, it was decided in 2005-06 to extend support to States up to 50 percent of the financial norms or to support 50 percent of expenditure incurred by them on supplementary nutrition, whichever is less. From the financial year 2009-10, Government of India has modified the funding pattern of ICDS between the Centre and the States. The sharing pattern of supplementary nutrition in respect of North-eastern States between Centre and States has been changed from 50:50 to 90:10 ratio. So far as other States and UTs are concerned, the existing sharing pattern of 50:50 continues. However, for all other components of ICDS, the ratio has been modified to 90:10 (100 percent Central Assistance earlier).

The following are the Supreme Court guidelines regarding the aanganwadi:

Order dated November 28, 2001:

1. Each child up to 6 years of age is to get 300 calories and 8-10 grams of protein.
2. Each malnourished child to get 600 calories and 16-20 grams of protein.
3. Each pregnant woman, nursing mother and adolescent girl to get 500 calories and 20-25 grams of protein.
4. Every settlement is to have an aanganwadi.

Order dated April 29, 2004:

1. All 0-6 year old children, adolescent girls, pregnant women and nursing mothers shall receive supplementary nutrition for 300 days in a year.
2. The number of aanganwadis shall be increased from 6 lakh to 14 lakh.
3. The minimum norm for the provision of supplementary nutrition shall be increased to ₹ 2 per child per day.
4. All sanctioned aanganwadis shall be operationalised immediately.
5. All SC/ST hamlets shall have aanganwadis as early as possible, and hamlets with high SC/ST populations should receive priority in the placement of new aanganwadis.
6. All slums shall have aanganwadis.
7. Contractors shall not be used for the supply of supplementary nutrition.

8. The Central Government and States/UTs shall ensure that all amounts allocated are sanctioned in time so that there is no disruption in the feeding of children.
9. All State Governments/UTs shall put on their websites full data for the ICDS programme including where aanganwadis are operational, the number of beneficiaries category-wise, the funds allocated and used, and related matters.

Order dated December 13, 2006:

1. Government shall operationalize a minimum of 14 lakh aanganwadis by December 2008.
2. All SC/ST hamlets to be identified and given aanganwadis on "a priority basis".
3. Rural communities and urban slums will be specifically targeted.

Order dated July 9, 2007:

The backlog should be cleared immediately and the centres that have been sanctioned up to September 2006 should be made operational and functional by July 15, 2007 in the case of all States except the State of U.P., where the last date is fixed to be July 31, 2007. Those centres that have been sanctioned up to January 2007 should be made functional by September 30, 2007.

Order dated April 22, 2009:

This is a judgement regarding revision of nutritional and financial norms under supplementary nutrition component of the ICDS.

Implementation of Anganwadi Schemes in Gujarat

The aanganwadi schemes have been most successful in Gujarat. Aanganwadi schemes are meant for pre-school and nutritional facilities for adolescent and young children. However, in Gujarat, certain additional benefits are provided for a girl child.

The aanganwadi workers provide aid to open any nationalized bank or post office savings account with ₹ 500 to newborn girls born to families after August 15, 1997. While getting education, a sum of ₹ 300 to ₹ 1,000 scholarship is added to their account. Till the girl child becomes marriageable or up to 18 years, she is eligible to get the sum.

For adolescent girls (11-18 years), the Kishori Shakti Yojana (KSY) was launched in 2000-01 as part of the ICDS scheme. The Kishori Shakti Yojana is being implemented through aanganwadi centres in both rural and urban areas. The scheme aims at breaking the intergenerational life-cycle of nutritional and gender disadvantage and providing a supportive environment for self-development. The objectives of the scheme are to improve the nutritional and health status of girls in the age group of 11-18 years. A group of ten girls in a batch, who would be expectant mothers in future, are given health check up by aanganwadi centres. They are also provided required literacy and numeracy skills, stimulation to social exposure and knowledge to help them improve their decision-making skills. The adolescent girls are given home-based and vocational skills, awareness on health, hygiene, nutrition, family welfare, home management and child care guidance with measures to facilitate marrying after marriage age of 18 years. They are encouraged for productive and constructive activities for their own development as well as for their family.

Facilities are provided for the aanganwadi workers as well. The aanganwadi helpers' children (maximum 2) studying in class 9 to 12 are provided a scholarship of ₹ 300 every quarter.

The recent progress in the aanganwdai schemes in Gujarat is noteworthy.

In 2010, the state of Gujarat launched India's first micronutrient-mix food programme aiming to reach around 40 lakh beneficiaries through the framework of the state's aanganwadi network. Introducing micronutrient pre-mix for 44,000 aanganwadis across the state, the Gujarat government aims to improve the health of malnourished children with a diet that comprises a pre-mix of soybean, cereals and pulses containing 18-20 percent protein and 600 gram kilocalories.

In March 2010, Gujarat Chief Minister, Mr. Narendra Modi, dedicated five aanganwadi mobile vans purchased at the cost of ₹ 12,35,636 for the aanganwadis of Chota Udepur, Dahod, Narmada, Bharuch and Panchmahals. As many as 245 trained widows, for self-employment, were given away widow aid kits worth ₹ 12.25 lakh. For the first time in the country, aanganwadi workers were given cooker, gas connections and burners.

In September 2011, The United Nations Organization announced its support for the aanganwadi scheme of Gujarat. The Women and Child Welfare department in an integrated approach would look after the welfare of 10 lakh children of age group from six months to three years in 41,484 aanganwadis comprising of 18,500 villages in 225 talukas.

In Gujarat, 256 ICDS projects and 41,984 aanganwadi centres (AWCs) are in operation. In all, 17,87,895 children up to 6 years and 3,37,037 mothers are getting the benefits of the programme.

Analysis of the Anganwadi Centres

It is seen that the aangawadis employ two functionaries in all the centres, one being the aanganwadi worker and the other the aanganwadi helper.

The ratio of girls to boys is 29:35. Hence, there are greater number of male children who are availing the aanganwadi services. However, the difference in the number of female children and number of male children attending aanganwadis is not despairing. The ratio of students enrolled and attending is about 70 percent.

The timings followed are 10.30 in the morning to 3 in the afternoon, everyday. The timings of the classes do not conflict with the household chores or other personal responsibilities of the workers. The regularity of the children attending the aanganwadi classes is about 70 percent of enrolled children. Further, a trend is observed that while students attend classes on most days, rain poses a problem and attendance drops considerably on days when it is raining.

The children are taught alphabets, rhymes and few simple reading exercises are undertaken to make ICDS more joyful; various toys and topo cycles are also provided by state. All the study material is in Gujarati.

The aanganwadi teachers are punctual and regular. The teachers do not receive any support from the Government or any other NGO.

The children at the aanganwadi centres are provided with 2 meals a day.

The quality of the food provided is satisfactory. The quantity is sufficient. The food items that are supplied are varied in nature. The food is provided regularly.

In all the Centres, there is no access to elementary education. Primary education needs to be availed from the neighbouring areas.

The basic amenities are average. Cleanliness and maintenance of the aanganwadi centres is satisfactory. The centres are small in size, and accommodate 30 students on an average in that space which might prove to be a little difficult. Also, the cooking area and teaching area are not noticeably distinct. However, the available place is well maintained. The building is a pucca construction in 70 percent of the centres, which is in good condition, and reasonable hygiene is maintained. The rest 30 percent indicate that centres are run in temporary structures which create hardship for the students in summer, winter and rains. This factual situation could be ascertained because the visit was a surprise visit without any intimation to the concerned heads of the centres.

There are blackboards in most of the classrooms. However, supply of study material and chalks is poor. Light and fan facilities are available in 70 percent of the centres. Drinking water facilities are also present. However, there are not adequate toilet facilities.

The CDPO officer visits the aanganwadi once a month. The health officer does not have a fixed time period between visits, and his visits are irregular. The supervisor visits the aanganwadi once a month. The supplier visits the aanganwadi once a month. Hence, generally, supervision of aanganwadi centres and supply of materials happens on a monthly basis.

The medical facilities and supplies are not satisfactory. Only 40 percent of the centres have reported regular visits by the doctor, both for the children, adolescent girls and lactating mothers. This also is a violation of the SC guidelines.

The nutrition supplementary food includes pre-mix packages, fruits and sweets. The food supply is delegated to SHG workers.

Caste discrimination is not prominent. However, the drinking water glasses for the children are separate for each caste. Also in some centres, separate divisions were observed for SC and ST children. This is a violation of Supreme Court guidelines. Further, having aaanganwadi centres especially for SC and ST communities is not properly focused and targeted.

The centres are not convenient for differently-abled children. The path to the classroom is generally a steep climb. In some centres, cycle facilities are provided to help differently abled children to commute to the centres.

The utilization of funds by the staff is satisfactory. This is gauged from the detailed accounts being maintained in all the centres.

APL and BPL ration cards have been circulated among the target groups. More number of people belong to the BPL category. Transparency is maintained in the affairs of the ration shops. The people seem to be satisfied with their services.

The aanganwadi centres are at a distance of two kilometres from the residential areas thus easily accessible to the children. The educational qualification of the aanganwadi workers does not adhere to the SC guidelines. They fail to undergo the mandatory training sessions. Average monthly salary per month is ₹ 1,250. They are not provided with incentives or basic health services. The aanganwadi helper undertakes both the cleaning and cooking activities of the aanganwadi centres.

In the food materials supplied, grams, rice, dal and vegetables are not supplied. Per child, 5 grams of oil and 65 grams of aata is utilized. Hence, 10 litres of oil is used for a period of 6 months. Cooking fuel is not provided, but firewood is supplied for cooking purposes. 9 kilograms of firewood is supplied per month.

A practice followed in some villages is that pre-mixed food packages meant for children between the age group of 0 to 6 months are sent to the homes of the children. In case of children between 3 to 6 years, if a child absents himself or herself due to illness, the parents can collect those food packets of the day or if the houses are nearby, food packets are delivered to those houses. In some areas, the food is supplied by mahila mandals. Hence, it is observed in some centres that the food is supplied by Government agencies and in some (slum areas) it is supplied by independent contractors. This is not in strict adherence to the SC guidelines.

Major Findings

1. Average age of kids who come to aanganwadi is 3.5 years.
2. In 4 out of 5 aanganwadis surveyed, girls outnumbered boys.
3. Overall attendance was fairly good at all centres.
4. Children came from families with similar economic backgrounds i.e. generally APL and BPL families.
5. Caste and gender discrimination is not a menace but does exist at a few villages.
6. Price rise is tackled by taking loans from banks.
7. Sanitary facilities at most aanganwadis is poor.
8. Provision for drinking water at aanganwadis is also not adequate.
9. Aanganwadi functionaries are efficient and regular even though they are not imparted proper training by the government.
10. Food requirement of children is well taken care of within

the limited budget per student allotted. The quantity and quality both are satisfactory but having scope for further improvement.

11. No cases of illness have been reported due to intake of aanganwadi food.
12. Parents claim panchayat plays no role to advocate the aanganwadi scheme.
13. As per the parents, the two main factors for which they send their kids to the centres is food and education.
14. Literacy levels of parents are very diverse. There are a few who are 12th pass and a few illiterate ones also.
15. Immunization and nutrition are provided to pregnant and lactating mothers in only 40 percent of the centres and adolescent girls are not properly counselled.
16. Education being imparted at the centre is very basic and uniform for the age group of kids attending it, spanning from 3-6 years.
17. Timings are convenient for both the parents and little children.
18. Government has not provided much of study material to the aanganwadi centres.
19. Record maintenance is transparent or proper at majority of the centres.
20. CDPO visits the centres regularly, however health officer comes rarely and only on events like Mamta Divas etc.
21. Sanchalak is not regular in monitoring the activities of the aanganwadis. The aanganwadi workers know not much about him.
22. Educational level of aanganwadi teachers is average of 12th pass and that of helper is the secondary education.
23. Average salary paid to teacher ranges from ₹ 2,500-4,000 and that of helper ranges from ₹ 1,000-2,000.
24. Helper performs various roles. She is the cook. She cleans the centres and also takes care of the children whereas the teacher only teaches the kids.
25. Panchayat claims that it supports the aanganwadi centres

in every possible way but could not be verified either by the parents or the aanganwadi staff.

26. Most of the aanganwadi centres in the area surveyed were started in and around 2000. They are about 13 to 14 years old.
27. There is not much difference in the aanganwadi centres of big and populous villages and small and less populous villages.

Personal Observations

Based on the survey, many discrepancies in what the government proclaims and what reality is, has been found. The first thing noticeable is that there is no proper infrastructure provided to aanganwadi centres. In some of the villages aanganwadi functioned in just one room, there were no separate kitchen and no storage room available. The packaged food was found lying there which could easily get affected by worms, insects, etc. There was no separate room for the kitchen too—the food was prepared in one corner of that room. There was no furniture provided to aanganwadis except of one or two chairs, with children sitting on the floor. Several other complaints regarding malfunctioning of ICDS include the visit of health officials for vaccination, which is erratic. aanganwadi centres do not organize regular meetings of mothers and adolescent girls. In some aanganwadi centres, no first aid kit was available. Aanganwadi centre in some of the villages was cut off and situated in a very desolate surrounding. In some of the other centres the infrastructure was supported by an NGO. Many aanganwadis claim they receive no funds from the Government.

However, it was heartening to see efficient and self-motivated workers putting their earnest efforts in developing each and every child. Food is tasty, nutritious and sufficient. Education is interactive with pictorial learning, songs etc. The main objective of the aanganwadi centres is to cater to the needs of the development of children in the age group of 0-6 years. Pre-school education aims at ensuring holistic development of the children and to provide learning environment to them, which is conducive for promotion of social, emotional, cognitive and aesthetic development of the child. From infant mortality to immunization, from pre-school education to women's health, the integrated child development services (ICDS) has policies on everything, which makes it a good scheme on paper. But the survey of aanganwadi centres and interaction with community revealed that this scheme has scope for much improvement. There remain a number of mismatches between designing and implementation within the programme, as well as there are some serious problems with the quality and willingness of its implementation.

In an overview of the Supreme Court guidelines on ICDS, concern is expressed for the 'not up to the mark' efficacy of aanganwadi centres in the state. On the contrary, southern part of the country, under this scheme—Kerala and Tamil Nadu—are the states where the diversity and nutritious content of the food is higher.

Analysis of Parents' Questionnaire

There are certain findings that were similar to all families:

1. Parents use the pre-mixed food packets.
2. They said that the aanganwadi timings are between 11 in the morning and 2 in the afternoon.
3. They are of the opinion that the aanganwadi centres are equipped with most basic amenities and most of them do not have any complaints. They also are satisfied with the teacher's regularity and teaching methods.
4. They said that their children are being taught alphabets and simple vocabulary and grammar in school.
5. Breakfast is served at 11.20 in the morning and lunch is served at 2 in the afternoon. The children are provided with two meals per day, and the quantity of the meals is sufficient. The children are also given vitamin and protein supplements.
6. Their children have not contracted any disease or illness

due to consumption of the food given at the aanganwadi centres. The food provided changes with seasons and is made appropriate to the prevailing season.

7. They became aware of the aanganwadi schemes through word of mouth. Ever since, they are encouraged to send their children and are satisfied with the returns they get by sending their children to the aanganwadi centres.
8. Families in general are not aware of any counselling facilities or programmes for adolescent girls. They also did not appear to be aware of the immunization facilities for lactating mothers.
9. The main reason the parents are encouraged to send their children is because of both the education facilities as well as the food they receive.

Family 1: Mr. Vardhman Singh Vaghela and Kinnari Veghela send their only child, 3 year old Sunny Raj Vaghela to the aanganwadi centre. Their educational qualification of is up to 10th standard. They are engaged in agriculture and their income is ₹ 20,000 per month. They do not have any financial problems and hence price hikes do not affect them to a great extent. They are satisfied with the teacher's regularity and teaching methods. Their son misses aanganwadi classes more than twice a week, the reason being the constant rains in the past few weeks. They have been provided with ration cards. They belong to the APL category. They do not suffer any inconvenience due to the aanganwadi timings. The aanganwadi is at walking distance from their place.

In their opinion, the children in the class are from all economic backgrounds, but most children come from families employed in the agriculture sector.

Family 2: Mr. Chawda Vijay Sirkumaiji and Chawda Ansaben send their 2 year old daughter Chawda Hansaben to the aanganwadi school. They have one older son. Their educational qualification is 10th standard. They are engaged in the labour sector. Their average income is ₹ 4,500 per month. They deal with price hikes by working for longer hours, and at times are forced to employ their children to work. In their opinion, no specific teacher has been appointed. The teaching is undertaken by the aanganwadi helper herself. Their daughter misses the aanganwadi classes once a week, the reason being the heavy rains. They have been provided with ration cards. They are BPL.

They do not suffer from any inconvenience due to the aanganwadi timings. The aanganwadi school is at a distance of 2 km. from their place, and they have to walk this distance. In their opinion, most children attending the aanganwadi schools are of middle class background. However, there are children who come from the below poverty line also.

Family 3: Mr. Sureshji Ganeshji Thakur sends his daughter to the aanganwadi school. He has two other children. His educational qualification is 10th standard. He is employed in the agriculture sector and his average income is ₹ 2,000 per month. He deals with price hikes by working for longer hours.

He is satisfied with the teacher's regularity and teaching methods. His daughter hardly ever misses the aanganwadi classes. He has not been provided with the ration card. An aanganwadi worker informed him of the aanganwadi schemes.

He does not suffer any inconvenience due to the aanganwadi timings. The aanganwadi school is at a distance of 2 km. from their place, and they have to walk this distance.

In his opinion, most children attending aanganwadi schools are below the poverty line. There are very few who come from middle class and well to do agricultural families as well. The satisfaction level of the parents has to be understood against their own level of expectations.

Since the majority of parents surveyed belong to the BPL and themselves having low levels of literacy, their levels of expectation remain low. Further, aanganwadis are the place where they can keep their children when they go out to undertake labour for survival.

Comparative Analysis of Aanganwadi, Parents' and Panchayat Findings

The first observation is that there is a small discrepancy with regard to the timings of the aanganwadi. While the aanganwadi workers claim that the timings are from 10.30 in the morning to 3 in the afternoon, parents said that the timings are 11 in the morning to 2 in the afternoon.

The second observation is that the parents are of the opinion that most basic amenities are being provided for in the aanganwadi centres. However, aanganwadi workers claim that chalks and some study material are not being provided.

Otherwise, there seems to be a general consensus regarding the overall working of the schemes. Two out of three families and both aanganwadi workers have availed the ration card services and they do not complain of any corruption in the working of the same.

It can be said that the aanganwadi workers and staff in both areas, are making optimum use of the available resources. The parents are also satisfied with the overall benefits they receive through the scheme.

The most distinguishing factor of the aanganwadi schemes is the package of services they provide. It is a scheme that aims to provide not only pre-school education, but also nutritious food.

One common factor that is observed in all the families interviewed is that all the parents are encouraged to send their children to aanganwadis, not only to avail education facilities or only to avail the food services. Parents are encouraged to send their children to aanganwadis to avail the benefits of both the food provided and also the pre-school facilities.

Hence, a general inference can be arrived at that, as the number of services provided increases, there is a greater satisfaction among the people.

To elaborate on this further, it was unanimously observed in all families that they sent their children to aanganwadi schools because of both, education facilities and food facilities.

Hence, greater the number of services provided through the same scheme, greater is the utility of the scheme. A corollary to this would be, if the utility of a scheme is to be enhanced, greater number of services or benefits should be provided through the same scheme.

As of now, the facilities provided in the aanganwadi schools are two meals a day and pre-school education facility. Consider that one more facility, say clothing facility, provision of uniforms, sweaters and rain coats, is also added to the scheme. The benefit of an additional facility would further increase the satisfaction of the parents sending their children to aanganwadis. This would in turn encourage more parents to send their children to aanganwadi schools as well.

Suggestions

As of now, the overall management and running of the aanganwadi schemes is satisfactory. However, in order to make it more far reaching, and to prevent children from dropping out in the future, a plausible course of action by the Government can be, adding additional facilities to the aanganwadi centres. This review is testament to the inference that, more services obtained from one scheme has greater utility than multiple services obtained from multiple schemes.

Further, focused targeting of the SC and ST children is essential. This focused target was found missing and in violation of Supreme Court guidelines. The role of mahila mandals needs to be made effective in terms of regular awareness exercise relating to all the dimensions of the scheme.

Other facilities that can be introduced in the scheme are simple English courses. It has been observed that all the study material and teaching medium is in Gujarati. Introduction of English courses along with the regular course would in turn help to attract more children from APL families. Or making the aanganwadi centres more convenient for differently abled children, will help to attract such children also to aanganwadi centres, so that they can also avail both education and food faculties.

One pertinent factor that has to be taken into account is the strain on the Government's resources in order to increase more and more facilities to the scheme. However, it can fairly be said that, adding further facilities and benefits provided to an existing scheme, would prove far more economical to the Government, than introduction of separate schemes for each benefit. Because, in such a case, the Government need not invest in land, labour and resources for each separate scheme.

There should be an increase in the expenditure allotment per child. It is a fairly difficult job to serve cooked snacks to children at ₹ 4 per child.

Raising awareness among the local female population about the benefits they can derive from sending their children to the aanganwadi could lead to an increase in enrolment.

Raising the honorarium of the teachers would provide an incentive for added commitment to the job.

Granting better infrastructure to the aanganwadi centres would help.

The knowledge and efficiency of AWWs should be enhanced through frequent lectures and on-the-spot demonstrations.

Working of the projects should be evaluated at regular intervals. Supervision and guidance should be provided to AWWs individually and concerned supervisors should evaluate their knowledge periodically.

Proper provision in terms of basic equipment should be provided for cooking, cleaning etc.

State and district coordination committees should be formed and their effective functioning should be ensured.

Efforts should be made to improve the coverage of children under-three in the scheme. This can be done by conducting exhaustive door-to-door surveys, encouraging consumption of food at the AWC, and enhancing mothers' awareness about appropriate weaning practices and supplementary foods.

There is need to experiment with some new innovative methods for imparting training to AWWs. AWWs should be trained in involving community members in the activities of ICDS. Voluntary agencies including mahila mandals should be involved to make the ICDS programme a success.

CDPO and supervisors should improve their attitude towards AWWs. Willingness on their part to listen and understand the problems of AWWs could go a long way in creating an atmosphere conducive for work.

Orientation courses should be organized regularly for grass roots workers and opportunities should be provided for discussion of day-to-day problems. Post-training evaluation programmes should be conducted to monitor the quality of training.

Frequent supervision should be undertaken by senior ICDS functionaries to establish and encourage a constant rapport between AWWs and the community. This in turn will educate the community at large and the people will become aware of the importance of health, nutrition and the services available.

Audio-visual aids like films, radio, television, exhibitions and charts should be used to educate people regarding health and nutrition.

An incentive or an award should be given to the best AWW or to those who show very good results to improve their work and efficiency. Improvement in the honorarium, job conditions and building facilities should also be considered.

According to the Supreme Court guidelines, every anganwadi centre has to organize periodically mother's meeting (expectant and lactating mothers) and community mobilization especially of mothers and adolescent girls. None of the centres organizes such activities.

Conclusion

Following the survey, it is possible to conclude that though the aanganwadis by and large follow the guidelines set down by the Supreme Court of India (apart from some important non-compliance), there is enormous scope of improvement. Most of the guidelines are not executed in a manner which would lead to maximum benefit to the community. Such lack of execution can only be improved through the provision of incentives to work and an upgrading of infrastructure.

The dichotomy regarding a state exhibiting a high GDP as well as high malnutrition rate can be resolved by looking into the different gaps between policy and implementation. The researcher states that though lacunas exist in the aanganwadi scheme in Gujarat, the study undertaken does not support the extent of malnutrition as declared by the Human Development Report of 2011. Given that the socio-economic and demographic profile of the different districts in Gujarat are much diverse, and the sample undertaken for this study is not a representative sample of Gujarat, yet the findings conclusively display lacunas in implementation but not all pervasive malnutrition to the extent of 44.6 percent.

Index

Index